AGAINST THE ODDS
FROM THE SLUMS OF SUMMER LANE

by

Thomas Lewin

Grosvenor House
Publishing Limited

This book is published by
Grosvenor House Publishing Ltd
Link House
140 The Broadway, Tolworth, Surrey, KT6 7HT.
www.grosvenorhousepublishing.co.uk

A CIP record for this book
is available from the British Library

ISBN 978-1-83975-276-6

For years I have wanted to put these memories down, clear memories from when I was two years old playing with the chickens and the ducks in Kingstanding.

Acknowledgements

To my parents

My mom and dad were good people, they never had a bad bone in their bodies. Would never judge people, would never slag people off. Some would not agree with that, judges, social workers, probation officers, but it's easy to speak and be opinionated from a lofty position. Mom and Dad brought us up to be free spirited and to find our own way in the world that was perhaps their only mistake, maybe they never allowed for how strong minded and opinionated we would be.

I often look back and try to imagine how hard, how difficult it must have been for them. My mother having to look after her mother who was seriously ill for many years before dying in her forties, plus five brothers from the age of 14 in the slums, the back-to-backs of Summer Lane, Birmingham.

Remembering my own upbringing, the hardship, the freezing cold, ice on the inside of our windows, pissing the bed and finding comfort in the warmth of that piss. Others might condemn them for their drinking most nights of the week down the local boozers, but my dad made his living in those boozers. My mom made her beer money by selling in the boozers. My friends, my peers suffered even more, one friend sat on orange boxes to eat at the table made up of boxes, he was caned on a daily basis for having dirty hands, yet he had to work in his father's wood yard, so he could never get his hands clean.

I had many friends who barely ate because their parents had no money or the will to cook, one friend would have a saucepan of gruel on the gas oven for when they left for school. His brother died at a very early age, for this and many other reasons I grew up thinking, as a family we were rich. In fact, we were in truth very well off. Living in Sutton I've known people struggle on a daily basis living far worse than us, the only difference is they live in a nicer house in a nicer area. In truth that is the only mistake my mom and dad made. My dad carried his bank around in his pocket, as did many others, I remember he carried a roll of some £500 in his pocket, when the average wage was £6 a week, he could have brought a better house with that money, but back then a lot of people thought it stupid to buy your own house, put a big milestone around your neck. I know people who had slogged their backsides off to buy a house, only to come out five years later with nothing and grateful to get a council house.

With little education, they got themselves a hawkers licence to sell fruit and veg from a barrer, in the old bullring. Dad would get up at 4am in the morning to get the barrer out, get his stock in and set up stall, come rain, snow or ice. After my mom had got us kids off to school she would take over the barrer, my dad would be down the boozer selling stuff and making a better living. Mom would buy a turkey frame on her way home from town. With the veg from the barrer she would make a two-gallon pot of good healthy stew that would feed us for three or four days at a time. With the specks and damaged fruit off the barrer we would get our vitamins which stood us in good stead.

I stand and look back with good memories of my mom and dad, hence my reasons for writing this book. They were true entrepreneurs of their day, their only downfall was their strict principles, they would never grass on anyone, it was not in their genetic makeup/ For that reason they were targeted, eventually they were looked down on by people. I have seen and known those who did far worse than they could ever do or would do. For that reason, I look back on them with fond memories and respect... people who live in glass houses I think is the expression.

My reason for this book is not the money, I have plenty, fame, I could have had that with the boxing, besides, I'm at the wrong age. I simply didn't want their memories to be forgotten, their little scams, their efforts to turn a few quid.

To Betty Jean Lewin

I can never thank my wife enough for everything she did for me. For all of us as a family. Without her backing, her wisdom, her natural talent, her loyalty I would never have had anything, Without her we would have fallen at the first hurdle. I can and will never be able to thank her enough... which I should have done more when she was alive. She was a diamond in the full sense of the word, yet all the time I just took it for granted. Accepting it at the time as normal. But she never was.

Once she was so hard up she crawled on her belly to nick some beans from the next door garden to give herself something to eat. As a child she was forced to live like a gypsy in a tent for two years whilst her parents were trying to make money from hop picking.

All this made her resolve to back me one hundred percent in whatever determined efforts I made to give us all a better life. She could have been a good hairdresser... I never paid for a haircut in my life. She was a good accountant having worked in an office doing accounting. She had a natural flair for shaving the pounds and keeping a tight but balanced budget. I trusted her one hundred percent with all the banking. All the handling of our money. I tried to tell our kids if you can't trust your partner then you have nothing. From not really knowing how to cook she leapt up to running a hotel. Cooking for up to 50 guests. Good wholesome home cooked food. She ran the hotel; she kept the books and she took the bookings.

Whatever business we took on she could and would run it. She had more ability in her little finger than I had in the whole of my body. Whilst I had the ambition and the goals Bet had the determination and confidence to follow me. all the time asking for nothing. When someone tried to put the poison in telling her she should take a wage in the hotel, or be paid for the work she was doing, she would just smile at them. A lot of people thought she was stupid because she went along with whatever I said or did, but all the time she was silently smiling at their utter stupidity. All the time she was helping me build up to a nice house, a nice hotel, living on very little, whilst they sat back with nothing.

How many were the times when people would turn to me, the roofer or the plasterer and say, "I'd love to get into this," or, "I should have done that before explaining how their wives would never stand for going without their regular wage packet coming in, or was not prepared to put up with living in a building site. But my Bet was. If it meant improving our life she would live in a derelict cottage, or a rundown house. Knowing the end result justified the discomfort. She was a diamond and I burst with pride and sadness. When I think of it. I only fully realised how much I loved her when it was too late, when she was gone… for all the mistakes I made. Silly. Petty and utterly stupid. It took her death to shake me up to see it, to see how wise she had always been. Much of it passed into me. When it was far too late

To my siblings. My brothers

Johnny. Reg. Billy, Kenny. As I go on with my life I just want you to know I love you all. All of us had good hearts, good genes. In many ways strong principles. Amongst many others who sadly didn't. My only real regret is that we didn't see that from an early age; recognised the abilities we had whilst seeing the mongrels amongst us… but I gain pleasure in the knowledge that you all did ok. Many others didn't; also love to my brave sisters Doris. Patty and Alma.

Our children

Andrew, Nicky, Louise, Rachael and Kristy know that I love you all. Perhaps this book might explain a few things. Maybe not. It's something I have wanted to do for years. Your mom also wanted me to do it. I'm sorry if it creates any problems. If it does deny all knowledge of me. I am proud of you all. Have a good life.

Lastly

I want to give thanks to all those who assisted me in putting this book together, with a special word of thanks to Diana Elizabeth Phillips, the administrator of the Nechell's forum, for her kind permission and help in choosing pictures for my book.

PART ONE

Against the odds - first memories

It's funny how the passage of time distorts our memory; when we were kids, every Christmas was a white one with deep snow falling on the ground. We always had the biggest Christmas tree in the road, so big it had to be cut down to fit in the front room, the fire big and bright with chestnuts roasting. The seasons were clear, the summers were always hot with a burning sun, and winters were dank and miserable with fog every night, so thick you could hardly see across the road. Every spring saw the trees blossom and the spring sun come out to shine. We knew everybody and everybody knew us. We played outside all day and never returned to the house until dark or night-time, our parents never worried, it gave them a break, and we ate worms and lived. We ran around barefoot or in ill-fitting shoes; it didn't matter because we were all the same; we only stood apart when we walked outside our area.

My mom and dad were born and lived their lives in Summer Lane. They were proper Summer Laners, loud, hard confident like many in the lane. Today, many people claim to have lived or been born in Summer Lane; the more successful they are, the more they boast about coming from Summer Lane. What they won't tell you is that when they were first moved out of the lane before and post-war at the start of the slum clearances, they denied all knowledge of it, of Summer Lane. To admit to coming from Summer Lane was to admit you were a slummer, a crook, a dishonest person, which most were if the truth be told, oh all would deny it. Still, no one refused something off the back of a lorry. Few wanted that stigma in their new terraced and council semis in King Standing, Kitts Green, and surrounding areas. Plus, there were the villains; I reckon Summer Lane had more criminals than anywhere else in the city; no one wanted to be associated with them. It was so well-known that it even had its own songs, its way of talking. Summer Lane had its own language, its own accent, subtle, but we all knew each other by the way we spoke.

When we moved to Chingford Road, it was a great place to live, trees lined the road, grass filled the verges, and the gardens were always immaculately kept with flower borders and mown lawns. Yes, Chingford Road was lovely. We had the Anderson air-raid shelter in our garden, ducks, chickens, and rabbits ran freely around. Mondays would be chicken stew, made up from the leftovers of the Sunday roast; Tuesday would be rabbit, and then duck. We always ate well; Mom made sure of that.

When the milk was delivered, Mom would always shout, "Tommy, Kenny, get up the hoss road and follow that cart. Here's the bucket, get the hoss shit".

Off, we'd run, our little legs racing to get there first. The still warm hoss shit would go into the vegetable patch at the bottom of the garden. Yep, our mom was enterprising all right, she also had a good heart. Many a neighbour would call round midweek to borrow a pound, or a bag of sugar, or a slab of marge until payday. Our days would be spent tearing around the garden chasing the chickens and rabbits, ragged-arsed without a care in the world.

Many a time, I would watch Dad with his barrow. "Oranges, come and get your lovely jubblies, only two pence a pound." Every now and again, he'd give me a look; a little smirk on his face and a twinkle in his eye; another few pennies in his bin. Yep, my old dad was clever all right. Every Monday afternoon, he'd come into the house carrying crates of old wrinkled oranges up to the bathroom, tipping them into the bath. When it was full, he'd fill the bath with water, covering the oranges.

I was perplexed. I couldn't figure it out. "What you doing, Dad?"

He'd give that little smirk, the twinkle in his eye," watch," and the next day I'd rush into the bathroom, and there would be the oranges, no water, just big juicy fat oranges, ready to be sold on the barrow the next day.

"Come and get your oranges, big juicy Jaffas, only two pence a pound, get yourself a bargain."

He always had that twinkle in his eye and a smirk on his lips, now I see why, he'd buy the cheap old oranges on a Saturday, fatten them up and the next day they'd be big fat Jaffas, same with the spuds. "Three pounds of best spuds, my luv."

As they looked at the spuds on display, he'd reach behind him, bringing out his spuds from a sack behind the counter. He always left a little bit of soil on the shovel to help the weight along; sometimes the punters would be on the ball.

"Ay, ay Jack, them on the fronts the ones I want, not, out the sack."

"Of course, my love," along with a little bit of soil.

I loved watching my dad work, every day was a lesson, he tried teaching my oldest brother Jonny how to run the barrow, but he wasn't interested. He'd wait until the old man had gone off to the pub, nick a few pennies out of the box, and off he'd go with his mates. He tried showing, Reg, the next oldest, but he wasn't interested either and preferred to go off with his pals playing snooker. Billy was different; he took to it like a duck to water. He could bullshit and talk on the stall until the cows came home.

Now, Mom and Dad could both go down the boozer. Mom with her dolly basket selling her goodies, between Dad's profits on the barrow and Mom's little earner of her basket, they could drink merrily until the boozers closed. If they got the taste, they'd buy a crate and carry on at home, bringing a few pals with them. Yep, it was a nice lifestyle, Mom and Dad worked hard; they had seen the horrors of life, seen the deaths from the First World War, served and fought and suffered in the second, who can blame them in their thinking that they deserved some good times? As did most people. And us? Well, we could do as we pleased.

Eventually, the complaints from the neighbours got too much. Mom was loud and full-on into your face; she just didn't give a damn about anyone or anybody. She had had to look after her mother from an early age and bring up her five younger brothers almost singlehanded. She had found from a very early age that there was no one around or willing to help them. Her dad had done a runner years before, never to be seen or heard again. They were alone and on their own. When she married Dad, she would argue, speak up for and stand loyal to him. He, being a bit shy, would stand back and let her argue or fight his corner. As we kids were born and were growing up, she extended her loyalty to us, fighting our corner with anyone who had anything to say. When Dad came back from a day's work on the barrer, he'd put and store his fruit and veg in the garden shed. We never went hungry because we always had plenty of food; our garden was full of chickens, rabbits, even the odd duck.

The neighbours didn't like it too much during and after the war, even so, many of them came to Mom regularly for a bit of sugar, a few potatoes, a bit of lard, even a few shillings when they couldn't pay their rent nor had nothing else to pawn. Mom had a heart as big as a mountain, and a mouth to match. After the war and during rationing, she would buy all their sugar rations, exchanging their ration cards for cash or other food. When their husbands were home, and as things started to improve, so did the neighbours, with a bit of money and the help of the credit lenders and unions they didn't need Mom anymore. The council came round and gave Mom a verbal warning. A few chickens were acceptable, but they couldn't run a business from a council property, plus there was a constant smell from the rotting fruit and poultry. Because of the years, she had been there; she never felt to heed it, just carrying on as before. Mom was Mom and spoke her mind; she didn't see the need to change or see why she should. Dad? Well, he didn't give a damn; either way, he just left Mom to sort it. In her ignorance, she just didn't see that the resentment from the neighbours was building up. Eventually, the council had had enough, following more warnings, Mom and Dad were given notice to quit, on the moving day the big van turned up, Dad did a duck. He had the barrer to run, leaving it all to Mom.

The removal men, hearing the story were a bit sympathetic. "Don't you worry love, one day, you will come back here with a fur coat on, and this lot will still have nothing." I don't think that was much consolation to my mom on the day.

Off we went to our new home, 259 Rocky Lane, Nechells, a big parlour house with the front door leading off the road into the hallway, no inside toilet here but we were luckier than most. We had our own outside toilet, unlike many others who had to share in the back-to-backs around us though. Yes, ours was a big house, alright, but it was still in the slums. I know Mom wasn't happy, it was a real comedown for her, but I don't think Dad gave a shit, there was a pub on every corner, and many of Dad's mates lived around us. To Dad, I'm sure this was just another business opportunity, more pubs, more people, and more business. Dad wasn't interested in dressing up to impress, coming from and growing up in the slums. Most people liked to dress up and impress, that's all they had, not Dad, he never felt that he had anyone to impress. He made good money, drank as much as he liked, a simple cravat was good enough for him. We knew even more people and had more friends in Nechells than anywhere. I don't think the fact that our house was a former doctor's surgery made a great deal of difference; a slum is a slum. To me and Kenny, my younger kid brother, it didn't make any difference. To us, Nechells was one big playground; already, the factories down

Schofield Street were becoming empty. Some of the houses were being emptied with the tenants being moved out to nicer posher houses. Yep, Nechells was one big playground for us to explore, all we had to do was find a few pals to explore it with.

Our house on Rocky Lane was a big three-storey Victorian mid-terrace. The hallway led straight off the pavement; off the hallway was the door to the front room, after that, a small lobby leading to the stairs. At the top of the stairs was a small landing, two rooms went off to the front and back room, also, off the landing was another door that led to the attic. Walking through the lobby at the bottom of the stairs led you into the back living room; this living room for some reason was always dark, even with the light on and the coal fire burning bright. At best, it could be described as cosy; sometimes, and off the back door, you went into the kitchen. This also was always dark and dismal with whitewashed distempered walls, a Belfast sink underneath the small window and a cooker. This kitchen was the storage room, washroom, and cooking room. Off the kitchen was the door to the back garden/yard leading to the outside privy and side entry, not forgetting the tin bath that hung on the wall. My mom must have been well pleased having moved from the slums of Summer Lane to the luxury of Chingford Road back to this. My dad? I don't think he was too bothered.

Kenny and I soon set about finding our feet, making friends and getting to know the area. I never heard the word slum mentioned until I was much older, but to us, Nechells wasn't a slum, if you lived in Sutton, we lived in a slum if you lived in King Standing, we lived in a slum. To those who had moved, it was quickly forgotten where they came from, but to us, the inner city was one big playground. There was always dust in the air because of all the demolition going on. But to us, that was just part of the excitement of the place. Nechells, like most pre-war properties, was made up of these tenement buildings, set into blocks, or squares. We were about three houses down from Schofield Street with Anthony's the grocer's shop on the corner, blocks of lard, margarine and sacks of sugar on the floor.

The opposite way led to Bloomsbury Street. It was a row of houses, a builders' yard, another few houses, then Frank Grounds, the transport yard, then more houses leading to "the Green". Why it was called this, I don't know because there wasn't a bit of green to be seen, just concrete and bricks. A bench was set into the pavement. People could rest their weary legs or just sit admiring the view across to the Beehive and the island with the phone box in the middle, not forgetting more terraced houses and the shops. Many people did use the bench just to sit and watch the entertainment. Truly, you could sit there any time of the day or night and be entertained. Street traders, hawkers, interspersed with people arguing, and fights. Hardly a day went by without a fight.

Schofield Street leads up to Great Lister Street with four blocks of tenements running between Schofield Street and Bloomsbury Street. Off the Green, Bloomsbury Street itself led up to Great Lister Street and on into the town. Schofield Street was made up of back-to-backs and terraced houses, in between these were entries leading to more back-to-backs set out in a square, to one side would be the toilet blocks. Eight houses with eight toilets. Nobody put a lock on their toilet so many a time, particularly over a weekend, people wouldn't be so fussy, someone would go to the toilet only to find it full of shit and piss from someone else on the booze the night before.

"FRED, FRED, get the fucking hell over here and clean this khazi, some dirty bastard's been and shat all over the place."

Whoever had made a point of keeping their gobs shut, the common name for the toilet was the shithouse, khazi or bog, we could see why.

It was the characters that lived around Nechells who made the place so rich. On the right, opposite Anthony's in Schofield Street lived Henry Taroni and his wife. Henry had a yard next to his house where he stored his lorry, which he used to make his living tatting. At the top of his yard was a big boiler that he used to cook the food for his pigs; there were always pig bins around full of waste bread. Henry would collect this, boil it up and feed it to his pigs. I used to think Henry did this to fatten them up for the dinner table until he told me it was to get the extra diesel for his lorry. Diesel was on ration, but Henry found out that by keeping pigs, he could claim extra diesel rations which he used for his lorries, course, he did eat the pigs as well. No doubt, Henry was the quiet one.

Further down lived Joe Taroni and his wife, Kitty. Joey and his family lived in a back-to-back fronting onto Schofield Street; his front door was off the side entry. No doubt, Joe was going to be a millionaire. Everybody knew it, and it was common knowledge, he had two or three lorries parked opposite on the "peck" and was a coalman. Next to Joe was the Asian that would come out twice a week and carry his chickens over to the peck. He'd chop their heads off, and we'd watch them flying all over the pitch until they flopped down lifelessly.

Further down lived Joe's dad, also known as Joe, his missus and daughter Sheila. Old Joe had worked on the coal all his life, but now suffered from his lungs. Between the two Joes lived big "Ginger" Harris, who would knock you out with one punch.

Usually, it was not long before the boozer was closing, everyone was getting merry and tongues started to loosen up. Suddenly Ginger would have enough and knock 'em out; he was never known to use more than one punch. He didn't need the booze, though. He worked for Joe off and on, and there was always a fall out over money. Mind you, Joe was always falling out with one of his workers over wages. Every Friday or Saturday morning would be the same, Joe would pay the wages, his blokes would whine they were short-changed; cue a few smacks and a punch up. Once word got around, us kids would always try to be down Schofield Street for around lunchtime. Soon Joe would turn up in his lorry, Kim, the

Alsatian standing proud on the back. Then another lorry, then another would turn up, into the little front room they would go. Joe would take the money, the others walking out and waiting outside, Joe would tally up, then walk out, giving each their wages, their faces would go down to their money, then back up to Joe.

"What the fuck is this? We're ten bob short!"

Then the arguments would start. Joe would tell 'em how they ain't sold enough coal, or worse, they've gypped him, soon, the punches would start flying, sometimes a bit of renegotiation went on. A few extra bob might be handed out; everyone was happy, or reasonably happy. Then off to the pub, they would all go, sorted. We all thought Joe was going to be the millionaire; he was making money hand over fist. Sadly, like my old man and many others, his fortune went in the boozer. The trick with being on the coal, like everything else, was to nick a bit, before setting out. We had to first load the coal on to the lorries in hundredweight sacks, on to the scales, then stacked into layers, once you went over the scales, the weight was checked you were ready to fiddle a bit for yerself.

Out you'd go, knocking on the doors selling coal, "a-n-y, c-o-a-l," you'd shout, someone would shout, "How much? Two bags, please." You'd hump it onto yer shoulder. Still, before doing so, you'd accidentally knock off a chunk of coal, maybe two, or even three, by accident of course. No customer would ever notice; two lumps of coal weighed a few pounds; it didn't take many lumps to make another hundredweight. We carried 50-60 bags on a lorry, sometimes doing three loads a day. Petty pilfering as it may have seemed, it could be an extra four or five bags of coal each load. Fifteen bags a day at ten bob a bag was £7- £8 per day and was the average wage for the week. No wonder Joe and the lads were always in the boozer, no wonder there was nearly always a fight, and a fallout come Saturday morning. Everyone had a scam; it was part of life, if you didn't have a little scam then you starved or rubbed your fingers to the bone trying to earn it. Didn't even Coleman, the mustard manufacturer, admit they he made his fortune on what people left on the plate?

Between the Taronies were some of my mates; Jacky Waldron lived up one of the back yards with his brother Danny and his mom, his dad had left years ago, and no one saw the sight of him since. Jack's mom wasn't very well and had her bed downstairs by the fire, and whenever I called round the fire was always blazing. Mrs Waldron would be huddled up to it legs purple and crisscrossed from the heat. She wouldn't say a lot, and I could tell she was not very well, 'He-e-ell-o, Tom,' she'd say, all weak and feeble. Further down lived my best mate John 'Bee-Bee' Beards. Bee-Bee also lived in a back-to-back with the front door leading onto the pavement. I hardly ever saw his old man, but his mom was a character in her own right, thin and scrawny with a big hook nose. One day I was outside Bee-Bee's when the debt collector called round. Seeing him coming, Mrs Beards dived into the house and under the table shouting to Bee-Bee, "Tell him there's no one in." the debt collector comes to the door, "Hello son is your mom in?"

Bee-Bee's standing on the doorstep and tells him, "Nah, she ain't in, mister."

Mrs Beards had forgotten to shut the door tight. Through the crack, the debt collector could see Mrs Beards under the table.

"Hello, Mrs Beards lost something, have you?"

"Uh, uh, uh." Mrs Beards came up from under the table quite embarrassed, stuttering. "Oh, I've lost me shoe." She held a shoe in her hands. "Anyway, I can't pay you this week, come back next week, alright?"

And off he'd go. This was regular up and down the street and around the area. Debtors calling around, people ducking and diving all over the place to avoid paying. Joe's missus Kitty had had some kettles and saucepans on the mace, the collector called round one Friday when Joe was having one of his bad days with his blokes. I wasn't too sure whether Joe knew his missus had had the kettles and saucepans on the mace but he well and truly flipped.

"Money? Money?" In he goes to his house and comes back out with a big sparkly new frying pan. "Money?" He shouts again. "I'll give you fucking money," and whacks the debt collector on the bonce. "Here, take your fucking pan with you and don't call round, here again, money!"

And with that, he bounces the pan off the bloke's head again as he goes running off down the road. The coppers usually walked in twos, and if they saw this or any fighting going on, they'd do an about-turn and walk off back down the road. Streetwise, as they were, how the hell some of my mates' parents thought they could hide in a ten-foot square room when the debtor came. They had nowhere to hide; the debtors knew it.

The area abounded with a colourful mix of people, most hardworking nine-to-fivers whose husbands went out to work, the wives looking after the house and kids. During the day they'd be popping out and about, over or into Anthony's for a loaf of bread or a slab of marge or lard, sometimes a few sweets, a little gossip; Mrs Anthony had it all. At teatime, you'd see the husbands come trekking home, heads down, weariness showing in their faces. That's it, you wouldn't see them again until the next night. Same at weekends, a night out to the Brit or the Beehive with the wife, a couple of hours with the lads, Sunday lunch, then off home, a couple of hours listening to the radio then off to bed ready to face the daily grind the next day. Everybody was either young or old, no in between. If you were young, you were bushy-tailed and shiny-eyed, or old and haggard looking and worn out like Mrs Jones who lived across the road. She was so big her legs could hardly carry her, veins and lumps sticking out all over the place as she struggled and hobbled across the road. Life was hard for some, alright.

School Days

I started my schooling at the Cromwell Street School, where it very quickly dawned on me that education wasn't for me. I tried and got my head down, but it was so bleedin' boring, plus, the teachers didn't much like me. Not just me either, they didn't like Bee-Bee, or my mate Robert, Turl, Turley. It wasn't too long before we started getting the cane and once that started, it didn't stop, and in we'd go, heads down at the desk.

Next, it would be, "Lewin, Turley, Beards, outside, go to the headmaster's office."

Mr Onions was the headmaster, and we never saw a smile on his face. Along, he'd come to look at us and tell us to wait outside his office. He'd walk back in ten minutes later, go into his office and leave us waiting, trembling outside for another ten minutes. We knew he was doing this on purpose, he enjoyed the anticipation, the fear we were going through. We would stand outside shitting ourselves, knowing what was to come. Eventually, he'd call us in one by one and whip our arses. The pain was terrible, and we'd be sent outside to wait, jumping up and down with the pain and crying, by the time the last one came out, our pain would have subsided. We'd start laughing at the tears and pain on the others' faces. Eventually, we'd be pissing ourselves laughing so much we'd forgotten the pain altogether. Well almost, I don't think a day went by when we didn't get a thrashing and none of us ever knew what for, yep, that Onions was a sadist all right, one day he went too far. Bee-Bee went home with wheals on his arse and legs, the next day Mrs Beards came storming into the assembly, grabbed the Onions' stick and started chasing him around the assembly room.

"Hit my son, would you?" Shouting her head off, it was hilarious. Onions running around the hall, Mrs Beards chasing him like a good un, shouting and bawling, whacking him on his back. Now he was getting a taste of the fear, and it showed on his face. Mrs Beards was our hero, she was a skinny little thing, and with that big hook nose you wouldn't think she had it in her, but she did all right, and it was a good few weeks before things got back to normal, and the cane reappeared. Our daily routine would be to turn up at school and sit waiting until we could finish and get out at the end of the day. I enjoyed reading, but when it came to maths, I just didn't have a clue, I wanted to learn, and I tried. Still, when I looked at those numbers in front of me, my eyes just blurred, and the numbers just blurred into each other. One day the teacher came over. "Now Lewin, 2 and 2 makes 4, 4 and 4 make 8." Smacking my head down on the desk in time with each number, well that was, I couldn't understand it, didn't want to understand it and just cut off, refusing to learn at all. Eventually, they would give up and not bother. The rest would turn up, sit down, shut their gobs and do as they were told, fuck that.

Come home time, out we'd run, straight over to the peck, mooching and climbing in and over the houses. There was so much to see and do that we hardly visited the same places twice. If we did, there was always something of interest that we'd missed before. It was fascinating to find what people had left behind in their excitement of leaving and moving into their new houses. We could play all day long, and did; we went out in the morning and never got back until dark. If it were summer nights, we'd get home for a bit of tea, then out again, if we got bored with one place we'd go off mooching to find somewhere else, sometimes it was a challenge to outdo each other.

One day I was taken ill and was taken into the general hospital with pneumonia. I was in there for six months, and there were always lots of visitors looking worried as they peered at me over the bed, deathly quiet. One day I was really bad, and I remember this guy all in black standing over me, I thought I was dreaming for some time until after my mom told me it was the priest come to give me the last rights, last rights? Well, I didn't know I was that bad, I never felt ill, no wonder it was deathly quiet, they all thought I was gonna croak. When I came home, Dad carried me all the way, I was too weak to walk, I didn't quite mind this getting ill too much though, I was well fussed over and being stuffed with boiled eggs on my first day, "Go on eat up. It'll do you good, we've got to fill you out a bit."

Well, I didn't feel too bad, my ribs were sticking out, and everybody looked away when I sucked in my belly, I thought, it was quite funny. If I sucked my belly in my front could touch my back, but nobody could look, I used to do it even more to annoy them, it took me a few years to get back to normal. I was that thin I could suck my toes.

While I was ill and off school, I spent a lot of time in bed. Mom making sure I had a big hot fire to wake up to, this was just as well as in the winter our house could be cold. I slept with Kenny and Patty in a double bed a sheet and Dad's army coat on top, we had to cuddle up tight to make sure we all kept under the coat. We'd learnt that there was no point in trying to grab it for yourself as no one would get any kip, better to cuddle up. Mom would always have the piss pot on the landing, but sometimes it was too cold, even to get up and walk over to that, never mind downstairs, through the cold house to the outside bog, far better to piss the bed. The piss was warm and sent a nice warm glow through the body, the next morning there would be hell to pay, but everybody blamed the other.

As I got a bit better, Dad would take me out on the barrer, where I'd stand and watch him work all day in the bullring. Sometimes he'd take his barrer out of town to West Bromwich or Blackheath. I never thought or questioned this at all until one day George Tooty Fruity Tuit Fewtrell, one of Dad's mates called round they had got a tea chest full of brown powder when I asked Dad what it was.

He said, "Snuff son, snuff?"

"Snuff, what's snuff?"

"Here stick some of that on the back of your hand and sniff it up your nose."

Well,' I did, and it nearly blew my bleeding head off, running around the room like the Asian's headless chickens, I didn't ask again. Dad and Fruit got a load of brick and smashed it into dust, once it was smashed enough and filtered through a sieve they mixed it with the rest of the snuff and made two tea chests, each full of snuff. Off, we'd all go, out of town and Mom would start packing the bags into two-ounce bags, while Dad would sell it on the stall for a tanner a bag. It was going down a treat, and Dad had got rid of most of one tea chest when one or two came tootling back.

"Gud afternoon sir, havin' a bit more snuff today, are we?"

They'd answer through blocked up noses. "No thanks, I'm all right for now."

"Good snuff though, ain't it?"

"Oh aye, just blocks the nose up a bit."

Well, I would have to dive down behind the cart, pissing my pants with laughter. Dad would give that little chuckle, the ready twinkle in his eye; Mom would duck her head and look away. Eventually, he'd move off, taking the barrer somewhere else until all the snuff had gone, there were always regular little "earners" as Dad called them. Some he would sell in his regular pitches, other times he'd take it out of town, if I asked where it came from, all Dad would do is touch his nose, give a little glint and tell me to mind it. I did, I used to hear a little bit about "off the back of a lorry" but what I didn't know didn't hurt. Dad's attitude was that if he didn't know, then he was doing nothing wrong. It was a common expression around Nechells; everyone bought stuff off the 'back of the lorry'.

The rules were clearly laid out in our house; Mom and Dad never had long and meaningful conversations with us. We were expected to watch, listen and learn, they were a throw-back to the Victorian period, children were to be seen and not heard. If the adults were talking, we were expected to keep our mouths shut, and that was it. Mom and Dad hated grasses, any form of grass with a vengeance; the rules in our house were dead straightforward, easy to understand. I thought it was the same in every household. My mom and dad weren't crooks or bad people; they were simply trying to make a living the best way they knew how. If you weren't a little bit bent, you didn't survive. If you weren't a little bit bent, you might as well get a job in a factory, on a building site; become an old man before your time, and die early in the process.

Up to Mischief

Saturday mornings we went to the picture house, it would be packed with us screaming kids, roaring on Gene Autry, Roy Rogers or the Cisco Kid. When we came out of that picture house afterwards, we were the Cisco Kid and off we'd go at a gallop down Rocky Lane and on to our bit of the Wild West, the bomb pecks. The flicks were our escape. For a couple of hours, we were transported to another world, another country; the world had just opened its imagination to other worlds. We had films about Buck Rodgers and his fights with the Martians and their invasion of earth. We would sit there, not a sound in the picture house, mesmerised by these little Martians invading us.

It was a natural progression for us to look for other means of excitement, from the houses and backyards to the factories. The demo down the bottom of Schofield Street was another source of excitement; it not only had a watchtower where we could see all around Nechells and up into town. But it also had a cache of air raid helmets that led to many nights of fun running and chasing across the rooftops. We would use the tower to fire rockets off at Bloomsbury Street nick, waiting until the coppers came out scratching their heads, trying to figure out why so many rockets were hitting their doors and windows with no one being about. One night we were up on the roof, and this kid started following us. Sometimes this is how you make and find new mates, but this kid was a bit dim, and we didn't want him around. We just couldn't get rid of him, we were running and hiding all over the roof, and he was still following us. Suddenly we heard this crash a loud yell and a thump, bleeding hell, he fell through the skylight. Over we go and look down through the skylight. Silly prat hadn't got the sense to keep to the main roof, fancy going across the glass. Looking down we could see he was as still as stone, he's dead, but we couldn't just walk off and leave him there. First, we thought we saw a movement, then wondered if we'd imagined it. Anyway, we decided to go down and make sure he was still alive alright but only just. We decided to lift him and carry him round to Bloomsbury Nick, with the clear understanding that he had to keep his trap shut. I don't think he understood us at all, I think he was completely out of it.

At any rate, we picked him up and started carrying him around Freemen Street down to Bloomsbury Nick. As we got under a streetlight, Kenny shot back and shouted look at his fucking foot, with that he ran back and said, "I'm off home." Bee-Bee and I looked down at the kid's foot. It was hanging off. I mean hanging off, hanging by a thread. This was big shit time; we were in big trouble all right. Kenny ran off home, and we carried the kid to the nick steps warning him again to keep his trap shut, knocked on the door and scarpered. A few weeks later, we saw the kid walking around Nechells regularly limping badly and dragging his foot. As we passed him, it was obvious he never recognised us. We weren't too inclined to tell him, after stopping in for a few weeks and keeping our heads down, we could start venturing out again, coast clear.

There was always a sense of danger to our shenanigans. Whether it was climbing onto the roofs of houses, into cellars or church crypts, factory roofs, buildings. One time, we were mooching around a factory down Schofield Street when we came across this big steel tank in the cellar. It was pitch black, just a bit of light shining through when we opened the door. We decided to explore in, and around the tank when Kenny, the silly prat, got stuck halfway down. I couldn't lean over far enough to reach him; he couldn't jump up. We could make out water at the bottom of the tank, but we didn't know how deep it was. Fuck this, we had no choice, someone had to go and fetch help. I sent Bee-Bee; if I went, no one would come. Bee-Bee ran home, next thing, our Dots turned up, opened the door, starts screaming and ranting, what the fucking hells up with her? We ain't in trouble and Kenny ain't fallen in the water. It was only after she had got Kenny out and gave him a good fucking whack around the earhole.

"You stupid little bastards, don't you realise what that is? It ain't water, its fucking acid, acid. Yes, you fucking idiots, acid, and that's a vat."

Fucking hell, acid, there'd have been nothing left on our bodies. The cockiness left us; we headed home, heads down, tails between our legs, this time for another right bollicking off from Mom. This time I got the whack around the earhole for leading Kenny into trouble. Fuck me, this was big shit, we didn't argue when Mom sent us to bed and wouldn't let us out for a couple of days. Then we'd be off again, things calmed down, the danger forgot.

Another source of great excitement was the canals or cuts. Birmingham was full of canals and a constant source of excitement, down the bottom of Thimblemill Road, was the gateway to the Birmingham and Fazely Canal leading to Cuckoo Wharf. The Birmingham and Warwick Canal and the Grand Union Canal branched off to lead all over the country; down by Cuckoo Bridge also ran "the runner". This was a deep culvert that took all the rainwater from all around Birmingham, the culverts were some 15-20 feet deep, and most days the water was just a trickle, but in a heavy storm, the water rose almost to the top of the wall. It was a frightening sight just to look at it roaring along, watching it would frighten the shit out of us. There was many a story of people being swept away and never being seen again. At the bottom of the runner it opened out to a big river, on the side was the lock keeper's house. We would watch him walking across the river and mudflats, collecting old bits of rubbish and stopping it from building up. We heard the bloke before him was doing the same when a storm built up. He got his waders stuck in the mud and couldn't get out. One story said he was sucked into the mud, another that he got swept away in the floods, either way, he was never seen again. We would sit there fascinated, watching the lock keeper for ages, waiting to see if he sank in the mud or was swept away.

Further along, the cut was the dark half-hour, so-called because it took so long to get from one end to the other. It was a rite of passage to do the run from one end to the other. The worst part was when you were halfway in between; if a flood built up, you were in deep shit, surely there would be no time to run and get out before being swept away. No one spoke, edging along shitting ourselves at every sound, if we heard a rumbling sound we'd stiffen up, pushing ourselves against the side walls, waiting for the inevitable. Still, it never came; we lived to fight another day. Each day was full of excitement.

Along Cuckoo Wharf were the barges, all tied up along the canal, mainly coal barges, some sunk and sitting on the bottom. In the summer we would take our clothes off and swim in the cut, it was filthy black and dirty green. But we didn't care; we'd dive in, hit the mud and come back up streaked with mud across our little bellies. The first time we did it, we soon learnt to dive in skimming the top just in case there were any broken bottles or dismantled bikes dumped in there. Keeping our mouths and noses shut just in case, we knew if we swallowed any of that shit we were done for, if we cut ourselves or landed on a sharp object that was it, we would be in the shit, the whole part of that canal was one big karzi.

We would then walk up the Walsall Canal from Cuckoo Bridge, passing through Witton then on to Perry Barr Park. To us city kids we were now in the country, green trees, open spaces and the park, then up past the locks at Perry Barr. We could feel the fresh air coursing through our lungs, we had the world at our feet, and all the time in the world, even the canals up here were cleaner and almost like a lake, just the odd dead dog or cat. We would take our clothes off and dive in for a swim; the canals were deeper here, not full of mud like down Nechells. After a swim we would go on the mooch, up and around the banks, looking into people's gardens. It seemed that every house along the canal had apple and fruit trees, the first time we'd fill our trousers and carry a few pounds in our open jumpers. Some gardens had raspberries, blackcurrants, after the first time we'd remember to take a bag so we could load ourselves up with fruit. Walking back home, weighed down and knackered we would be rewarded by Mom making a few apple and fruit pies. We'd gorge on them until our little bellies were choc-a-block, content and ready for bed.

Over on the Walsall Canal, we could see over to the Hampstead Colliery and watch the lifts going across the sky from one end of the colliery to the other. This seemed a really exciting experience to us, me, Kenny, David Parry, Jonny Beards and Turley. We decided to go down and have a mooch. At one end, they were loading these skips up with coal, off they'd go to be tipped onto mountains at the other end, sneaking through, three of us dived in one skip, three in the other, as we took off we popped our little heads up over the lip. As we climbed higher we could see for miles, into the back gardens, over to the canal we had just swum in, over to the end of the line where we were going, it was then that it fucking hit us, how the fuck do we get out? We thought we would just reach the tip of the slag heap at the other end and jump out, a couple of feet. Well, we jumped alright, but it was at least ten foot. We all started screaming and shouting. All of us shitting ourselves with fear, looking around there was no one to save us, no one to come to our rescue, we were in deep shit. I looked at Kenny and realised that we only had the one chance and that was to jump. I shouted the same to the others; three of us jumped and hit the side of the slag heap. There was no stopping us as we gambolled and slid nonstop to the bottom at 100 miles an hour. At the bottom, safe, we looked at each other with a sigh of relief, we were alive, looking up we could see Bee-Bee, Turley and Parry, ashen-faced, mouths open, screaming. "Fucking well jump," we waved our arms as it started to go round, if they didn't jump quickly it would start to tip if they got caught in the tip they would go down anyway with a ton of coal and slack on top of them. We started pointing to the ones in front that had already tipped. They started screaming again, this time they jumped, seconds before the skip tipped. Down they tumbled screaming their heads off, me, Kenny and Dukesy pissing ourselves laughing. When they got down, brushed the coal dust off and stopped shaking we all started to laugh and puff our chests out, full of bravado, we had done something no one else had done. We went back to the canal diving in with our clothes on to wash them, walking home as the sun-dried our clothes and no one was any the wiser.

Another time we were walking back along the locks from Perry Barr when we noticed the big mound spread over the land at the side of the canal. Climbing over the fence, we figured it was some kind of council tip and decided to explore it. Climbing up the sides, we saw it was quite steep, and when we reached the top, it flattened out and was as big as a football pitch. This was most interesting. We couldn't figure it out as we walked across the ground seemed to be a bit soft and moved under our feet, further and further, we walked across the centre when before we knew it the ground was even softer. Suddenly I came to a full stop, looked back at Kenny with a fear rising in my stomach, fucking hell, this is dangerous. Worse, I noticed steam or smoke coming out of cracks in the ground, fucking hell, the fear was getting worse now. It was our worst nightmare, something was burning underground, and one wrong move and we could be sucked in and down, burnt to bits and no one knowing about it. Worse, if Kenny went down, how could I tell Mom? I looked at Kenny, and he could see the total fear in my face and eyes. I said to him turn around and go back the way we've come stepping in the exact places coming over, he turned around. I followed, slowly, cacking ourselves with fear. Eventually, we got to the edge and climbed down to the canal where we stood shaking. Kenny looked at me, face blank, "What was all that about?" When I explained, I saw the fear and relief rise in his eyes. We never went over on that trip again and made sure none of our mates did. In truth, I think we were the only ones fucking stupid enough to do it in the first place. Some things are just too dangerous.

Jacky Waldron had decided that we should all go down to the mines where the coal was being brought over Hampstead Colliery. We arranged to meet up the next day: me Jack, Eddie Ginger Dukes, and a couple of others. I couldn't make it, they didn't give a shit and set off without me, getting on the bogies stacked with coal going down from the mine entrance there were only a few inches above their heads. One young lad, Ernie not realising, raised his head only to hit a steel girder in the roof. It split his scalp straight off, tore him backwards, breaking his legs, hips, and Lord knows what else. Jacky was the hero of the day; he managed to drag Ernie out of the mine into the daylight. He was taken to hospital where he stayed for months. Jacky had a big picture taken of him sitting on his bike leaning on the lamppost in his courtyard. Yes, Jacky was the hero of the day, worshipped by us all, he was my hero, and I was dead jealous. Ernie's parents weren't so forgiving and blamed Jack for putting their son in a wheelchair. He was in that wheelchair for life. I never mentioned it to my mom.

Keeping your trap shut and not being a grass was buried deep within us. One day Kenny was walking along Cromwell Street when a lorry mounted the kerb knocking Kenny off his bike and crushing his hand. All hell let loose with Mom and Dad rushing out and up to Cromwell Street. The driver was drunk and was very apologetic and terrified of losing his job, Dad told him to piss off and sent Reg up later to smack the bloke. This was ok I suppose, but it didn't seem right to me, the bloke kept his job, but Kenny's hand was smashed to bits, I thought the bloke should have got nicked, but if Dad said that's it then that's it. Dad's explanation was, what's to gain? Ok, squeal on the bloke, the bloke gets sacked; Kenny didn't get his hand back. No winners, all round, seemed logic.

Kenny certainly had his run of bad luck, one night we were just climbing over the wall of the back-to-backs down Schofield Street. Off he falls, leg broken, in plaster for two months, as soon as he gets better he falls off another wall and breaks his arm, another two months in plaster, another two months off school. Even on a nice quiet day out in Sutton, Kenny would get hurt. We were climbing from tree to tree, air raid helmets on our heads when Kenny fell, easily 20 feet, head first, landing on his bonce in the stream below. We shat ourselves. As I looked down, I saw him straight upright like a rigid arrow in the ground, fuck me, he couldn't have survived. We dashed down to him, holding our breath, by now he had stood up in the water, dazed and shaking his head. We looked in astonishment and disbelief, fuck me, he was all right, the little fucker was like a cat with nine lives.

I swear there was never a day went by when there wasn't a nugget of excitement going on every day around Nechells. There was the penny-winkle man that came down the Green selling his penny-winkles for sixpence a pint pot, delicious; Mom would give us a tanner each. We'd spend a few hours picking the winkles out and eating them, just like big bogies.

Also, there would be the flower sellers – "Buy a bunch of daffs, two pence a bunch."

Then there were the medicine men, selling their wares and cures – "Roll up ladies, roll up, back pains, rheumatoid aching knees and joints!! I have the elixir that will cure them all." He'd hold up his bottle and shake it with a wave of mysticism and conspiracy; a brown liquid that would cure all ailments. He sold loads of bottles, and we would listen to him for hours, fascinated.

Our older brother Billy would be round on his scrap wagon – "Any iron, any iron", shouting at the top of his voice. Another day it would be any rags, any rags, all collected in exchange for a coloured chick, a goldfish or a budgie. My old dad would buy the budgies by the hundred. Our front room was filled with cages from floor to ceiling with budgies. Until one day, Kenny and I were alone in the house and decided to have some fun with the budgies. Fetching a couple of pillows down from the bedroom we let the budgies out, one cage at a time, swiping them as they flew around, seeing who could hit the most. Soon, most of the cages had been opened, and most of the budgies were lying all over the place. It took us a bit of time to realise that most of 'em, weren't just lying there exhausted but were dead with broken necks before the reality hit us and we were in deep trouble. We put most of them back in the cages and pretended that nothing had happened when Mom and Dad came home. We never thought or had the brains to realise that we had forgotten the feathers from the pillows, they got mixed up with the budgies' feathers, but Mom and Dad clocked it ok. I blamed Kenny; it was all his fault. Mom chose to believe Kenny, the little runt, she always believed him, I got my arse smacked again, Dad never got any more budgies.

Old Bill

By now, Dad was a fully-fledged general dealer, buying and selling anything to make a living. Our front room was his shop, full of toys and fancy goods; Christmas would see the room full up, chock-a-block with toys and fancy goods, electric fires and sweets, if it made a profit Dad would buy it. On a Saturday, various people would call around; either giving orders or picking up stock. Among these was Joey Wragg, Joe was a nice bloke who had a shop up Park Road Aston opposite HP Sauce. Now I quickly caught on to what Joe was up to, he had his regular job delivering bread and cakes to the local shops, his missus ran the shop daily. Joe had it sussed at work, so his last pick up on the van was for himself. The first delivery would be to his shop with a few trays of bread and cakes, all buckshee, before carrying on with his normal deliveries. He would call around to our house down Rocky Lane to buy some more stock from the old man. A few shirts, some teddy bears, toys, etc., walking into Joe's shop I would see all my old man's stock amongst Joe's cakes and other stuff, the customers were always calling in to get a bargain. It was a proper Aladdin's cave. Joe showed me one day the nice detached house him and his missus had bought over Great Barr, I was well impressed. Still, I couldn't help but wonder why he was buying such a nice house, yet my old man and Billy, who made far more money lived in a shit hole council house in a shit hole area.

The problem was Billy, and the old man thought it was stupid to rock the boat. Yes, the old man was earning a great deal of money, blimey, when the average wage was ten pounds a week. He was spending that on a good afternoon in the pub, course, anyone who brought a house and lumbered themselves with a mortgage were mugs. In one respect, they were right. In reality, they were the fools themselves. Times change, circumstances alter. During those times people struggled year in year out to pay their mortgage on a house that hardly rose in value.

What none of us also realised was the cops were watching us and putting two and two together, then coming up with nine, because my brothers mixed with villains, and Johnny was joined at the hip with Ray Kirby. The cops must have had this thought that our house was an Aladdin's cave full of nicked gear. I think even the neighbours must have had their thoughts. This came home to me one day when I picked a nice compact up out of Dad's shop and took it round to Patty Morgan, who lived in Schofield Street with her sister Christine and her mom and dad. Patty was a few years older than me, but I was quite infatuated. Patty took it off me with quite good grace and a smile, but within two hours, her old man was round the house like a shot. He must have thought the compact was nicked. That was the problem and if the old man did get nicked, then Old Bill knew he would never have had a leg to stand on. He had no shop because he wasn't allowed to run a business in a council house. Worse, he was not at work or registered for work - he was fucked all ways. All Old Bill had to do was embellish it a bit. And they did. I was yet to find all this out.

Joe was also very shrewd I'd noticed he'd got a few days growth on his face.

"I've had the taxman call round the shop questioning the takings and demanding to see the books." With an air of boisterousness and defiance, he said, "Well I've told 'em, I ain't taking a fucking bean in the shop." I don't know why I bother letting my wife run it, it's that bad I'm having to go out to work, working my bollocks off just to make a living. He got away with it as well, crafty bleeder was making a right few quid, buying a big house as well, I'll have to remember that little trick, don't visit the taxman in a nice suit and looking prosperous.

Georgey Stevens was another character who called every Saturday morning. George was a nice guy who also lived over Great Barr. George would come in; pay the old man for the stock he had had the week before and pick up his new supply. George worked in the factory for the Rover Car Company. He had built up a nice little clientele supplying goodies and taking orders from the workforce. Reg Chance was another pal of the old man's who lived over Castle Bromwich. Now I always thought Reg was a bit of a snide, I always thought he felt he was a bit of a cut above everyone else as well, he always spoke in a quiet, almost laboured whisper, " Well, Jack, what have we got this week then?" Now Reg liked his snuff. He would walk around with his light brown expensive Crombie overcoat with its black velvet collar, shoulders hunched over. Now and again he'd pull his little snuff box out, take a dip, put a pinch on the back of his hand and take a good sniff. First the right nostril, then the left, then holding first one side and the other he would take a good snuffle, sucking up every last morsel of the powder, then pulling out his hanky, stained with the brown shit and take a good blow, clearing out whatever was up there, the dirty bastard. One day I turned around to the old man and told him, "I think he's robbing you." Typically the old man gave me one of his crafty little smiles, I don't care, if they all nick ten percent off me they think they're making more, but they're making me money as well. We had people coming from all over different parts of the city, most would call on a Saturday morning, look at what stock Dad had got, strike a deal and buy a few items to sell again or just one item for themselves, people knew when they came to our house, they would get a bargain, want a watch? Thirty bob, in the shops it was two pounds ten shillings. Dad was happy with just a little bit, better a little bit than nothing at all. That's why our front room was always full.

That was typical of the old man, he wasn't a crook, he just wanted to lead a happy life with his mates drinking the days and nights away, making a nice living that enabled him to do that with little effort. Where he was quiet and shy, he was a complete opposite to Mom, who was loud and prepared to speak her mind. But he was selfish when it came to our mom and us kids, he would never worry about us, or what clothes we wore, we walked about with our arses hanging out, not a pair of underpants to our name. He would have plenty to buy a drink all night long for him and his mates. If Mom wanted to have a drink, she had to make her own money. This she did by sitting in the Little Brit or the Beehive with her dolly (laundry) basket, full of little toys, sweets and fancy goods, she would sit there in her seat, "Don't sit there, that's Alma's seat," drinking her half of ale, selling the odd toy during the day or night.

Mom was desperate to be respectable and have a shop, there was a hardware shop up Nechells Park Road that Mom was desperate to have, "Come on Jack, buy the shop, we can make a go of it." The old man was having none of it, he's got a good thing going, our front room was a shop, he had no hassle from the taxman, why should he spoil a good thing, it didn't make sense. Then she'd try to work on Billy. Billy was also making a nice few quid, but there was no way he was going to risk his money in an unknown venture, sadly, the old lady had no choice but to carry on selling from her little basket and drinking her pale ales. I couldn't understand it either, why were we living like this when we were earning so much money? Why couldn't we have a nice shop like Joey Wragg and be respectable?

To me, it all seemed to be straightforward and a choice between two options, you could either be a bit bent and make a nice living or work your balls off, beating yourself into the ground on a building site or the factory. I had enough mates to see how they lived. I didn't like what I saw, some lived with orange boxes for chairs, others were skin and bones, going without food, many having vitamin-filled orange on prescription, most living in shitholes without a fire. I thought we struggled, but that was because of the old man spending his money on booze, we still ate well with good healthy food. I considered ourselves rich in comparison, most of our neighbours thought so too. It didn't take a lot of brains. I never considered my dad a crook, to me he was a businessman, a businessman who had the sense to see the pitfalls of taking on the costly burden of a shop and all the risks it entailed.

Dad was savvy enough to see where a deal could be made, how much to pay for something and how much profit could be made. If someone came up to him with a bundle of shirts, or a few suits and asked if he wanted to buy them, he didn't ask where they came from, his main and only concern was can he buy them at the right price, could he find a buyer and how much could he get for the item, or items. Anyone who didn't do the same is telling lies. You don't turn around to someone who is offering you something and say, "Is this stolen?" Course you don't, it's cheap; it's a bargain, that's it. One day, Dougie Hardiman bought some bloke over the house; he had some stuff to sell and wanted to buy some shoes that the old man was selling. The next night the coppers were banging the door at one o'clock in the morning, seems this little toerag had got nicked with a bundle of cash on him, squealed that the old man had given it to him for some goods that he had nicked a few days earlier. Well, the cops found no goods in our house; the old man denied buying bent stuff, said he'd bought some shirts off him and sold him some boots. Somehow, the cops found some evidence and Dad got done and was sent down. It was the first time I had seen Pip the Planter and heard about fitting up. More about this fitting up later.

Many of my dad's and brothers' friends were ex-army soldiers, they had done their conscription service in the army and come out to what they were led to believe was a country fit for heroes. That quickly turned out to be a load of bollocks; the country was in the depths of depression with misery, hardship and starvation all around. People were trying to keep warm or feed themselves any way they could, it was only as my older brothers and sisters left home that we had managed to have blankets on our beds. When I was younger, I can remember my dad's army coat being thrown on us to keep us warm. Me, Patty and Kenny sharing the bed, and still we were fucking freezing, windows rattling, ice on the insides, no wonder I almost kicked it with pneumonia.

To me, these were not bad or evil people, they were loyal to their friends, and had strict principles, not for them robbing defenceless old people or poor people from poor backgrounds. Anyone who stole from a church or the elderly was looked on with contempt, as were pickpockets or shoplifters. Each would have their team and would find their resources or tickles, if anyone came across a tickle that they couldn't do, they would pass it on to another team who might consider it of interest, sometimes, it might not be their bag, some didn't like factory breaking, safe breaking or breaking into shops. My older brother Johnny worked with Ray and Tubby Kirby, and then there would be others like George Crow or Billy Henry, big Jock. If one came across a little tickle, he would approach one of the others and see if they were interested. Sometimes one or a few of them would get nicked and have to take a bit of porridge if they got a six or twelve-month sentence it was considered a price worth paying.

As it happens, a bit of porridge was not that much harder than being outside, once in, those on the outside would do their bit by bunging the wives a few quid. To me, I had my doubts, but I admired and respected these people anyway. Johnny and the Kirbys had been friends for years, went to school with each other down Summer Lane, their dad had been British flyweight champion, Bert Kirby, from sparring and training together my dad and Bert had been friends ever since. To me, the Kirbys were loyal and sound people, yet they had a notorious reputation. Although not one of them was over or bigger than 5ft 6; this mainly stemmed from the sheer size and number of them. It seemed to me that there was a Kirby on every street in Birmingham, if there wasn't a Kirby there were offshoots, of relatives, the family was that fucking big they didn't know each other half the time, but you could always tell a Kirby by their distinct square heads and tipped up nose.

It was common knowledge that old Bert would go into a fight with a mob of his brothers in the crowd geeing him on, as his opponent came out they would surround him and threaten to break his fucking legs if he won, few won. This method of sticking together spread to all the other Kirbys, so whenever there was trouble, they would all go steaming in.

Mainly they were robbing shops and factories, loading up with stock hauling it away, then flogging it on, when they had a nice tickle it would be drinks all around for a few days. When Ray and Johnny discovered gelignite, we were getting gangs from London popping up overnight. They started on the safe breaking, with factories the main target hitting the safes with the payrolls in. Quite often, a safe would be unloaded and the door blown off, one day Johnny handed me some dark brown soft, gooey stuff and told me to go and wash it down the toilet. When I asked what it was, I was told, gelignite. One night, an argument had gone off in one of the nightclubs up

Soho Road. Someone got offended, and a few nights later someone put a bomb against the nightclub door, it hit all the headlines in the mail. The message was made.

In their expensive suits, they all looked the business, Johnny always wearing a nice smart black blazer and slacks. Sometimes, they would be having a tot in one of the boozers when a local shopkeeper or factory owner would come over and see if there was a deal to be had. It was a nice happy little circle with everyone benefitting, sometimes the shopkeeper would buy a load of stock at a knockdown price for his shop, it might be shirts, suits, shoes or games, if it were booze, it would go to one of the clubs or boozers. Sometimes a shopkeeper or factory owner would sidle over and ask if one of them would be interested in turning his place over. It was all described and made very easy for them, so simple it was like taking candy from a child. The deal would be that the team could help themselves to whatever they wanted.in the shop or factory, the owner would make a claim on the insurance for treble the amount, get a nice pay out, even giving the lads a bung as well. This enabled the owner to build up his stock, put himself in the black and put a few quid in his pocket as well, why, I knew of one factory owner up Summer Lane, who had a fire every few years, each time, the stock got a bit bigger. The owners upgraded their cars; soon there were nice e type Jags and Mercedes on the forecourt, great big signs all over the place, no smoking, please.

My uncle Jimmy (Pussyfoot) Littleford was another sharp, but deceptive character, he was nicknamed Pussyfoot because everyone thought he pussyfooted around, but in reality, he was a right shrewd bleeder, who looked like a little gnome, short, chubby face and a Buddha's belly. One time he got a flat directly opposite the dog track in Perry Barr. He made up a roulette wheel mounted on a table with pram wheels. On the side of the roulette wheel, he had a button fixed in so he could slow or stop the wheel at will. On race nights he'd head across the road to the dog track car park and set up his wheel, he had a couple of lookouts with him who also acted as decoys playing the wheel to bring the punters in. Slowly, one by one the incoming crowd would start sidling over, seeing the decoys winning a few quid they would start to place a few bets themselves. Pussyfoot would let them win a few quid until the crowd had built up with everyone fighting to place a bet, then Pussyfoot would let out his little belly, slowing the wheel and stopping it where he wanted. No one sussed it, and his only worry was the Old Bill coming over, the decoys would be on the ball, give him the nod, and as quick, as he had got there, he was gone, back over to his flat. No one any the wiser and a good few quid made. Pussyfoot had little scams like that coming out of his ears and would spend days looking or trying to figure out another scam.

.

Weekend Entertainment

Saturday nights were another source of excitement around Nechells, this was when everybody came out to play and have a drink. The working pecks who had toiled in the factories or on the building sites, put on their best suits, many having just been redeemed from the pawnbrokers for the weekend, the young studs up into town, starting off with a couple of halves in the Beehive, or the Brit. A steady pub-crawl up into town and Yates' Wine Lodge, Saturday night was when the married men would take their wives out, they'd gently stroll down the Beehive or one of their favourite corner pubs and settle themselves in for a good old night ending with a singsong, it was the same songs every weekend. Hardly anyone ever finished a song off before starting another one.

Roll out the barrel; we'll have a barrel of fun,
roll out the barrel we've got the blues on the run
zing boom tararrel, ring out a song of good cheer
now's the time to roll out the barrel for the gangs all here.

Chorus repeat,

Chorus repeat

Da-da-da-da,da-da-da-da
da-da-da-da,da-da-da-da.

we'll meet again, don't know where don't know when
but I know we'll meet again some sunny day.
Keep smiling through just like you always do

until the blue skies drive the dark clouds away
so, will you please say hello to the folks that I know
tell them I won't be long
they'll be happy to know that as you saw me go
I was singing this song.
we'll meet again, don't know where, don't know when
but I know we'll meet again some sunny day.

During the early part of the night, old Maggie would be standing outside the Beehive, waiting for a punter to turn up. "Give us a half-crown, Joe, and I'll give you a fuck." Eventually, somebody would give her a tanner for her first half, she'd take them round to the pub toilets, give them a quickie and would return and into the boozer, she'd go, sinking her first half. We'd see her come out four or five times and take a bloke round to the bogs before disappearing back into the pub, at closing time, she'd stagger out off home, it was a wonder her poor little legs could carry her.

I felt sorry for her son who was one of my best mates, he only lived up the road and had to see his mom performing like this every night. Jesus, I was lucky, at the end of the night the fun would start, the pubs closed at ten with a strict ten-minute drinking up time, ten minutes to ten everyone would start queuing up to double up on the pints. My old man only drank halves so he would end up with six or eight halves in front of him, he drank halves because as he said a gentleman don't drink pints, only labourers drank pints, that was it then, I knew my old dad was a businessman, he was also a gentle-man, quite.

At ten o'clock the heavy drinking would start with everyone downing their booze before kick-out time, by the time people started walking out there a steady and staggered walking back to the drums, most times there would be a fight of some kind, Kenny and I would watch with excitement and anticipation.

Smack!! "Don't talk to me like that!" With the booze in them, it was normally over with one punch.

Then there were the parties, Stanley Wooten and his clan would have a party every Friday or Saturday night. They'd either stock up beforehand or blag the landlord to sell them a crate or two if it were a spur of the moment knees up, the Wootens were like family to us as Sylvia was Patty's best mate, so we could just wander in at ease. One night they'd got a crowd in, Stanley, his wife Beryl, Tommy Hewston and his missus Sheila, Stan's sister, some of the Turners, who were cousins, big Eddy, and the Bellaby's, John and George. Now John and George were twins and looked like a couple of little monkeys. Their young brother Malcolm was also my best mate, and he looked like a monkey as well come to think of it, most of the Bellaby's looked like monkeys, but they were great people, good fun, loyal and funny too. The party got off to a good start, and everyone was having a good time, lots of talking merrily by all, plenty of singing "Roll out the barrel." Everybody sang that song, being younger, some of them would start singing rock-around-the-clock, old girl Peg would duck off to bed, taking her two dogs with her. After the party had been going full swing for a couple of hours a knock came on the door, it took a few minutes for it to sink in before I shouted to Stan that there was someone at the door, to the door Stan goes, and there's a bloke there.

"I've come to join the party," he says in an Irish accent.

Well, Stan turns around before realising that nobody knows who the bloke is. "Fuck off," says Stan.

Well, the bloke's a bit persistent and insists on walking in and joining the party. Stan pushes the bloke out onto the pavement and into the road where he puts one on the bloke's chin. The bloke goes down on the ground, and Stan walks back into the house. Two minutes later, the door goes again.

"I'm the yank, and I want to come to the party."

This time Tommy Hewston pushes the bloke out, onto the pavement and the road, puts one on his chin and down he goes again. By now, Kenny and I are out in the street full of anticipation relishing what was going on. As Tommy walks away, the yank gets up again. Jesus, this bloke is hard. Now the Bellerbys join in; George first punching the bloke, then John. Still, the yank gets up; bloody hell, this bloke is hard.

"I'm the yank," he says again. "No one can beat me or put me down."

I was beginning to think he was right; he'd been hit four or five times, and each time he still got up. I thought this yank's dangerous. Who's the yank? I'd never heard of him before. Tommy comes over again and gives him another right-hander; eventually, I think he got the message; he wasn't going to get into the party.

He stumbled off, shouting, "I'm the yank, no one could beat me, no one can put me down."

Well, he was right, no one could put him down, but off he went. The party started to slow down after that and people started going off home. A good night was had by all and the Bellerbys? Well, I was well impressed, small they may be, but they had a knock and against a bloke much bigger than them. And the yank? Fair play, he kept getting back up.

Most people, after the boozers had closed, would go straight home and tuck themselves in for the night. For us, young as we were, the weekend heralded only fun and excitement. If there wasn't a party on at ours, it was someone else's. When we had one, it was always a crowded affair, Mom had a piano in the back room, especially for such nights. Jacky Willis had a shop up Railway Terrace selling pets and pet food and was a professional on the piano. He wouldn't be in five minutes before Mom had him up on the piano.

"Do us a plate of stew, first Alma, I'm starving."

Mom would dish the stew out, and everyone would get stuck in. I swear, Mom's stews were famous, and she always had a large pot on the stove. Jack would then start on the piano, Billy Henry would get his spoons out and start rattling them off on his legs and arms in tune to the piano, I guessed that playing the spoons was a cost-free way of entertaining yourself in the nick. Timmy Marnie and his brothers would join in, Big Jock and broken nose George Crow would be looking on, I don't think he could sing too well because he was a bit punchy. Dennis Woodhall, Raymond, Jonny-Ragpot and Tubby Kirby would be standing there in their tailor-made suits, all enjoying themselves at the moment, together with my brothers Raggy-Reg, Jonny and Billy, and their wives, Jimmy Moore, the flower seller and his wife, June and the singing would start.

See the palm trees swayin' way down Summer Lane
Ev'ry night there's a jubilation, you c'n hear 'em singin in the 'Salutation'
There ain't no snow on Snow Hill, no need to catch a train;
To a sunnier clime, where the weather's fine,
'cus it's summer in Summer Lane.

As the booze flowed, some would forget the words, sing a few verses, then start again on the same song, trying hard to keep the rhythm Mom would get on to egging up June Moore to sing. Now June was noted for having the best singing voice in Birmingham and was always in demand to sing a song or two, after a lot of persuading. But not too much, June would take a deep breath, a little self-satisfied smirk on her face, waiting until everyone had quietened down properly, paying due respect to her efforts. When everyone was duly quiet, the atmosphere built up, she'd then start, the first line drawn out slowly, for everyone to appreciate when I was a millionaire! I didn't have a care, and on she went.

Well, Kenny and I soon caught on to the fact that perhaps June - bless her heart - wasn't as good as they all thought, maybe it was the booze, but she always sang the same song, it, and her singing it was in hot demand.

Kenny and I worked hard to learn the words to a couple of songs, the first one was,

> Dennis, the menace, he's a <u>bundle</u> of dynamite
> Oh, the <u>things</u> he says and the <u>things</u> he does
> ·Will make you <u>shake</u> with fright
> (Beware of) Dennis-the menace

We'd learnt it at the Saturday matinee, and the first party after, making sure everyone was well pissed we asked if we could do a song, well that was it, big Jock put us on the table. Everyone looked with due attention, the old lady gave a big smile, the old man pushed his belly out with pride, off we went, "Dennis, the menace, was a bundle of dynamite." We couldn't remember all the words. Still, no one noticed, when we finished, everybody dived their hands into their pockets and brought out all their spare change; there was loads of it. They didn't bother to check or count it out, a cap was bought out quick, and it was soon filled with silver threepenny bits, crowns, two bobs and coppers, Kenny and I shot off to bed, vowing to learn a new song every week, we were rich.

Sad Characters

Old Albert was a nice old bloke; he'd served in the Second World War and lived through the first one. He lived between the Beehive and Brett Ford's, the paint shop. During the day, I would see him walking around doing his shopping. Sometimes he'd be seen sitting on the bench opposite his house, others he'd be standing on his doorstep, looking up and down the road, watching life go by, always dressed the same in a shabby suit and tie and a flat cap peaky blinder on his head. Many times, I would talk to Albert, and he would tell me about his life in the army, the suffering he had endured, the fighting and the Germans he had killed. "I've killed a few, son, killed a few."

I never tired of listening to his stories and his accounts of the war, I never asked if he had a wife if he did, I never saw her, he never seemed to smile, night two coppers walked up the Green from Bloomsbury Street nick.

Old Albert started shouting at them. "Got nothing to do?"

The coppers looked at each other and smirked, this was like a red rag to a bull to old Albert.

"That's it, you no good buggers, idle that's what you are, got nothing better to do than walk around doing nothing."

Still, the cops did nothing, infuriating Albert even more, I reckoned he didn't like authority from his time in the army, suddenly he ran back into his house and came back out with a house brick, running into the road he shouted at the coppers, "Here you are you idle buggers." With that, he threw the brick into the clothes shop by his house, glass splintering all over the place.

The cops walked over and casually grabbed him by both arms. "Come on, Albert, down to the nick." Off he walked, both arms held out. The cops led him away down Bloomsbury Street to the nick, this shocked me a little bit, and I was saddened to see the old boy being led away. I saw him again a couple of days later, but he shuffled away inside his house, giving me a half-hearted wave as he looked down at his feet. It was the last time I spoke to Albert, thinking it was better to keep out of his way for a bit.

Billy Clark lived in a two-up, one-down up the yard where my mate Jacky Waldren lived. Sometimes I would go into his house, and his mom would be sitting on the chair, worn out, wearing old rags and looking knackered. His old man would be at the table, sifting through hundreds of nubs, breaking the paper and turning the tobacco onto the table, he'd mix all the tobacco together and place it in his tin as I looked on in fascination. I'd see him walking around Nechells pushing a pram. When he walked, he always walked at a slow pace, eyes searching slowly back and forth if he saw a nub he would dive down quick as a flash, pick it up and examine it before putting it in his pocket, I never saw him throw one back down. On he would carry always searching, picking up pieces of coal dropped by the coal lorries and put them in his pram, he spent all day like this, street to street, all around Nechells, eventually finding enough to keep his fire going at night, I never spoke about it to Billy. He never said anything to me; actually, he never really said a lot at all, always with a vacant look on his face and his mouth half-open. I didn't spend a lot of time with Billy, but it made me dead grateful I had a mom and dad who could earn a living and not be like that. Lots of strange things went on in different streets, you learnt to keep your gob shut, see all, hear all, say nothing. My mate Robert Watts lived by the El Greco in Bloomsbury Street, a well-built lad, a bit eccentric and missing a bit in the brain department. Maybe it was because of his lack of education that he developed the eccentric side. Maybe he just liked a bit of attention, to be liked. At any rate, he always had something to make him the centre of attention. One time he'd got himself a little blackbird that sat on his shoulder, he must have spent some time training it because he loved nothing more than to walk around the Green with the bird on his shoulder, head swivelling left to right, Rob would bring little nibbles out of his pocket feeding his little pal. He didn't worry about the shit dropping on his shoulder, and no one passed any comment, Rob loved the attention.

Another time he had a little white mouse that sat in his topcoat pocket. If there was an audience, which was most of the time around the Green, Rob would feed the mouse little nibbles of cheese before gently poking his head down into his pocket before walking off. How he got the shit out of his pocket, I don't know. One day I caught Rob hobbling around the Green with shoes on but no socks. What's up, Rob? Rob takes his left shoe off to show me proudly a gaping hole in his foot, measuring about half an inch in diameter. A clean, fucking hole straight through. I jumped back in horror.

Looking at Rob, I saw a shadow of a smile. He was dead proud of it. Oh, I got it on the coal the other day, put a pitchfork straight through it, I was fucking horrified and couldn't believe what I saw, Rob didn't have a care in the world. Rob, you need to get that seen to. You'll get gangrene. By then I'd got to know a bit about the perils of gangrene. Rob was just oblivious to any danger. I saw him a few days later, and he's got a bandage around it, but the green was starting to show. A few months later I saw Rob with a crutch hobbling along as usual. This time without a foot, oh they've amputated it. Giving a slight shrug of his shoulder. Beneath all the bravado I could see Rob was looking a bit concerned with a sense of fear penetrating his brain. Oh, the hospital said by taking the foot of it might save the leg. Eventually, Rob had to have his leg off, a few years later Rob had both legs off. He would end up being pushed around in a wheelchair down to the local pub where he would sit on his arse all night before dying, a sad look in his face as he slowly realised the predicament he had put himself in, a fucking shame.

Mom and Dad

Normally money for the matinee would have to be earned fetching the coal for Mom. This was something Kenny and I hated and would always try to get out of it.

"No, I ain't giving you a tanner until you fetch some coal."

Off, we'd go round to Thimble Mill Lane to Powell's Coal Yard, now Powell's Yard was next to my mate Dave Parry's house. It wasn't too far to walk, but it was the barrers that you had to push back. Powell's barrers were little square solid wood boxes blackened with all the coal, sat on little cast metal wheels. Old man Powell would be loading the barrers from different piles,, and we'd go in, order our coal, we would have to pay for the coal and a deposit to bring the barrers back. I would push the barrer and Kenny would pull from the front, it would break our backs pushing and shoving, the cast wheels trundling along the road making such a racket you couldn't hear anything else in the world. You never spoke cause you couldn't hear each other, we'd just give the odd shout to each other, "pull you, little git, pull." The little git would shout back, "you bloody well push you, idle bleeder," even shouting was hard work so we would just knuckle down trying our hardest to outwit each other. It was bloody murder, and it was a welcome sight when we finally got to the front door and tipped it in the coal cellar, after a rest, we'd trundle it back, or more like I would, cause Kenny would collapse on the floor, "I've hurt my stomach," the little git.

Sometimes, Mom would decide to have coke. We'd have to push a pram down to Saltley Gas Works to fetch it. The coke wasn't so heavy and going downhill was the easy part, all we could think about was getting our tanner and in the excitement never thought about the haul back. It was only when the pram was full, and we got outside the coke yard that the size of the hill in front hit us, now it wasn't a hill but a bloody mountain. As that we didn't have to take the pram back. Within an hour, the pain was gone, and we were off to the flicks, a tanner in our pockets and another world waiting.

Mom's routine was set out; she'd get up in the morning and make the fire up, tidy the house up a bit then get Kenny and me up for school. The only problem was we didn't want to get up, we were comfortable in our pits, and school wasn't something we looked forward to. Under force, we'd pull our kegs on, run downstairs, have a quick swill under the cold sink then run out. We never had anything to eat, relying on our school dinners to fill us up. Mom would go out and do her shopping for the evening dinner, or stew, then she'd take her basket, full of toys or sweets, down to the Beehive, drinking a half of mild and selling her goodies, Mondays were usually washday. She'd be in the brewhouse, stoking the fire up before filling the tub with water. She'd carry the washing up the garden, get the dolly going, shoving it around the tub, pushing and pounding until all the dirt was out before taking it out and putting it through the mangle.

Some of the neighbours would polish their front steps with cardinal, but Mom never bothered. Some of the neighbours would put their rugs out on Monday morning to air, hanging them out the front bedroom windows for all the neighbours to see, Mom despised them, calling them two-penny-halfpennies, they only put them out to show they've got a carpet she'd say. Mom would make her own, buying a sheet of Hessian. With Patty, she'd cut up old coats into strips and thread them through the Hessian. They would spend night after night doing this until they had a nice big comfy rug about three feet wide by six-foot-long. I always hoped we'd get one on our bedroom floor to take the chill of the cold floorboards, but we never did.

One day, my mate Dave Burton, who lived next door, invited me around to dinner after school. Well, I say mate, but Dave wasn't a mate, he was just a next-door neighbour, and I was a bit surprised to be invited, but I looked forward to a good nosh up. School finished, Dave met me at the gate, and off we walked, down Rocky Lane, past our house into his next door. Their living room was much like ours, but much warmer and cosy, the table was laid out in front of the window and on the table were plates of sandwiches. I was dead impressed with how posh it all looked and stood with my eyes bulging, twiddling my fingers behind my back.

Mrs Burton said, "Hello Tommy, help yourself to a sandwich then." Well, I was wondering where the dinner was, perhaps this is only the starter? I grabbed the plate handed to me and started eating one of the sandwiches. I like jam, but I couldn't eat them, they were disgusting and sickly. I tried to ask Mrs Burton as politely as possible what was on the sandwiches. "Just butter and jam, Tommy," well it was making me feel sick, I liked my jam straight on the bread, not with thick butter on it, I tried to force the sandwiches down my throat waiting for the "dinner" to arrive, it didn't, and the sandwiches were the dinner. Dave turned to his mom and asked to use the "toilet". Toilet, it was the karzi, bloody hell, toilet, they were posh.

As soon as I could, I made my thanks for inviting me and walked back next door. "Mom, Mom, give me summat to eat, I'm starving.

"Starving? I thought you'd been next door for dinner?"

When I explained, Mom got a bowl out and filled it up with stew, handing me a chunk of bread. She said, "Here, have summat proper."

Dave never invited me again, and I never went around his house again, I could never figure out why he invited me to dinner if it were to impress me; it didn't work. We were rough and ready in our house, but we ate proper food. Mom would go up to Lewis' on a Monday or Saturday and buy a turkey frame. In the deli, shop workers would be cutting meat off the frame and selling the slices. Once the meat was cut off, the frame would go behind the counter, and Mom would buy it for a shilling. Once she was home, she'd cut a few more slices of to make a few more sandwiches before putting the frame in the pot to make a stew.

If we didn't have stew, it might be pig's trotters, which were delicious with vinegar and a drop of salt and a chunk of bread. Another day it was chicken's or a sheepshead, sometimes Mom would buy a few slices of cows udder, cooked in milk and served with bread, good basic food that filled us up, that's all that mattered. We were lucky, I had a lot of friends who had very little to eat, some were thin and scrawny and always starving. It was a fact that there were very few fat kids around Nechells. Come to think about it, I didn't know any fat kids. You never saw a fat kid around Nechells. Well, I never saw a fat kid in Brum.

FUCK 'EM ALL. I sometimes think that it was my mom's favourite saying.

"Mom, the teacher says I need some new shoes?"

"Did he now?" Down she'd look at my feet. "No, you don't, fuck him."

"Mom, Trevor's dad says can he have his ten bob back that he paid for that dog the other day?"

"He says it's died."

"Died, died! He's had it four fucking days; no he can't have his money back, fuck him." Mom could be quite harsh, savage with her tongue. Maybe it was the upbringing she had had, maybe the hardship. Her mom Annie Louise Milne had been a beautiful woman, yet she died at a very young age. Her husband Fred had done a runner; no one knew where no one had heard from him or where he had disappeared to. Annie's dad was a horse soldier, served 22 years before retiring. Fred was a joiner, carpenter, as was his dad also named Fred, all the Hipkisses passed the names down through the generations. Freddy named his eldest son Freddy, went back generations, great-great-granddad Freddy's mom was a schoolteacher whose dad was the famous painter Henry Lark Pratt from Derby. His painting hangs today in Chatsworth house, maybe she had married beneath herself when she married a Hipkiss, these things happen all the time. Certainly, my mom's pride and arrogance came from somewhere. She wouldn't take shit from anyone if anyone around Nechells wasn't afraid; they did their best to avoid a tongue-lashing from her. God help anyone that picked on one of her kids, don't you pick on my boys. It was a no brainer. Fuck em all.

As a parent, you do your best for your kids within your capabilities, my mom and dad felt that education wasn't all that important. If you had an ability, you could make your way in the world. To all those who would criticise I would say, stand back, look at yourselves, let he who is without sin cast the first stone, people who live in glass houses shouldn't throw stones. In many ways, my dad was right. That's why I will never knock him or his memory. The only thing he never allowed for was the majority of us kids at school were taught zilch.

Given different personalities, we could have been different. As it was, with a bit of help, we were allowed to grow wild. Each day we sought to find different avenues of excitement, not for us the boring and mundane routine of, getting up, having breakfast, going to school, coming back without homework, then off to bed at 9 pm like most kids. Jesus, what a miserable existence, how could they live like that? Fuck it, fuck em all; I would watch the dads coming back from work, knackered after a hard day in the factory, or on the building site, worn out before they were 40. My old man had a smile on his face every day. By 12 he was in the boozer, earning his money as he supped a half, he had packed up the barrers by now, becoming a general dealer. Summer, it would be toys, fancy goods, shirts and winter, it would be toys, fancy goods, electric fires and woolly jumpers. Mom would be up and ready to get out by 12, a big basket hanging from her arm, full of goodies, over she'd go to the Beehive, makes her way to her chair, no one dared sit in Mom's chair; half a mild would be ordered, the basket sat down, and the sessions began until 2 o'clock. People would come up, buy a few items, a toy, a pair of socks, my mom's beer would be bought. Of course, there would be the occasional but regular barny, Mom would ask Dad for extra money to get some food in.

The old man would refuse to pay, arguing that Mom had her own money, earned her own money and had to pay out of her pocket. Sometimes, the arguments would go on for hours. Most times, Mom had to wait until Dad went to sleep on the sofa, his coat draped over the settee, before leaning over, dipping her hand in his pocket, before slipping off a bluey. Kenny and I would watch this with eyes wide open. The average wage was eight pounds a week, Mom was nicking a bluey without a blink. We'd wait for the old man to wake up and find her out, he never did. He had that much in his bin that he never noticed. Sometimes we'd watch him draw and check his roll, to us, he was rich. His roll being some 500 quid at any one time.

Once, Randolph Turpin was defending his world title that he had won the year before. He had won it that easy that it was a cert that he would win it on his defence. Dad was so convinced, he bet 500 quid that Turpin would win. Turpin lost, so my dad lost his 500 quid. No one knew that after Turpin won his title so easy, he thought he was invincible.

Women were throwing themselves at him, he sated himself on everyone. By the time he got back in the ring, he was knackered. I think Dad was pissed, he gave Mom a hard time, cut back on his money and never gambled again.

Dad would tell me little snippets of information, education. Go to school, get a bit of education, and end up on the building site or the factory. He would tell me stories that opened my mind up to other possibilities or ambitions. When he was a kid he put an advert in the local paper for coat hangers, sixpence each or three for a shilling, a bundle for half a crown, when he got the money he would send out a bag of nails, and a block of wood.

Well, I didn't believe that for a second, no one would stand for that, but he was telling the truth. The papers couldn't stop him, he was advertising them right, and in truth, once the nails were knocked into the block of wood, you had a coat hanger. He told me the tale of the night he was in the Brit and a pal walked in, sat next to him and asked if he wanted to buy a car. It was an old Austin 10, well, the old man wasn't interested, he didn't drive now, but a deal was a deal.

"How much do you want for the car?"

"£10," says his pal.

The old man says, "Look, I'll give you a fiver."

The bloke was skint, the deal was done, the bloke handed over the logbook of the car. The bloke next to the old man, another pal, asked what was going on. Dad told him, except the price paid. His pal says how much do you want for it? Well, the old man sold it to him for a tenner. Over the night, that car went around the pub, each time a few quid added on, each time someone made a profit, the last bloke paid £25 for it, went outside, had a look, paid his money, and was happy with the car. A pint of beer cost just over a shilling, so everyone had a good night. I thought this also was a bit far-fetched, but it was the kind of thing that could and did happen. Money was easy to come, easy go. These were, to me, shrewd people. Entrepreneurs, people prepared to take risks and back their abilities. No one got hurt.

No one was short of money, every Friday, Saturday night was party night, friends would come back to the house. They lived a lifestyle we could only envy, nice suits, or black blazers and trilby hats, piles of money in their pockets, always a few pennies for us kids, except our older brothers though.

"Gis a bit of pocket money, John?"

"Fuck off."

"Gis a bit of pocket money, Bill?"

"Will you fuck off!! You scrounging little gits."

We thought everybody gave their kid brothers or sisters a bit of pocket money. All the money our brothers had yet getting a shilling was like trying to pull teeth, fucking hard. Many, if not all of them spoke out the side of their mouths. If you were on their right, they would speak out of the right-hand side, mouth pursed tight dropped at the corner. At first, I thought it was because they were or thought they were gangsters. I used to watch the gangster movies on the pictures, and Al Capone and his gang spoke like that, I didn't feel like asking too much, and if you did, you'd get told to fuck off, again out the side of your mouth. Eventually, I pulled old Georgey Crow, who was an amiable and easy-going bloke, George.

"Why do so many of you talk out the side of your mouth?"

Well, George looked at me to see if I was taking the piss or not, then he told me. In the nick, when they were let out for exercise, they weren't allowed to talk, they had to march in twos along the paths, without saying a word, they had no choice but to talk out of the side of their mouths, gangster fashion. If they didn't talk right or were too loud, the screws would shout out, "No talking."

I found all this fascinating and built up a bit of a romantic image of what it must be like to spend time in the clink, everybody seemed to have a joke or a tale about some experience or screw in the place. It'd got to be a bit of a habit after that that we would look for the ones who spoke out the corner of their mouths.

"Look, he's done a bit of porridge."

Of course, to gain kudos, some people who had never been to prison would also talk out the side of their mouths just because they thought it made them tougher, you could even see 17-18-year-olds walking around talking out the sides of their mouths, a bit of a frigging joke.

Sometimes, Mom and Dad would take us somewhere for the day out. Maybe it would be to the circus, no one could ever forget the circus. The big top, the horses, the elephants, clowns, lions and tigers, for a couple of hours we were transported into another world, our home, school. Nechells forgotten as we were, lost within all the excitement. One day, a mate of Dad's named Jacky Willis turned up in his big bread van, all emptied. He had put a table in the back and six chairs, and two armchairs. Mom had spent all night, making the sandwiches, ham, cheese, pickles, etc. Off we would set in the morning, all us kids in the back, driving a few miles out of town until we came into the country. Our kids and I didn't know where we were except it looked nice and exciting. Well, it was the country, anything was more exciting than the grey of Nechells. The gates were opened into a field, and we all jumped out, setting the table and chairs on the grass, Mom sent us over to the farmer to buy a pitcher of milk and Mom duly boiled the kettle for tea all round. Sandwiches were bought out, and everyone settled down to relax and enjoy the day, except Kenny and me of course. We had spotted the cows in the field, a little bit of exploring soon taught us that the cows were frightened of us. Up we'd walk and away they would walk from us, soon we were in all our glory, chasing the cows down the field. Our little legs were going like good uns, this was real cowboy stuff, and I was Davy Crockett until we got to the bottom of the field, then the cows stopped. Having nowhere else to go, they turned around and gave us the meanest fearful look you could get; this was serious. We knew they meant business, they must have sensed the fear in our faces because the next thing was they were chasing us back up the field, Kenny and I were shitting ourselves, our little legs going like the clappers, we were screaming for Mom and Dad, they were sat there, laughing their heads off, bloody great.

After a couple of hours in the field, we'd set off down the lane to a nearby country town where the grown-ups would find a pub and disappear for a few hours. We kids would have a happy afternoon walking around the stalls, visiting the shops, enjoying the strangeness of it all, all this was a million miles from Nechells, Birmingham.

These trips out were few and far between. We didn't expect much, what we got we were grateful for. Sometimes, once a year there might be a school trip out, to the Cotswold, or the sea at Llandudno, these were also exciting times, and we all looked forward to the big day. Sometimes, even the teachers enjoyed themselves a bit, but you knew it was all part of their job, and it was done under sufferance.

Another event to look forward to was the Christmas party. Before Christmas, we would start collecting stuff for the Christmas treat, tins of fruit, cakes, biscuits etc. We would spend weeks cutting up the crepe paper into 8" lengths by 2" wide sections before linking them together with glue and making long Christmas chains. Little groups would be organised to play musical instruments, and I always got the cymbals, looking around it was always the least musical who was placed on the cymbals or the castanets. It was all great fun and very exciting, on the day, we had to bring our plates, cups and spoons, one for the sweet, and one for the soup, I always thought it was the school giving us this food and providing all the goodies, it never dawned on me that we were paying for our own Christmas.

If we strayed too far from our patch we felt uncomfortable, in our area, we knew how to act, we dressed our way, we could shout and be loud, we were confident, but outside it was different. One day Mom and Dad took us to the Old Horns in Kingstanding. It was a hot summer day, and the beer garden was crowded, Kenny and I were standing there, minding our own business when a few kids came over and started playing with us. It was just normal fun, and we were playing for about 20 minutes when the lad's mother came over, gave us a right withering look, grabbed hold of the eldest kid and in a real sharp voice with looks to kill, told him to get back to his family and not to move. Kenny and I looked at each other, but couldn't figure it out. Kenny was on his walking sticks from when he'd fallen off the wall and broke his leg down Schofield Street. Maybe it was because we were a bit scruffy. And dirty? Well, it wasn't worth too much washing ourselves around Nechells, within ten minutes, we'd be filthy again, and anyone should know that.

Occasionally, a customer or friend of Dad's would pop round to do a bit of business, now and again, they would bring their sons, and we would become immediate friends. One day, we had spent a few hours with this lad when his dad came back and invited us to stay with his son for the weekend at their home. Kenny was having none of it, I ain't going to no stranger's house, and I don't like him. That was settled then, I thought this was an exciting adventure, and off I went with my new friend in his dad's car. His house was on a posh council estate, and immediately I started having doubts, I shuffled into the house and started looking around me, for a few hours it was fine as we played in the garden, but then we went inside, and my new pal took me up to show me his bedroom. I was shocked and straight away felt sick, it was like a palace and far too posh for me, nice wallpaper on the walls, clean sheets on a made up bed that was so white my eyes hurt. I couldn't stay and told my friend that I had to go home; much as he tried to persuade me, I was having none of it. I wanted to go home, and that was it, after a bit, his dad put me in the car and drove me home, nothing more was said, my new pal's dad never said a word. Kenny was right, I shouldn't have gone, it was a no brainer, but I never saw my new pal again.

The Teenage Years

Charles Arthur Street School was a drudge. I couldn't do my tables. If I looked at any kind of arithmetic in front of me, the numbers just blurred in front of my eyes. I just couldn't understand numbers and sums, and when the teacher started talking decimals, percentages, well, I just went fucking numb. The teachers didn't give a shit anyway and just ignored us, concentrating on their little favourites. The fact was no one gave a shit about us, so we didn't give a shit about them. The routine was the same, sit there trying to pass the time until lunch, or teatime. If it got too boring, we'd try to occupy ourselves by talking or joking, this inevitably led to us being told to get to the headmaster, Mr Troop's office where after a short wait, we'd get the cane across our arses, we just went round and round in circles.

One day, a black teacher turned up to teach, a black teacher. How could a black teacher teach? It's a known fact that black people had got no brains. Well, we could see he was nervous, so started giving him some stick. His name was Mr Robinson, black as coal dust and very shy, he kept having days off, which made us think he was lily-livered, he didn't last too long and soon left, we were all quite pleased, it wasn't right us being taught by a black bloke.

Charlie, that's our school, Charles Arthur Street consisted of the main building, with the classrooms set around the big hall, which acted as a gym, assembly where we said our morn-ing prayers and general meeting area. It was built during the

Victorian period, and all schools were built to the same design, more or less, Loxton Street, Elliot Street and Bloomsbury Street. The only one that was different was St Joseph's the Roman Catholic School, and none of us ever got in there to have a look around, to be honest, no one wanted to have a look. It frightened the shits out of everyone I knew, what with those priests lined up, walking down the avenues, saying their holy words, chanting, waving their little candle holders with smoke coming out, all dressed in long flowing garbs. Fuck that for a lark; even the kids seemed different.

One day I met this beautiful girl; long dark hair, proud, upright, mysterious, beautiful long slim legs, and most amazing of all, they were tanned a lovely light brown. Now, this seemed very exotic to me, no one, but no one in Nechells had tanned legs, no one in Birmingham had tanned legs, this was film star stuff, they were so beautiful she never even wore stockings. We fell in love and started courting each other a bit. Well, I fell in love with her, she told me that she stained her legs with tea and gravy browning, but I didn't care, she was beautiful, and that was it for me.

Talking one night, she told me a few of the secrets of St Joseph's School. They had communion where they all had to sip a mouthful of wine, this was all something to do with God and the Last Supper. They had their christenings, where they had to swear allegiance and devotion to God or Mary, I could never figure that out. They had the confessional, every Monday they would have to go into "the box" and confess their sins to the priest.

"Father, I have to confess to stealing some crayons off my sister, Bridget and hiding them."

"Did you commit any further sins, my child?"

"Well, yes, Father. I spoke back to my mother and gave her some lip."

You didn't have to be exact in your confession. For instance, she didn't have to admit to the priest that she had had sex with a boy, she could skirt that a bit. She could say she kissed a boy and did embarrassing things, or things that embarrassed her, and that was enough, cough, cough. When all her confessions were made the priest would say, "It's alright child, you have been a naughty girl, and you mustn't cheek your mother. Now I want you to say three Hail Marys and when you go to bed, tonight say a prayer of forgiveness." With that, the priest would wave his hand back and forth, up and down. "Say Hail Marys and you are forgiven, child."

I looked at her in astonishment. "Is that it? You can commit any sin you want over the weekend then just go into church on Monday, say three Hail Marys, confess your sins and all is forgiven."

It's a fucking joke, it also sounded great to me as well. If I was committing a crime every day of the week. Imagine, being able to confess every Monday and coming out clean and innocent.

I said, "Does that mean anything?" Well, I don't know what she thought I meant, I think she thought I meant something different to what she meant.

She turned and looked at me funny and said, "We can confess to anything and be forgiven."

Well, I don't know what she was saying. I knew that girls had sex. Still, I never had, that was something that kept popping up, but never really bothered me, I heard stories of one or two girls, doing it, but it just didn't interest me. I liked this girl a lot, she was a dish. Still, I couldn't imagine her doing something like that, only slags did that, and she was not a slag. Still, it bothered me for months after that. She was saying something, and I was missing it. As with all things, our friendship didn't last long, and we went our separate ways, I never saw her again, but she taught me a bit about the Catholic Church.

At the bottom of the playground, siding on to Rupert Street was the science lab. This was where we learnt how to light a

Bunsen burner and do little things like cut a frog up or dissect a tadpole if we weren't doing that we were being shown how to mix some ingredients that created a flame or something. All useless and I just couldn't see the point in any of it. What fucking good is it ever going to do me to know how to cut a frog into bits. The only interesting bit about this was the teacher was a fairly young bloke who thought he was something special. The rumour was flying around school that he was knocking it off with Lorraine who lived in Charles Arthur Street. Lorraine was a beauty and had a model figure, all of us boys fancied her, but knew that we didn't stand a chance. Lorraine was too good for any or all of us, so it wouldn't surprise us if she were knocking it off with a teacher; Lorraine was ambitious and wanted better things in life. Next to that was the domestic science room where the girls were taught all about cooking and preparing meals and sewing, it was all about teaching them how to become good little wives. Across to the other side of the playground was the woodwork shop.

The woodwork shop was run by Mr Lloyd, a Welsh bastard of the first order. Our first day was the benchmark for what was to come, there we were, lined up to attention next to our workbenches, Mr Lloyd stood in front, reaching behind him, he pulls out this massive, wicked-looking cane and starts bending it one way then the other.

"Right then boys, this is the world-famous whispering Willy, and when I say famous I mean famous. I have had boys leave here and talk in awe about this and spread the word far and wide."

Well, that was it, we all stiffened up, shitting ourselves with fear, this was the last thing we wanted. Without further ado, we all set about to keep our mouths shut and pass the time as quietly and quickly as possible, none of us learnt anything, but I at least avoided the cane. Well, we did learn how to make a teapot stand, but that was about it in the three or four years we were there.

There I was, talking quietly to my mate Dave on the opposite side of our workbench, each bench is set up for two. Suddenly I saw Dave's eyes open in shock, felt a drop in the atmosphere, then a whoosh. Instinctively tilting my head and moving aside, the big heavy planer came whizzing past me hitting my mate smack bang on his nut, right on the forehead, he went spark out on the floor. Lloyd came running over, white as a ghost and shitting himself. This was serious, the bloody plane was heavy and could have killed my mate, worse, I knew the plane was meant for me. Dave hadn't said or done a thing, bleeding hell, even I was only talking quietly; the man was a raving fucking lunatic. The word went around that he was an ex-copper who had had a few good beltings and hated all villains. Well, that was it then, no wonder he hated our lot, the man needed fucking certifying.

It was with great relief to all of us when within a few weeks someone broke into the woodwork class and put a match to the wood store underneath the class itself. I think the whole school gave a cheer of relief, well, us boys did. Lloyd, the bastard, disappeared, and we were transferred to a one-afternoon session a week for woodwork lessons at another school. Suddenly, I realised and discovered my love for woodwork. The teachers were great, showed us how to do mortice joints and dovetails. I had discovered a craft and job that I thoroughly enjoyed and loved, and why not, both my older brothers Billy and Reg were skilled carpenters. My mom's brothers the Hipkisses were skilled carpenters and joiners going back years, sadly, it was too late; too much time had passed before I had this opportunity.

Most of the teachers were not too bad, none of them was interested in us as human beings, most just ignored us outside school hours, obviously clocking in to do their jobs. The PE teacher, Mr Bevan, was a nice quiet bloke, as was Mr Colley. Mr Walker was a square-headed tyrant who loved all things,

German. He had studied the war and Hitler. He paced back and forth in front of us like he was on a march, arms swinging from side to side, face stern on that big square Germanic head of his. As far as I was concerned, I knew exactly what part of Hitler's Germany Mr Walker liked, the SS. I could feel his eyes burning into us. The longing for us to be his concentration camp victims as if we were in Germany, and he was in power the thought of what that bastard would do to us didn't bear thinking about. There was Mr Hughes, another Welsh bastard, steely grey curly hair that matched his steely cold eyes. He wore Pince Nez glasses on his nose and looked down it at us poor little sods. I could never lose the feeling that he looked at us as if we were a bit of shit on his shoe.

One day, one of the girls had the temerity to put her hand up and ask about job possibilities when we were all to leave school. That was his opening; it was as though he had been looking for this opportunity, waiting to fire out his venom. Quietly but firmly, he put down his piece of chalk and turned to face us, gathering his thoughts. He put his arms behind his back, looked out of the window for a moment before facing us again.

"Well, he started, in measured tones, no doubt, most of you girls will get a job at Woolworths or one of the local shops for a couple of years before getting married. I will expect most of the boys will find work on the building sites or in the factories. Some of you, if you are really lucky, might even get yourselves an apprenticeship, serve your time and after five years get a city and guilds. Some of you," and looking around, I swear his eyes rested on me and Turley, "will no doubt end up in prison."

No one asked any more questions; Mr Hughes returned to the blackboard and picked up his chalk. I think the class was a bit stunned; trying to let it sink in a bit, everyone fell silent. Sick no doubt, that's our future laid out on a plate, exactly what the teachers thought of us. Bastards. What possible chance in life did we have with these people teaching us? They had no interest in us; they had no ambition for us. We were never told we could do, nor have whatever we wanted in the world if we worked hard enough for it. No, it was clear to most of us that they were here under sufferance, just for the money. Only the odd one had any illusions, and even they had their horizons limited. If you did well, passed a few exams you might get a job in Woolies before you got married.

Then there was Miss Smith. She was a big starchy woman, built like a brick shithouse, stern and not a smile on her face. Miss Smith, not the first in the queue when it came to giving out looks, was the music teacher. She would play the piano and teach us English. Listening to her playing the piano was bad enough, what good was it going to do us to play the fucking piano. English was boring, so most times because I enjoyed reading. I would just read a book. One day, I must have said something Miss Smith wasn't happy about.

"Thomas Lewin, get out here in front of the class."

Well, it was humiliating; she made me sit down on the floor with my back to the class, looking at the chalkboard. Seeing the chalk, I turned around to see Miss Smith's big square arse right in front of me, grabbing the chalk I wrote in big letters – FUCK OFF. After the lesson, she walked out, and the school was in an uproar; half the kids laughing before she was bustled away by one of the teachers. It wasn't long before they all sussed it was me, and I was summoned to Mr Troops' office again. By this time, he had decided that it was a waste of time giving me the cane so decided to expel me.

The only problem was no other school wanted me. I thought, OK, fuck you, so off I went to upper Thomas Street School. The headmaster called me in, told me no thank you, so off I went to Loxton Street, he came up with the excuse that I was too far away. I spent a few days twiddling my thumbs and keeping out of the old ladies' way before Mr Troop called me back into his office.

"Lewin I am not going to expel you after all, but you will not go back to your own class. Miss Smith is a lovely woman and is very upset. You will go to Mrs White's class until you leave." It was made worse by Mr Colley. For a week or so, I had been put into Mr Colley's class. He was a lovely old bloke who taught English; one day we all walked into class from break and there on the blackboard, written in chalk was the words FUCK YOU. Well, that was it; Colley looked around, cast his eye quickly over me and said to the class, "Well, we can only guess who wrote that disgusting word, can't we?" Contempt was written all over his face. As I looked around at everybody in all innocence, the effort of not looking at me by everyone made it clear that they thought I was the guilty party. Fuck me, that's it, I had done one thing, then I get blamed for everything. It was obvious someone had drawn on the board to get me into trouble; this was to become the story of my life.

Well, Mrs White's class was two forms up from mine. I couldn't do fuck all in my class so in hers, I had no chance, so was told to sit at the back of the class and read, or do whatever else I wanted to do as long as I was quiet, kept my mouth shut and didn't disturb the others, Jesus Christ, roll on break time.

The weeks strolled on, me learning nowt, Mrs White was giving me pitiful looks; it was getting more and more difficult to keep myself occupied. The other kids were years older than me, in reality just a year older, but a million miles away from me, but that's how it felt. So, after a few weeks, someone had a brainwave, we were called into Dan Troop's office. Me, Bee-Bee and Turley, heads bowed, trying to look humble, we stared at the floor as Mr Troop came up with a suggestion.

"OK boys, it's obvious you're not learning anything and are not interested in learning."

We turned and looked at each other from our bowed heads, giving each other a knowing glint. Oh, he's caught on to that then.

Mr Troop continued, "So what I propose is this, how would you like to clear out the workshop at the bottom of the playground? Putting all the rubbish outside and tidying the place up. There's no rush, you can take your time and just do a good job, ok?"

Well, we only had another six weeks to go before we escaped from this torture house, so this suited us a treat. Clearly, from the relief on Mr Troop's face when we said yes, it suited him too. Off we went to the bottom of the playground where Mr Troop showed us what needed doing, once sorted, he walked off and left us to it. We looked around with big smiles on our faces. This was going to take us weeks, weeks, right up until we left school.

It was about now I discovered my love for boxing; Kenny had joined the Morris Commercial Boxing Club down Saltley. Being naturally fit, we both took to it like the proverbial duck. Boxing has a routine and discipline that I immediately loved. First, a few light exercises to warm up the body and make it supple, then on to the skipping ropes. After a good warm-up and exercise on the ropes, it was on to the punch bags, swing ball and shadow boxing, then into the ring for a bit of boxing itself. Watching Kenny, I could see that he was good, he had a natural body movement, good shoulders and a natural punch, and I was pleased. Some of the other boxers I knew, Norman Parish, my mate lived in Long Acre by the school. Danny Baker lived up the top of Rupert Street and was also a mate who had only recently started at Charlie. Danny was a real handsome kid, great physique and I gather his dad had been a professional boxer, Billy Monagh had turned pro, but still came down to the Morris to train, along with Johnny Prescott the midlands heavyweight champion. I quickly realised that the Morris was one of the best clubs in Birmingham, if not the whole country and had a well-respected reputation. The main trainer was Wally Cox. Wally had no kids, a lovely wife and devoted his life to boxing, he had been a very handy boxer as a youth himself and I soon realised, to him, we were his kids, he loved us all.

One day, Miss Smith came down to the workshop. "Lewin, would you like to do some work in my garden?"

Well, I looked perplexed. I was nearly expelled for writing fuck off on her arse, I'm stuck down here in this shed, and she wants me to do some work on her house? I couldn't figure it out; still, I was up for it, especially as there were a few pennies and a dinner thrown in, so it was agreed. Miss Smith would pick me up from my house after school, take me to her house in Boldmere Road, Sutton if I liked it and we were both agreeable, she would give me the bus or train fare, and I would return once a week to work on her garden. Miss Smith was old; I wouldn't ask, but we were told she was retired and just came into school once or twice a week to top up her pension. Not only was Miss Smith old, but she was also not one of the prettiest ladies, she had never been married because she told me, but she also devoted her life to music and the piano. At one stage, she had ambitions to play in the philharmonic orchestra. That may have been true, but I think her looks had a little bit to do with it, that and her bossy, domineering manner. Miss Smith was an only child and had been used to getting her own way. Still, she was the boss, she was paying and feeding me to do a little bit of work, which I enjoyed doing anyway.

Miss Smith had a beautiful long, immaculate garden rising in three tiers, and spread over 150 feet with an air-raid shelter in the middle. Our relationship progressed to her either picking me up from the house or giving me a tanner to get the bus or train at Aston up to her house. Her house was one of three in a block set aside in Boldmere Road. A builder had built the three, retaining the detached house for himself and selling the two semis, Miss Smith's parents had bought the large four bedroomed semi; when they died, she had inherited the house, now she had converted the top floor into a self-contained flat that she rented out to give her another source of income. I took most of this in as she told me over each visit, sometimes a Sunday, sometimes midweek and at nights. Sometimes she would play the piano, which was absolutely fucking torture, but I suppose I had to put up with it. Other times, she would take me to see one of her friends and introduce me. Another time she would take me to see a neighbour further down the road and play a game of whist. Each time I felt slightly humiliated and couldn't escape the thought that she was introducing me and talking about me behind my back as the poor slum kid from Nechells who she was trying to lift up in life.

After a bit, the gossip started; first, it was my old lady. "What's going on with you and that old battle-axe? Why is she always round this fucking house?"

"I don't know, Mom, she just keeps asking me."

No matter what I said, I kept getting the dirty looks. For God's sake, what the fuck are they all going on about? She's an old lady. One day, the old man had had enough.

"I know what you're up to you dirty little bastard, and the next time she comes around here, I'm going to see her."

Well, one day, Miss Smith turned up at the front door; the old man was asleep on the sofa sleeping off an afternoon drinking session.

As I made my way to the parlour, I said quite loudly, enough for the old man to hear. "Oh, that must be Miss Smith, I'll bring her in." When I got to the door, I said in my loudest voice. "Ahh, Miss Smith, my dad, would like a word with you."

Well, the old man might have heard me the first time, but I don't think he thought I was going to go through with it. As Miss Smith marched into the hallway, I heard the old man coughing and spluttering. As I got to the back room, he was struggling to get up off the sofa, heaving and swaying, face bright red, split between giving me a dirty look and forcing a smile on his face for Miss Smith who was directly behind me. The years of drinking had taken its toll on the old man; he was only five ft. seven and was double his weight at 16 stone.

All he could do was splutter and choke. "Oh, hello, Miss Smith, nice to see you."

I could feel Miss Smith recoil behind me. "Hello, Mr Lewin, so nice to see you," in her loud, clear, high-pitched voice.

With that, she turned and marched out, she never uttered another word, neither did the old man. A few weeks later, my mom met Miss Smith also on the doorstep and stepped back when she realised that Miss Smith and I were not up to anything and that whatever her misgivings Miss Smith only had my best interests at heart. I think it helped sway things that Miss Smith was not only old, but she wasn't a raving beauty.

It didn't stop the others going at it though, one by one, the whole of Rocky Lane clocked on that Miss Smith was always picking me up and taking me away. The gossip went into over-drive, although my mom and dad were now satisfied the rest of the family were not convinced. My sister Dot and sister-in-law Tresa knew for a fact that we were up to something and didn't hold back with making it clear to all and sundry, "Course he's knocking her off, the dirty little bleeder, why else would she be giving him money, no one like her class comes around here unless it's to do with the law." It got worse, Rodger "the Dodger" Hardiman who lived across the road was also convinced, "Ay Tommy, how much are you getting out of that old bag?" Stanley Wooten down the bottom of Rocky Lane also pulled me, " Are you fucking her Lewin? Do me a favour will you." "No, I ain't." "Well, the whole street's talking about it so something must be going on."

Work and Boxing

I had got myself a job as an apprentice bricklayer with Emlyn Williams of Aston. I had a bike, and the first job was based in Solihull working in a bank, I would get up in the morning to reach Solihull which was ten miles away going through Sparkbrook and up the Stratford Road into Olton before reaching Solihull. The ride was great, and because I was boxing, it helped keep me 100 percent fit. My apprentice wage was the princely sum of £3 a week, the foreman touted me as a prime example to all the others as I was always first in and they came by car and bus. If I'd have had the brains to work out the bus fare I might have had second thoughts about it there and then, but I was there six months before I started to realise I was more of a labourer than an apprentice. I couldn't see this going very well, and when the site bricky turned up one day and started discussing his wage packet of £10 per week, I got a sick feeling in the pit of my stomach. £3 a week for five years, then only £10 per week. One of my mates was working as a plumber's mate for a firm in Aston, he was getting £9 per week plus travelling expenses, fucking hell, that was almost as much as the bricky. I went to the firm quick sharpish, got a job and packed up with Emlyn Williams the same day. In those days, you could get a job in the morning, pack up at lunchtime and get another job down the road for one o'clock. There was always plenty of work around.

In between work, Miss Smith was still picking me up and doing odd jobs for her, I was also getting into my boxing and looking forward to training twice a week and Sunday morning.

The first time Wally set me up for a sparring session I started prancing about and flicking out punches with my left hand, followed by a flick cross with my right, Wally would get me back on the bag where he explained I wasn't punching properly.

"Look, son, you're flicking out your right hand like a girl, now look, put your left foot forward, lean back on your right foot and when you throw a punch, bring it up from your right foot, right? Imagine the punch coming up from the sole of your foot, through your body, into your shoulder, so when you throw a punch, you're punching with the whole weight of your body."

Well; it took me a bit, but when I got it, it was a revelation, I had a fucking punch I didn't even realise I had. Soon, Wally put me in with Danny Baker, well, Danny was a great boxer, I'd seen him give Johnny Wright, a local bully a good boxing lesson, so I was a bit nervous.

"Now take it steady Dan." Danny looked at me with a smile, "Don't worry, Tom, I won't hurt you."

With that, the bell went, well, I couldn't believe it, I knocked poor Danny all around the ring, there was just no stopping me now. I sparred with everyone and anyone, light-weights, middleweights, heavyweights, it made no difference, the more I sparred, the better I got. Even better, I discovered I could take a punch, there are two things you have to have in boxing, the ability to give a punch, and the ability to take a punch, without one or the other you were knackered, Danny Baker was a beautiful boxer, handsome with it he looked great in the ring, but he couldn't punch. Same with Norman Parish, clean, tidy boxer, no punch, I loved boxing and saw myself going somewhere with it, Johnny Prescot was my hero, great boxer, handsome and a heavyweight, I was big for my age, 5-9; and ten and a half stone, I had no doubts that I would be a heavyweight just like Prescott.

The weeks rolled into months, it was work, boxing, in between I was still doing jobs for Miss Smith, and she was still taking me out now and again. One day she took me down to Mr Richards in Boldmere Road, he had the bike shop, and Miss Smith felt that I could get to work easier and quicker if I had a bike, with that in mind she bought me a small 125 BSA Bantam motorbike. This was great and nervous as I was I soon learnt to ride and handle it. Of course, I also quickly found out that Miss Smith could call on me more often to visit her house and do some work, I was now even more at her beck and call.

The mere sight of me on this bike fired the gossip up around Nechells even more, I reckon the tongues were rattling that fast everybody's ears were burning. I was getting it regularly, "how did you get the bike, Tom?" Everyone knew the wages were that low few people could afford anything other than a pushbike, the old man had given up and just shrugged his shoulders and sighed. The old lady guessed what Miss Smith's motives were and that it was to help me and keep me on the straight and narrow, but the rest of the family? Well, they all knew I was giving Miss Smith one, and as such, I was a dirty little bastard for doing such things with an old lady. No one wanted or had the bottle to confront the old lady, though.

Stanley Wooten blagged me again outside his house down Rocky Lane, now Stan was married to Beryl and had two kids, they lived with his mom Peggy, daughter Sheila and Sylvia, and her two little dogs. Peggy had the back room, Stan and Beryl and the two kids had the front.

"Ay Tommy, don't come the bollox, are you trying to tell me that old schoolteacher of yours bought yow that bike for fuck all? Who are you taking for a cunt?"

The disbelief on his face plain as day, well, I looked at him in astonishment that anyone could think differently, shoulders hunched, hands out in all innocence, "Look, Stan, it's nothing like that at all, she just likes me and wants to help."

"Bollox, don't tell fucking lies. I'll tell you what then if you ain't fucking her, take me up her house and I will, if you can get a bike, I'll get something."

Oh well, I thought, if I take him up it would at least stop the gossiping around Nechells. With that, I rang Miss Smith, "do you want any jobs doing Miss Smith?"

"Well, no thank you, Tommy, but if you wish, you can come up Tuesday night and have some tea."

"Can I bring my friend Stanley up, Miss?"

With that I told Stan that I would pick him up at six o'clock Tuesday night, now Stan was about 26 and a full adult, I was intrigued, maybe Stan knew something that I didn't, well, we'd soon find out. At six, I picked Stan up and off we went up Nechells Park Road and off into Sutton, arriving at Miss Smith's for six-thirty. Miss Smith had laid the table, and after I introduced her to Stan, she invited us to sit down and have a cup of tea. I'm sitting there with my tea waiting for Stan to say something or do something, looking for signs of I don't know what. After 30 minutes, Miss Smith mentions that she has some nice fresh strawberries for tea that we might like, Stan nods his head in full agreement.

"Well Tommy, I have no cream so could you go down to the corner shop and get a carton of whipped cream and we shall all have fresh strawberries and cream."

Well! This was all very interesting, and I'm straining my brains trying to figure out what I am missing, I know I'm missing something, but I couldn't see it, Miss Smith hands me the money, and I set off, afraid to look back at Stanley in case I upset something. Well, I'm mystified, the shop was a good quarter of a mile walk to the bottom of Boldmere Road, and I didn't have to force myself to go slow. My brain was trying to keep up with my footsteps.

Walking back, slowly, I'm still in a whirl, brain trying to function and figure it out, why did Miss Smith ask me to go and fetch some fresh cream. Why hadn't she got it? Maybe Stan was right, maybe I had been missing something. My uncertainty and doubts were soon answered as I approached and started walking up the long drive. There was Stan in the window, desperation and pain etched all over his face, what the fuck's going on here, Jesus, he's tried it on, and she's put him right in his place. As I got closer, his arms started going, waving frantically and crooking his finger, get in fucking here; then I heard the piano going full blast, I burst out laughing. After our tea and fresh strawberries and cream, we got to the door and said goodbye to Miss Smith. By now, I was pissing myself laughing, Stan hadn't even tried it on, as soon as I had left the house Miss Smith asked him if he liked the piano, like a prat he admitted he did, from then until I got back she started playing him classical music. After I dropped Stan off, he never said another word, whenever I saw him after that he'd give me a funny look, but he never brought the subject up of Miss Smith ever again. Still, he was just one; all of the Green still thought I was up to no good with Miss Smith.

Mischief-makers

Boxing gave me new confidence, the great thing about boxing is it's a great leveller, it teaches you so many things, firstly discipline, a sense of camaraderie, of belonging, of loyalty. An old mate Big Maccy Clayton from down Scofield Street turned up to do some training one day, now Mac was a big bruiser of a bloke, morose and sulky, after a bit of warm-up and training, Wally told me to get in the ring and put the gloves on with Mac. As soon as the bell went Mac came at me like a fucking steam train, no stopping him, he was pounding into me, lifting me off the floor and knocking me all around the floor, I was a welterweight, and he must have been heavyweight if not much less. I didn't mind the pounding, I could take a punch anyway, but I was a bit puzzled as to why he had to knock the shit out of me like that, after all, I know we weren't close mates, but I did think we were mates. Wally pulled me to the corner and took the gloves off me; he then called one of the bigger, more experienced lads into the ring. They had all been watching, the bell went again, this lad tore into big Mac, knocking the shit out of him to be sure, but this time knocking the shit out of him, Big Mac was going all around that ring, and I tell you, Wally never pushed that bell until he'd had a right good pasting. Big Mac never spoke to me after that, he put his clothes back on and left the gym, never coming back again. No one likes a bully, and that event taught me a valuable lesson about loyalty. And bullying.

It was the bank holiday, and all us Brummies' liked nothing better than a day out at Stourport, known to us lot as

74

Stourport on Sea. It was a thriving place when we got to the café on the bridge with a big outside leisure area, where lots of the kids would rock n roll to the jukebox. Many would drink in the various pubs around the river, some would go on the riverboats for a cruise up and down, and some even hired their own little paddling boat or do other things like playing games along the grassy banks alongside the bridge and river. I had gone with deaf and dumb Johnny Hardiman, and his brother Rodger the Dodger. All our mates were there, almost everyone from Nechells, Johnny had gone off up to the boozer, and I was walking along the riverbank watching everything that was just going on, relaxing and taking it all in. Someone kicked the ball across and I kicked it back into the crowd of lads, it seems I had made a mistake because the next thing I know I see Micky Taylor running towards me like a fucking wild bull, snarling and snorting, eyes wild, what the fuck's going on here? Oh, I get it, it was his ball, and I had kicked it to someone else?

Mick was a big stocky kid, built like a brick shithouse and wild with it. He and Stanley Tarony used to hang around together in Nechells, bullying anyone they thought they could get away with; I once saw them walk over from the El Greco Café in Bloomsbury Street to a young but big lad standing across the road by the bus stop. Stanley pulled a knife on him, and Mick gave him a few words before smacking him, all this because they thought he was looking at them. In truth, it was just plain bullying, and they were trying to build up their reputation, Mick also had an Alsatian dog that he walked around with threatening anyone within reach.

A year or so earlier he had grabbed hold of me and threatened me before smacking me, snarling and spitting in my face, in truth I was shit scared of him, like a few others. And here he was, charging at me like a fucking wild pampas bull.

But this time, I had learnt to box, as he came over, still frightened, I subtly shifted myself into a boxing stance, left leg forward, right back, arms relaxed and to my side. As he came to within a foot of me, snarling and spitting, he knew in confidence that he was going to give me a hiding in front of all his mates, only this time he didn't. I gave him a beaut of a right-hander, smack bang on his chin and he went down like a pole-axed bull, I was that fucking shocked I couldn't even believe it myself, being good in the boxing ring is one thing, you're boxing or fighting under controlled conditions, often by bigger lads, better lads who are holding their punches. In the real here and now it was different. Spark out he went on the grass, looking up I could see the open-mouthed astonishment on everyone's faces as they came over to watch, getting myself together sharpish I decided to press home my advantage and gave him a good couple of kicks to the head, making him cover-up in fear like the coward he was. You try that again, and I'll fucking splatter you all over the place, with that, and as much pride as I could muster, I walked away, arse tight in and stiff, unable to believe what had just happened and what I had just done. That was another valuable lesson for me, never be frightened of a bully.

The better and more confident I got at boxing, the more trouble seemed to seek me out or come my way. I didn't look for trouble, but neither did I shirk it if it came into my face, maybe it was the way I walked, I was confident, maybe a bit arrogant, but I didn't ask for trouble. Walking up Nechells Park Road one early evening, these two lads sidled out of a shop doorway, both pushing themselves up to me in a threatening manner. It wasn't about demanding anything, it was just about letting me know I was on their turf, in their neighbourhood and they wanted to let me know it. I stood for it for a bit, but the more I tried to ignore them, the more they thought they had me at their mercy. I recognised the one as Donald Houghton, the other as Eric Reece, now I thought Eric was normally a nice quiet kid, but this time, this night I think he was determined to let me know he was the boss. I couldn't put up with this crap for much longer, I gave Eric a quick smack on the chin, down he went like a fallen log, Donald jumped back quick in shock, I put my mitts up and asked him, well; do you fucking want some? Well, Donald quite sensibly didn't want any that was it, I put my mitts down, adjusted my jacket and carried on, that was that then, sorted.

A few nights later, I had gone to bed at about ten o'clock. Shortly after I heard some commotion outside, and my mom came into the bedroom, "Now listen, you two, shut up and stay in bed." Well, Kenny and I looked at each other in the dark and thought, what the hell's going on here? Coppers what? We heard Mom go down the hall and open the front door, raised voices came from outside, and I heard the old lady shout "fuck orf," to someone, that someone shouted back, "shut your fucking gob you old slag, or I'll cut you up."

Well, that was it, no one will insult my mother like that, down the stairs, I flew, and the first one I saw shouting his gob off was Donald Houghton. All I saw was a red mist, I flew at Houghton, fists flying and within seconds he was on the floor, I turned around to see someone out of the corner of my eye, with a knife in his hands; fortunately, my old mate Nobby Hall had just come out the boozer and was walking up Rocky Lane. He slowed down as he got to mine looking at the excitement, the geezer with the blade was coming for me as I was sorting Houghton out, intent on giving me the blade in the back, Nobby grabbed hold of him from behind. Having sorted Houghton out, I then turned to his mate, come on then? Nobby threw him towards me, still with the blade in his hand, watching his knife with care, I circled him a bit before giving him a strong right-hander, the knife was dropped, and I laid into him. I was fucking furious, not only do these toe rags come to my house, insult my mother, but they also try to stab me into the bargain, I gave that kid a right good belting, when he went down on the floor I gave him the kicking of his life.

Eventually, my mom got hold of me, " Get to bed, son."

Exhausted I went up to bed, oblivious of what was going on outside, someone had called the ambulance and taken the kid away, Houghton had sloped off somewhere. The next day all was quiet on Rocky Lane, the old lady didn't say a word to me all day, she didn't have to, I knew she was proud that I had defended her honour. That night, at six o'clock, the door went again, it was Houghton, this time he had bought a bunch of flowers for my mom, giving them to her he apologised for the trouble he had caused the night before, Mom accepted the flowers without a word, honour was restored fully.

I don't know who Houghton's mate was, never sought to ask him, I didn't care, I didn't think he would bother me or come around again. A few days later, Bonny, that chief inspector Bon, from down Bloomsbury Street nick bumped into my dad in the Little Britt, "That son of yours gave that kid a good belting the other night Jack. He was that bad no one could recognise him," chuckles all round at that. "He must have deserved it then." Well, the old man just gave his three monkeys look and a smile. That was it; the subject was never mentioned or brought up again.

A few days later, I'm sitting on the bench on Nechells Green with Turly, little Malcolm Bellerby and Dave Parry when these two big brick shithouses came walking over, fucking hell, they both must have been six feet tall and wide with it. One had a bomber jacket on, which made him look even bigger, "Are you, Tommy Lewin?" Well, I'd never seen them before or recognised them from anywhere, who the fuck are these two clowns, well, that was it, off it goes, and I'm having a right tear up with the one, knocking him all around the Green. He's bigger than me, and I just couldn't seem to be hurting or having any effect on him, my one advantage was my boxing skills, but he was that fucking big I was tiring myself out trying to hurt him. Eventually, he went down on the deck where I struggled to lay a few more punches onto him to make sure he got the point. I had felt something or someone come up behind me and saw Nobby Hall grab him and throw him under the bench, putting his foot on him, so he didn't move, the bastard had only tried to put a knife in me while I was on the floor with his mate. Exhausted, I walked over to Nobby, the two lads pulled themselves together and shuffled off, never saying a word or looking back. I never did find out who they were, what they wanted, what for or why, someone had sent them to sort me out, or they had heard about me and wanted to put me in my place. Fucking treat ain't it.

It's also interesting how things or events come in strings, fall over, you start tripping all over the bleeding place. Now I was getting into little scuffles regularly, me Turly, Bee-Bee, Dave Parry and a few lads were sitting on our little bench on the Green one day, minding our own bleeding business when this adult started walking up with his girlfriend. I didn't hear Turly say anything but the next thing this bloke comes across and grabs Turley by the collar and pulls him off the bench

"Yes, you little bastard, just watch yourself." It was only a copper in plain clothes, he must have misheard or thought Turly had said something and was trying to impress his girlfriend, well, I couldn't have that. I stood up and said, "Ay, don't get picking on him."

That was it, the prat then made a dive for me, too late, and a bit too slow I sidestepped and put one on his chin, that shook the dickhead a bit but it was too late now, he couldn't back down or stop in front of his girlfriend, especially against a bunch of young kids. Off it goes with me giving him a boxing lesson all around Nechells Green, it was a fair old sight to behold, and people came out of the Beehive pub and nearby houses to view the spectacle. I was teaching the mug a right lesson, when Tony Williams came over and dragged me off, whispering in my ear, "leave it, Tommy, he's a copper." I could tell that the idiot was done for; he stood like a wounded bull, panting and embarrassed. Tony started to walk me up home, and as we reached the door, the copper came up behind me, girlfriend in tow, standing a bit behind him, head bowed in embarrassment. Well, he didn't want to give up, shouting his mouth off about how he was going to have me, I went to give him another hiding when Tony grabbed me again, "Leave the cunt alone, Tom." Eventually, he walked away, tail between his legs, I tell you, some of these coppers are a fucking joke, just because they have a uniform they think they can boss people around all the time.

Another time I'm walking along Railway Terrace towards the Prince pub, minding my own bleeding business with my little pup. Now this pup was a beautiful little thing, barely three months old and not even a foot high, on the left you had got Newton's factory and on the right was a row of terraced houses before I got to the boozer. Before I knew it, and out of nowhere came this geezer, at the run and with one mighty kick booted my little pup three foot into the air, I stood there in fucking shock for a bit; I just couldn't believe someone could do that to a defenceless dog, a pup at that. No reason, the dog didn't even shit outside his house, the bastard had just seen the pup walking past his entry as he came down it, I didn't have the dog on a lead. He must have thought it was a stray and a chance to get some of the nastiness out of his system. Well, I weren't gonna stand for that, I could feel the anger rising in me, worse, the cheeky bastard stood there, cocky as you like as though he had done nothing wrong said, "That mongrel should be on a lead." Without much ado I gave him a good smack on the chin, no boxing match this time, I just laid into him giving him a boxing lesson he would never forget. Before I knew it, his missus had come down the entry, and there was a nice little crowd circled us, a few of them recognised me and were giving me curious looks.

Suddenly it occurred to me that they must be thinking I was just belting this seemingly respectable bloke for no reason, I pointed to my little pup that was still sitting there in the gutter, head down, in pain, "that bullying bastard just kicked my little pup for no reason at all," I shouted to them. Worse, he was another copper. His missus grabbed him and started to turn him back up the entry, that was it, over, but not before he turned shouting," I'll have you." Fuck me, that's another one. I think the crowd were more bemused than anything that I was a young kid knocking the crap out of this grown man.

Round Nechells coppers were considered the lowest of the low, most of them ex-army who hadn't the brains to get a proper job after the war, most of them were bent, and if you were poor and skint, you were seen as fair game, what had happened to me just gave me no reason to think otherwise. Most people might think coppers are there to protect the innocent, if you're skint and poor, you're fair game for them to have a pop at, bully and rob.

Another night, I had just got home from work and was still in my wellingtons and donkey jacket. There I was standing on the doorstep of Wimbush's on the corner Nechells Park Road, minding my own business as usual, out the corner of my eye I noticed a few kids running across from the Green, passing me and up onto Nechells Park Road, they were being chased by a copper. II recognised it was Turley, Dave Parry and another kid, I also knew they didn't cause any trouble, so as the copper passed me, I just said to him, "Leave 'em alone." That was it, a red rag to the bull, the copper came to an immediate stop and did an about-turn, "Mind your own business, you little bastard."

That was it, he obviously knew me, or thought he knew me to say such an offensive word, now I knew what a bastard was, and I was no bastard. I had a mom and dad and was offended by the word, I stood out in the road, and he made a grab for me, well, I gave him a few punches to the chin but found it very difficult to move in my wellingtons and donkey jacket. The copper clocked this smartish, threw his arms around me and grappled me to the floor, I realised I had made a rick, I relied on my fists and feet and my ability to move around to defend myself, the fucker grabbed on to me like grim death, suddenly his mate came over, a plainclothes copper. "Hang on, hold him there, I'll get help." He didn't want to involve himself- my old mom's standing outside the Beehive telling me to be still, I'm shouting for him to let me up so I'll punch his fucking head off.

Next thing, the Black Maria pulls up, half a dozen cops crawl out and whip me down to Bloomsbury Road nick, putting me in the holding cell, the head dick Bunny pulls over, "What's going on over here then?"

Away they go off, saying nothing in front of or to my face. I said, "He called me a bastard for no reason, and I ain't a bastard." Shortly after, another copper walks in, I looked at his face, oh fuck, I'm in trouble now, it's the mongrel who kicked my little pup a few weeks earlier, that's it, I'm fucked, I've got two coppers onto me now.

Bunny turns to the copper who's in plain clothes. "Is this the one you mentioned?"

Well, blow me down, the copper turns and says, "No, that's not him."

I could hardly hide my disbelief, the old lady came to the door, "I saw what was going on, my son was doing nothing wrong."

With no explanation, no one saying a word, I was told to piss off, Mom following me up Bloomsbury Street giving me the verbal nonstop all the way home.

I couldn't figure this out, I had just belted a uniformed copper on the Green, another copper denied I had hit him and then let go. The only conclusion I could come up with was my age, they were too embarrassed, to charge me because I was too young, how would it look for a 15-year-old kid to be taken to court for belting two coppers, or more? I thought I was a right smart arse, What I didn't realise, or see, was that I was building up problems for myself in later life, these bastards ain't bothered about you or anyone else getting away once or twice, they have a little book stored away in which they write your name.

Laying Low at Agricultural College

Miss Smith must have known this too and suggested I get out of town for a bit one day. She told me the police had visited the school and she asked them how she could keep me out of trouble. Their reply was I would always be in trouble, my only alternative being to get away from Nechells and my family, as such, she had got me farm work on a trial course in Lichfield during the school break, I loved it, I loved the open air, the cleanliness, the healthy hard work. After giving it some thought, Miss Smith came up with a college over in Burton upon Trent that offered a six-month intensive agricultural course. Why not, I'll give it a go, on the weekend, I packed my bags, what little clothes I had and Miss Smith picked me up in her little Morris Minor,

It was an agricultural college situated just outside Burton on Trent, a big house standing in its grounds of a few acres. For four days a week, we were shunted out to farms around the area gaining first-hand practical experience. It was great, it was an ordered existence of getting up early in the morning, having breakfast, and then a group of us would be herded into the college van and taken off to our allocated farms. The farm I was allocated was a mixed dairy and arable, that means the farmer had a few cows, a few pigs, poultry and the rest of the land was set aside for crops, wheat, potatoes, etc. The farmer was a lovely old guy, short, wiry and amiable, didn't talk much or say a lot but I could tell within a couple of days that he was happy with my work. His wife was to me typical of what a farmer's wife should be, short, buxom, with a chubby little rosy face that didn't smile a lot. I took to the work with no trouble at all, I loved hard physical work, and I loved farm work because it was so varied. One day you could be planting corn, the next, fixing and replacing hedgerows, in between feeding and milking the cows, collecting the eggs and a million other mixed and varied jobs.

Now and again, the farmer would kill a pig, hang it and gut it, he would then cut it up into quarters, chopping of the hind legs, front, head and body, and he would then hang it up in the smoke room, a small shed kept just for smoking. Once smoked, he would hang one side of bacon in the cold room next door, again about the same size as the smoke room, about 3ft x 5ft. Before breakfast every morning he would go into the cold room, cut off a chunk of bacon, take it into his wife who would then slice it up, cook it and serve it with our breakfast. It was a great experience, and I enjoyed learning every aspect of the farming experience. I learnt they didn't have a bull like a lot of farmers, so they would bring in a vet to inseminate the cows when it was their time. The cows would all be lined up in the stalls, the farmer would come up from behind, lift their tails stick the big syringe up their Annies, and give the rubber ball a big squeeze shooting the white stuff deep into them. I thought the lifting of the tails was to get the aim right, but there was another reason for this. By lifting the cows tail it disabled her from kicking out, never approach a cow from behind, especially if she was a kicker, always go to the side, tickle her little soft bit next to the tail just like the bull would, and she will lift her tail. I spent many a day, tickling the cows' soft bits, watching her eyes light up, then saying no bull for you today Daisy.

When he'd got too many pigs, we'd herd all the suckling piglets up into a pen. One by one, he'd tell me to grab a piglet and bring it over. Sitting on a stool, he'd grab the piglet, flick it over onto its back, grad its little nuts between his finger and thumb, pull out his little razor-sharp knife and slice each ball. The piglet would give a little squeal, its two little balls would pop out, and he'd let the little piglet run off, turning to me and gesturing for another.

At the end of the day, the college would pick us up, one by one from each farm, for an hour, we would attend the classroom reading and studying the theory of farming. To me, this was a great and easy way of learning the business of farming. The work was fascinating and rewarding, the classes just enough to educate us in the theory side without boring the tits off us. The time flew quickly, and we made good friends with each other, most of us knew where we wanted to work and we were given a choice of which part of the country we wanted to go, some chose Derby, others Yorkshire, me and another kid liked Wales, to me, I'd always loved the wild country and rugged mountains. Farmers from around the country would apply to the college for trainees, and we would be allocated to that farm. The little old farmer I was working for wanted me to stay with him and his wife on his farm, we had all got on well, they liked me and knew I was a good worker, but I wanted to work and experience Wales, and I think I had unwittingly fucked up.

Although I got on well with all the kids at college, there was one big fucker who liked to rule the roost. He was big and built like a brick shithouse; he knew it too and lorded it over the others who weren't so big. I had kept my eye on him from day one when his bullying became a bit obvious. Thankfully, he never went over the top with his bullying, just enough to let everyone know he was top dog, and thankfully, he either kept out of my way or avoided me. That was until the day he decided to sit on my table in the dining room. The college had dormitories where we would sleep, maybe four or five to a room, there were about six rooms and about 24 to 28 of us kids.

The dining room was one big square room facing onto the lawned gardens. We were sharing four to a table, and the tables were set around the outer edges of the dining room, three or four of the teachers sharing a table right in front of the big windows. I was on my table with another three, right opposite and in view of the teachers. Only this day, the big fucker, the bully, found his way on to our table, worse, right opposite me, I tried to ignore him, but unfortunately, this prick, like most bullies mistook my avoidance for fear, the more I tried to ignore him, the more he kept giving me the grief. I could feel my temper rising and was dying to give him a smack on the chin. I couldn't, I knew I couldn't, not only would I show myself up, but I would also show my nasty side, which of course I didn't want anyone to see.

Eventually, it became too much, to avoid trouble I went for the better option, I picked my fork up, put on my fiercest and hardest stare, put the fork to his throat, and said, "Listen prat, say one more word and I'll fucking cut your throat from ear to ear." Well, the poor fucker went white as a ghost, I bet no one had gone back at him like that before; he shut his mouth and never said another word. I was dead pleased with myself until I happened to look across at the teachers; they were staring open-mouthed and in shock, none of them saying a word before turning their heads and concentrating as hard as they could on eating their meal.

Fuck it, I had tried my hardest to avoid this mug, I had handled it in such a way that not only had I avoided a violent incident, I had also put the shits up him enough to make him stop bullying people ever again with a bit of luck. I had never used a weapon in my life, I had never had the need or urge to use a weapon. I had seen one or two in my life use knives and in every incident had realised that they were cowards, now, because of this prick, I had put myself in a bad light with the teachers. Hopefully, it might die down, but I bet they must think I'm a right fucking nutcase, especially as they must know I came from a rough area of Birmingham. Needless to say, for the short time I had left, I noticed the teachers gave me a wide berth and didn't talk to me a lot.

A couple of weeks later our time was up, we all gathered to say our goodbyes, to each other, to the teachers and to the farmers who had been so good to us, my boss and his wife was sad to see me go, I could see that they were nice people. I started having a few regrets to whether I was making a mistake by going away; I liked it here, got on well with the farmer and his wife, would I regret it. Too late, I had made my choice; the van came up the next morning to take a small group of us to our allocated farms. The six or seven of us in the van had mixed feelings of fear, trepidation and excitement as we set off. Dropping one off in the Derbyshire dales, then another, then over to Wrexham where we dropped another lad off at a sheep farm, straining to look as he got out and walked up the farm track, sheep scrambling on the rocky mountains to get a foothold. I didn't fancy that, then down into Shropshire dropping another kid off to his farm in Salop.

Then we were off to my allocated farm between Newtown and Welshpool, a little place called Sardou, the countryside was beautiful and mainly flat, the Black Mountains in the distance, up a long narrow lane we finally reached the farm gates and pulled in. As we got out of the van, the farmer walked towards us, well, I say walked, he loped, and he was built like a fucking bull and walked like a gorilla. My heart sunk in my chest, I know why they've done this, they think I'm a fucking nutter, don't put him with someone small, let's find the biggest bastard we can, well, they found him all right and lumped me with him. The teacher wished me well, shook my hand and without another word or a backward glance, he was off. Oh well, I'm in it here, nothing I can do, I'll just have to try it out, if it doesn't work out I'll be off somewhere else or back home.

Farming with the Welshman

Mr Phillips the farmer wasn't too bad, he was a sulking morose fucker no doubt about it, didn't speak a lot, just grunts and groans, really, a typical farmer, but we seemed to get on, and I think he was impressed with my keenness to learn and work. I enjoyed farm work, I loved getting up in the morning at the crack of dawn, witnessing a difference each time, the silence was deafening, even the birds weren't up that early, just waking and chirruping as we moved along. I had never had the experience of getting up early in the city, in the slums, even if I had; it wasn't the same as out here in the country. There was a briskness, a freshness in and about the air that was exciting and different every morning, even if it rained, which it regularly did in Wales it didn't spoil the beauty of the morning.

Our first job, before any other was into the cowshed, where through the dimmed lights we'd make our way through the stalls, each cow had a name, and I soon learnt each one, each cow had their own personalities. In the city, you look at a cow, and it's just a piece of meat on four legs with a big tit. Here, in the country, it's an individual; it would turn its head in that cow like docile way, recognise you, then just carry on chewing its cud. Our first job would be to wash its big fat teats with a wet rag, of all the dirt or shit around them, and then we'd push on the pumps, turn the switch and let the machine start pumping out the milk. Setting up about four at a time the first to finish would have its pump taken off, and then pushed onto the next cow in line, each cow having its teats washed in readiness. Everything ran smoothly with Dolly, Daisy and

Gertrude giving up their milk without any fuss or bother, each cow giving around two gallons per session.

The farm was mixed arable, with about 30 head of cattle and this farmer kept his own bull. Like most farms, the barns and cowsheds were set around in a square with the farmer's house standing central overlooking all angles. In the nearby field stood the hen house with about 400 laying poultry, the rest of the land was set aside for crops and feed. Mr Phillips proudly pointed out that he had 140 acres and his farm was worth about £40,000. The cows were good quality Friesians, black and white, most English farms kept either Hereford or Friesians for milking.

As the cows gave up the milk, I would take it over to one of the churns in the corner of the shed, pour the milk in then on to the next cow. Once all the cows were milked, the churns filled, we'd go and let each cow loose and lead them down the field. Every cow knew their routine, it was like a trade-off, we gave them a warm shed, food and corn, then a nice day in the field eating as much grass as they liked, they gave us a few gallons of milk. Once the cows were in the field, the gates locked, it would be back to the farmhouse for breakfast cooked and prepared for us by the farmer's wife.

Mrs Phillips, the farmer's wife was a good looking woman, quite tall and statuesque, it took me a while to figure it out because I wouldn't have considered the farmer the best of catches they looked definitely at odds. It seems Mrs Phillips had been a model in London, how the fuck does a stunted little farmer from way out in the sticks find a nice looking model for a wife. It took me a few weeks to put it together, Mr Phillips dropped out little clues, travelling to London to meet his wife, the distance involved, she'd never lived in the country etc., etc. Then I clocked it, he'd found her in a lonely hearts club, he wanted a wife to cook and give him children, she wanted security and home, I think as part of the deal he'd had to take on her widowed mother into the bargain, not only was she a widow but also a battle-axe to boot. She hardly ever said a word, but her pointed nose and beady, bird-like eyes were everywhere. That poor fucking farmer might have thought he was the boss, but the real one was the mother, no one or nothing would get past her.

After breakfast, it would be back up to the cowshed, fork the straw over a bit, shift the shit out, then start on the gullies, shovelling the straw and shit down, into the wheelbarrow, then out into the centre of the yard where it would be tipped onto the ever-growing pile. It never occurred to me how different this was to city life, we lived in the slums a real tip, yet I could never imagine piling a few tons of cow shit right outside your door, yet here, in the country, it was the most normal thing in the world. Put me next to a lump of dog shit, and I will be spewing up all over the place, and human shit other than my own would have me gagging and retching until my eyeballs popped. But here, in the farmyard, I'd think nothing of picking up a pile of shit with my fingers, tip it into the barrow, then go over to the urn and help myself to a liberal helping of lovely warm pure cow's milk, I could drink two or three pints a day without a thought.

After the cowshed was cleaned and washed down, it would be looking for other duties around the farm, fixing dry walls, repairing broken fences, breaking, turning and seeding or planting crops. The sheep would be tended to and as the spring approached readied for lambing, then dipped for diseases then sheared. Mr Phillips, being Welsh, and a typical mean bleeder at that, didn't believe in paying out if he could avoid it so did his own shearing, cutting the odd sheep in the process. That was something I just didn't fancy and had no interest at all in learning.

When the cows were in heat, the farmer would lead them out, one by one, tether them to the post then bring the bull out. Well, this was a sight to behold, I had never seen anything like this at all, even at my training farm where it was all very clinical and tidy, a two-foot syringe pumped into the cow's fanny, a squeeze on the rubber ball and that was it, all over. Here it was a different ball game, everybody knows that bulls are dangerous and this was no exception, he was snorting and snotting, and his eyes were fucking red with anger. I could see that Mr Phillips was a bit nervous, to say the least, and he made sure that he kept a firm hold on the rope tied to the ring in its nose.

He had recently told me the story of a farmer in the next village who had gone to get his bull out, the bull had taken a turn and crushed the shit out of him in his stall. Well, fuck that, I kept well out of the way as the farmer started on his business. First, he would lead the bull around, bringing him past the cow's arse so he could have a whiff; this could take several passes before he got the scent; apparently, the cows give off a scent from their fannies that drive the bulls crackers. All the time the poor cow looks wildly first to one side, then the next, becoming increasingly more nervous by the minute, eyes bulging wildly, snotting and snorting in fear and anticipation.

Once the bull gets the sniff, his dick comes down, and what a dick it is, I've seen horses dicks, and donkeys, so I expected the bull to have a monster. Low and behold, it was only like a pencil and about two-foot-long, I really couldn't see what the cow had to fear. With his dick out, the farmer would bring him to the back of the cow. After a few tries the bull would do the leap, get up on the cow's back and with a little help with grabbing the bull's dick and helping it in, the bull was away, in, push and... that was it, all over, no thrusting, no pumping. The farmer would take the cow back to the shed or the field, bring out the next and start all over again. Once the first one was out of the way, it became simpler, the bull knew what he was doing, and with no further trouble, six or seven cows were serviced. The cows would be released into the field, the bull following where he could choose the rest of them as he pleased, now he knew what to do.

In many ways farm life was an idealistic lifestyle, the farmer was happy with my work and gave me an extra ten bob a week after a few weeks taking my wages to the princely sum of thee pound ten shillings a week. After a few weeks, he even managed to find me a bike, so I could get down to the local village, or Welshpool, eight miles away. On a Friday night, I would take a walk or bike down to the local village, buy a couple of pints and smoke a cigar. For a bit it was great, I enjoyed it, some days the farmer would take me for a ride on his tractor down to Welshpool market where we'd spend a few hours. After a bit, the boredom started to get in, after tea, I would go up to my room and play my mouth organ, learning a few tunes to while away the time. I popped my head into the living room one night where the witch was watching the telly; one look was enough to tell me that I wasn't welcome to share it with her. The farmer and his wife had their own cosy little room on the other side of the house; that left me every night in my little room, except for the Friday night.

I had got to know the farmer in the next village on the other side of the hill, he must have been told that I was a good worker so asked if I knew of anyone else who would be interested in a job in farm work. I got in touch with my mate Dave Parry down in Longacre and painted a nice rosy picture of farm life to persuade him to come over, as there was a job waiting for him, he didn't need much persuading, I was glad of the company.

Between the farmer on the other side of the hill and our farm was a smallholding with about an acre of land, the bloke who lived in it was the farm manager, foreman for the other farm. Walking up the lane one Sunday, I stopped and got talking to him, he was a nice bloke with a wife and two kids. As a perk of his job he was allowed the farmhouse to live in, this was known as a tied tenancy, he was also allowed to keep a bit of livestock, a lamb, a few chickens, even enough garden to grow a few vegetables. This was all very impressive, and I fell in love with it, I couldn't think of a better way of living and a place to bring up your kids. The more we chatted, the more he would tell me, how one day, he hoped to have his own farm.

I asked why he'd want his own farm when he had such a lovely way of life here. "Oh yes," he said, "But this isn't guaranteed, if I have an accident, or one of the farmer's sons grows up and wants a house I will have to get out."

I could feel my eyes rise in terror, "What do you mean, get out, where would you go?"

"Oh," he said a matter of factly, "I'd just have to go to the council and ask them for a council house." Well, fuck me with a duster, I looked at him in shock, he didn't seem to be in the least bit bothered this was all perfectly normal to him, so the farmer brings you in, gives you a house, then when his kids have grown up, its fuck you sunshine. As I started to walk on up the lane, the shutters were starting to lift from my eyes, idealistic lifestyle. This was striking me more as cheap labour; worse, as soon as you had served your purpose, learnt the business inside out that was it, out you go. No wonder old Mr Phillips was a grumpy old bastard, yes, he'd given me a ten bob rise, even loaned me a bike to get about, but all the time he had his eyes on his lads; eventually, I would have no job anyway. The light had entered my brainbox; even the arrival of my pal Dave couldn't extinguish it.

It was great having Dave with me, Dave enjoyed working on the farm, and the farmer found him a good worker. We'd meet up at night or weekends, go down the local pub, take walks, forage around the nearby countryside, for both of us it was a million miles away from the Green. But after a bit, even that began to pall a bit, and I started to clock that Dave was getting a bit worse, it seemed he was being treated almost as bad as me, only being allowed to associate with the family in small doses. Eventually, after a few weeks, Dave had had enough, "I ain't sticking around here no more, Tom, my fucking brain's about to explode with boredom." That was it; he left.

I tried seeing if I could make a few friends in the nearby villages, no one wanted to know or be friendly. In Welshpool one sunny afternoon, I called into a café for a coffee, tried talking to a lad on the next table that seemed disinterested and carried on reading his paper. I'm working on a farm over in Sardou, I said to open up a conversation.

"Yes," he answered back in a bored and disinterested voice, "I noticed the straw in your hair."

Fuck me, did I still have straw in my hair? Fuck, it took me a few seconds to realise he was just being a clever prick. That's it, stone dead. No friends here.

I started to wonder if there was a boxing club around the area and with a bit of spare time set off to Sardou one Saturday afternoon, making a few enquiries I was told about Dennis Powell, who lived around the village, I had never heard of Dennis Powell but was told he was known as the Welsh lion.

Dennis told me he didn't have a gym in Wales, but he would come over to the farm and set up a gym in the barn attic. He duly arranged to call over on the following Tuesday night, Mr Phillips the farmer was more than happy to let me use the barn as a gym, it kept me occupied and happy as far as he was concerned. It didn't take us long to set up a gym, keeping fit was no problem, so when Mr Powell turned up, all we had to do was fit-up a punching bag on a rope from the ceiling, and that was it, we were away. Following a bit of warm-up, I would go on the bag and do some boxing moves, I never thought about next week or next month, as far as I was concerned I just concentrated on the now, thinking that Mr Powell was interested in training me, possibly for a few future fights. What I didn't even realise was Dennis-the lion-Powell, was the former British light-heavyweight champion. One of his most memorable fights being against George Walker the London boxer, further, he hadn't come to train me because of his immediate liking for me but because he had a professional boxing gym in West Bromwich, and was weighing me up as a potential stablemate.

After a bit, Dennis asked me to put the gloves on and put the pads on his hands had me boxing around the room. Unexpectedly, I had moved in one direction as Dennis moved in the other. I gave him a right-hander, and down he went, I felt fucking mortified, I couldn't apologise enough. Here's the bloke coming to help me do a bit of boxing, and I put him on the deck. Dennis was even more embarrassed, even to the extent of getting a bit narky with me, don't bloody apologise, don't ever apologise in the boxing ring.

Dennis couldn't get over more than once a week, sometimes not even then, so I was left to my boxing and training routine in the barn. After a few weeks I had decided I'd had enough, I had been on the farm seven or eight months, and I'd got about £70 saved up in all that time. Fucking hell, all I was spending was about seven bob a week on a couple of pints. I looked at the farm manager across the road then looked at my little post office account, it's going to take me a lifetime to save enough money to buy a house, that means no chance, and where am I ever going to meet a girlfriend, girls around here were like fucking hen's teeth, I hadn't even met one. The only females I met were the cows.

Very soon I just couldn't take any more, I got my suitcase, walked down to the village and got the once a week bus to Welshpool then from there back home, the flags never went up neither did the bunting or the welcome home signs. My family just wasn't like that, "Oh, your back home then, ok, no big deal." I think most families in Nechells were like that.

Dennis Powell had given me his phone number so after a few days, I gave him a ring, and he said he'd pick me up on Tuesday night. Mom was sitting on the doorstep as was usual sometimes, Dennis pulled up in his nice new car, called hello to Mom in his normal cheerful voice, Mom just looked back in her normal unsmiling cautious and distrustful way as we got in the car and started to drive off. Dennis observed, "Your mom looks like she's had a hard life." With that, I looked back at my mom's face, I had never even considered her thoughts or feelings before, Mom was Mom, and that was it. Seeing her now, looking back, with Dennis saying that, I looked at her afresh, her clothes were cheap and tatty, her long dark hair, matted and straggly, her eyes sharp but tired, her face drawn and haggard. Poor Mom, she had had a hard life.

When we got to Dennis's gym, it was a small smoky sweaty place above a boozer. I wasn't much impressed, after a few warm-ups and a bit of shadowboxing, Dennis put the gloves on me and told me to get into the ring with one of his boxers. Well, the bloke was a bit heavier and older than I was and a bit overweight, so I thought I'd best take it steady with him, he must have thought the same with me, so we just shadowed for a few rounds with each other. After a few rounds, he turned to me saying, you're ok, which I took as a compliment. Fuck me if I'd known I was on trial I would have let rip. Dennis asked me to come back regularly, and I agreed but, once I left the gym, I felt a little bit let down and disappointed, I didn't see any future or prosperity there, only hardship and sweat. The Morris Commercial Club with Wally Cox was a proper gym, and that wasn't even professional, no thanks, Dennis-the Welsh lion-Powell, and his club was not for me I'm afraid.

Back to Nechells

Getting back to Nechells was getting back home, Nechells was a shithole and a slum, but excluding the beautiful countryside, I didn't see a great deal of difference between my house and the farmhouse, they were both grim, but at least mine was home, I knew where I was, I took comfort being within my own family.

Walking back into the Morris Commercial Boxing Club, seeing Wally Cox, and the regular team of boxers only added to my feeling of comfort. Most of the team were still there, Peter Hewitt, Johnny and Dezi William, Billy Monagh, Brian Ward, Charley Taylor, all talented boxers, all modest. One or two had left to turn professional, Danny Baker had turned pro, but one or two others had taken up their places. Billy's brother, Danny had joined the club, the Morris had the best reputation in Birmingham for its boxing, a big black guy had joined the club, built like a brick shithouse but just a gentle giant. Paul Brown was a nice guy, one of the nicest blokes you could wish to meet, Paul just didn't say a lot at all, a hello, how are you going and that's about it. When he smiled, his face lit up like a Belisha beacon, his goodness shining out for all to see.

As with all the boxers, we would take it in turns boxing and sparring with each other, a typical training session would be me sparring with Brian Ward, then a couple of rounds with Billy or Danny Monagh, a couple with Paul Brown, before winding down with a shower and a linseed oil massage by Wally.

But unbeknown to me, and a few others, the storm clouds were closing in, and our little worlds were about to be disrupted. With the competition from abroad in the car industry, the Morris could no longer keep the building going, so it was more cost-effective to sell it off, the building itself was a massive complex and our boxing club, great as it was, was just a small portion of it. There was no way around it, we had to go, there was no discussion, no debate, we were out on our ear. The alternative venue for us was the Nechells Green community centre, this was one of those ugly block buildings on the corner of Melvina Road and Saltley Road, there was no character to it at all, and it was almost depressing just turning up to the place. At the Morris you turned up to the door knowing you were the only one with the other boxers walking into the place, here, it was bedlam. First, you had to walk through the café social room, where different groups of different ages congregated, then we would go down to the dismal basement to get changed into our kit, then back up into our allocated sports hall. Our time slot was six-thirty to eight-thirty, after that was the five a side football team, before us, was the netball team, and in the next hall was the judo team.

Still, we had Wally, his co-trainer had left, but now Ernie Holt and Charley Lewis had come on board. Charley and Ernie had been two talented boxers, were okay blokes but I didn't think they were much good or experienced as trainers. I wasn't too much bothered, to me, Wally was the boss, he was the club, he made the club, that's all I cared about, the atmosphere wasn't quite the same though. A few of the boxers had left, Danny Monagh, the William brothers, even Brian Ward had left for other clubs, I just hadn't got a clue, how do you find a better club? A better trainer, I'd feel totally disloyal to Wally if I were to leave the club, his club. No, I'd stay here until Billy came along, it must have been good for him to come being the professional that he was, so did Paul Brown, although he had just turned professional, there was enough here to keep me in my comfort zone.

Soon, Wally started to talk about getting me a few fights, but first, it was about finding me the right opponent. I was, after all a novice, but I was good. I knew I was good, I could hold my own with anyone, but there was a whole world of difference between my training in the gym to a proper fight in the ring, quite rightly Wally didn't want to knock my confidence back before I'd got started

One night Wally had put me in with Billy Monagh, we had sparred around six rounds with no punches pulled, we had gone hell for leather, and the sweat was running off both of us in buckets, as we wound down, shaking our arms and legs. As we walked around the hall, Billy turned to me and said, "That was a good session kid, you know, if you keep this up, you will be better than me." I looked at Billy in amazement, this was high praise; indeed, I half wondered if he was just bullshitting me, but no, he was serious. Billy had fought some of the best in the country, before turning pro, he had fought and won most of the titles, even fighting for England. As a pro, he had even fought the world champion Terry Downes, rated one of the best. I could feel my little chest puff up a bit with pride, not too much though, there was nothing worse than a cocky boxer.

Another night I had done a couple of rounds with Billy, we had got the ring set up, and Wally shouted to me.
"Tommy, you get in the ring with Paul."
In I go and as I did, I noticed this big blonde kid with an older bloke walk across the floor to the opposite side of the ring. We often had this, so I didn't think much about it, a few people came into the gym, most just to watch, some to weigh the club up before joining. Within seconds, Paul and I were going hell for leather. As usual, I was flying all over Paul; he

was a heavyweight, me a welterweight. Against Paul, I know I always felt and looked like a champion. He was a bit slow and ponderous, but I also know Paul held back with his powerhouse punches, one good punch off him would have left me sparked out. We did about four rounds, and at the final bell, we both got out of the ring satisfied with a great session. Looking across the ring I could still see the big blonde kid looking intently at Paul, I had seen the same look once or twice during the training session, it was only after they had left that Wally started discussing the two strangers. The young kid's name was Joe Bugner, good looking, blonde hair; he had just turned pro and had come to size Paul up in the gym. Their next fight was to be their first against each other.

Wally had started to get me a few fights, and before each one, I would shit myself, for the first one I thought it was because it was my first, walking through the crowd to our dressing room was nerve-racking enough, you don't know who your opponent is, what he looks like, how big he is. As you walk around you try to scan the faces, he looks handy, I wonder if it's him, your stomach tied in knots, and with the best will in the world, Wally is shaking all over the place. For fuck's sake, he's the boss, he's the trainer if he's nervous what the fuck am I up against? If he's shaking what chance have I got? All kinds of thoughts go through your mind, okay, shadow box, do a bit of shadow boxing to warm up, and doing so I look out the corner of my eye, the first opponent's in from his fight, he's looking a bit pissed off, he's lost, oh fuck. The stomach tightens up a bit more, then, it's your turn, old Wally starts bustling about all nervous and jumpy.

"Okay, Tommy, here we go, out you go." Gloves on, feet skipping on the floor, I'm walking out, through the crowds and into the ring, looking across, I catch a glimpse of my opponent, he doesn't look any bigger than me, he's moving around, throwing punches in the air, I'm still trying to figure out how good he is or how weak.

Before I know it we're called out into the centre of the ring, the referee gives us the rules, shake hands, we touch the gloves, and that's it, we're off, with a flurry of punches we're all over the place, fighting for real. In the ring, it's different from the sparring I did in the gym with my mates, Billy, Paul, Danny. There I always felt comfortable, everything seemed to click, punches were passed smoothly, one to another Here, I felt awkward, every bloody punch I threw seemed to miss, where I was supposed to have this big punch, in the ring it felt ineffective. Before I knew it the round was over, back into my corner, sit down, a drink was thrown into my gob, then the bell goes again, and I'm off into the next round. Very quickly, the fight was over and low and behold, I was declared the winner. Elated, I walked out of the ring over to the judges' table where I was presented with my first prize, a Chinese tea set, and then, back to the dressing room. All over, that wasn't as bad as I thought. Wally was behind me, sweating and bustling as normal.

This was my first fight, and Mom and Dad were there to watch me. When I gave Mom my Chinese tea set, she took it off me, head held high with pride. She put it in her favourite china cabinet, still in the box and wrote on the outside, Tommy's first fight.

Back in the gym, everything went back to normal, no big dramas, just mild congratulations and that was it, no big deal, just another fight. There were no prima donnas in boxing, we were all equal, no one better than anyone else, we were all fighters, we were all having fights. It was a case of just getting back to practising, sparring, training and learning from our mistakes. Soon, another fight came up, then another, each one I won, each time it seemed to get a bit better, but I still felt awkward in the ring maybe it was something to do with the time in the ring. We would spar for 5—6—7, rounds, by the second round I had settled into the fight, I knew the opponent, I knew we would spar for three minutes, then on the shout of

–last ten, we would give it our last shot and go hell for leather for the last ten seconds. In the ring I was thrown in against a total stranger, I didn't know his moves, how he fought, how he moved, by the time the third round came along I was only just getting used to him, I felt stiff, stilted.

Paul had had his first fight against Joe Bugner and knocked him out. It was not only the talk of the gym, but it was also the talk of Birmingham. I thought back to that night in the gym when Paul and I had been sparring. I know Paul and I had had a really good sparring session that night, as we usually did, but that night, Joe Bugner had walked in to watch Paul, look out for any weaknesses, find fault in his boxing. He must have thought Paul was a big lumbering giant with no punch.

Wally had got me on the pads a few nights later, after the usual - last ten seconds, a final pounding on the pads we broke off for the one minute break. Walking around, shaking my arms to loosen up, Wally came over, looked at me and said, "You know Tommy, you won Paul that fight the other night." I didn't know what the hell he was on about, I looked at Wally in bafflement, he gave me a cheeky smile, "It's true, do you remember the tall blonde kid who came into the gym a few weeks ago? That was Joe Bugner." "Well, of course, I knew that his name was mentioned on the night." "Yes, but what you didn't realise was that he'd come to size Paul up, he was watching both of you over the rounds, you looked good, and because Paul was taking it easy with you, as he always does, you made him look stupid." On the night of the fight, Bugner went into the ring full of confidence, no doubt the words ringing in his ear from his trainer, who had also seen us spar, that it would be a walkover. Well, it was a walkover, but not for Joe, again, that was a nice bit of praise of Wally, but I don't think anyone else felt the same if they did, no one said anything, but that's to be expected in boxing, did you win? Congratulations, good boy, that's it, carry on.

We were training away one night, Billy Monagh was train-ing next to me, Bill was great, although he was a professional he would still come down and train with us, spar with us and take us out running. Billy's problem was that when he laid off training, he liked a drink and just piled the weight on and bloated up like a balloon. So, there he would be, two or three layers of black plastic bin liners on with a big thick woolly jumper on top, sweating it all out with extra training.

Billy trained up at the Trees Public House in Hockley, alongside my hero Johnny Prescot, and Brian Cartwright the British featherweight champion. Their manager was George Biddles, George was one of those old fairground showmen, a conman and salesman, a good businessman and sharp as a flute, always with a nice expensive Crombie and a trilby to top it off and chomping on a cigar.

We were both skipping away next to each other and in line when Bill cut off to talk to Wally. Now I wasn't eavesdropping, but I could hear Billy was having a right good moan. "It's no good Wal, I've had enough, don't get me wrong, I've got nothing against Johnny, we're mates, we train together, but George is getting him all the plum fights, I've had ten fights now Wal. I've won every one, yet all I'm getting is a couple of hundred quid a fight. I've fought the British champion, yet George is concentrating only on Johnny, and he's making big money."

Wally was just listening, nodding his head in agreement; this was most interesting to me as I saw my way to making it as a professional in just a few years. Now here's Billy, a man and a boxer I had great respect for, moaning that he was getting nowhere. Fucking hell, this was the bloke who was only recently telling me how good I was, how I would be better than him if I kept it up, and he's moaning because Prescott's getting all the money, all the glory, not forgetting all the girls, and Johnny was getting plenty of girls.

I looked across at Billy talking to Wally, in contrast, Johnny was dead handsome, he had film star looks, and a beautiful smile, although he wasn't a natural heavyweight, he had built himself up to be one. Billy was a cruiserweight, not much bigger than a middleweight really. Even bulked up, he would never make it in the heavyweight division, also, and I regret to say it, Billy wasn't the first in the queue when good looks were handed out. Billy wasn't ugly, he had a lovely big face like a squashed tomato, a nose equally as squashed, no doubt because of the boxing, spread across his face, his face and cheekbones shiny with the punches it had taken over the years, but he wasn't handsome like Prescot either. When Johnny got in the ring, everyone loved him. He was glamorous, the woman alone filled up half the rooms to come and see him, he was a film star and hero to us kids in Birmingham, to everyone from Birmingham, and to us he was a shining beacon of hope to what we could all be, he was a Nechells kid done well. But it also gave me food for thought and something to think about, his words didn't immediately sink in that night, it was over many nights and many months.

In the meantime, Johnny was in the news almost every week, even better, he was around us all the time; Johnny lived at the back of my sister Doris, Dot, in William Henry Street. He lived with his Uncle Tommy and Aunty Mary in a little mid-terrace council house. Playing on the streets in Rocky Lane we would watch as Johnny would come driving up and then down towards William Henry Street, great big white flash convertible, top down, and a blonde or a couple of blondes beside him, a big wide smile on his face. One day we recognised the blonde as Many Rice Davis, and the other as Christine Keeler, the two glamour girls who had just bought John Profumo the politician down and caused Stephen Ward to kill himself. No doubt about it, not only was he, my hero, I think he was everyone's hero. No one disliked Johnny, he was a friend to all, a nice bloke who everyone liked, he even bought jewellery and watches off my old man, if he were in the pub he would buy you a drink, he wasn't flash or a big head, in fact underneath he was quite shy.

He was lined up to fight the London glamour boy, the blonde bomber Billy Walker from London, well, we all thought he hadn't got a fucking chance in hell, Walker was a big brute of a bloke, a proper heavyweight, built like a brick shithouse with a punch to go with the build. Every opponent, he fought, he knocked out within the first couple of rounds, Prescot hadn't got a fucking chance and much as we prayed for a win, we knew he hadn't got a chance, I made sure I was watching the fight on the night. Not only was Billy Walker a big bastard he had the advantage of having for a brother the former British light-heavyweight champion George Walker, who had fought my trainer Dennis Powell, the Welsh lion. Certainly, the odds were against Johnny.

But on the night, both boxers came out to the centre of the ring, eyeing each other up. We were sitting there looking for the tell-tale signs, Walker standing head and shoulders above Prescott, bigger and wider, more menacing. Both boxers came out for the first round, sizing each other up, letting a few punches go before going for it full blast, hell for leather, first-round over with little in it, we all looked at each other in wonder, maybe he does stand a chance after all? No, he'll get knocked out within the next couple of rounds, but he didn't. Both boxers came out for the second, and the third, then the fourth, no boxer giving way, each one giving it his best, it was a war of the regions; the cockney blonde bomber against the Brummy film star. No boxer would give way, each one giving it their all. Walker knocked Johnny down a couple of times, and we thought he would lose it, but he kept getting back up and coming back, sadly, Johnny lost the fight on the final round.

Another fight was arranged fairly quickly, this must have been a real big money-spinner for George Biddles, and he wasn't going to waste it, Billy Walker was being touted as the next big white blonde world champion. The Arena, an even bigger venue than the first one was full to the brim, this time it was Johnny's turn, after a hard-fought ten rounds, he won on points. No doubt about it, Johnny Prescot had cemented his position in Birmingham. To us, not only was he a hero, he was a champion who had done all us Brummies proud on the world stage.

Wally had left the club, whether he left of his own accord or whether he was pushed I don't know, but now it was down to Charlie Lewis and Ernie Holt, two ex-boxers who had now become the trainer managers. I carried on training, but my heart was going out of it a bit, I loved Wally, and to all of us he was a father figure. We knew without question that he loved us all and was devoted to us. Wally trained us because he loved us and he loved boxing. He arranged and got us fights that he knew were right for us, not that we would win easily but ones that we wouldn't get the shit knocked out of us either. Charlie and Ernie, I felt didn't give a shit, either way, it couldn't be the money as we were only paying a shilling a session and there was only enough to pay for the hall hire. I could only assume it was for the glory or the take from the fights when there were amateur fights on at the hall filled up with everyone paying a couple of quid.

At any rate, a lot of the boxers left, Brian Ward, the William brothers, Peter Hewitt, Danny Monagh, new kids were coming in, but it just wasn't the same. Wally had lined me up with a few fights before he had left; one was with Jacky Turpin, nephew of the legendary Dick Turpin and Randolph Turpin. Jacky Turpin was up and coming, and Wally was trying to figure out if I was ready yet. The problem was, and I knew it myself was that I was inexperienced.

To move me up a bit, Wally had entered me for the ABA boxing championships, just the thought of it made my bottle go, but with Wally at the helm, I didn't feel too bad. My first fight was for the Birmingham championships, I was shitting myself, but shock of shocks it was a walkover, the next was for the West Midlands title, I won that also on points, even that was easy, then on to the North East where I fought the current British army champion, I beat him too. Each time, Wally was there at my side with me, cajoling and urging me on, giving me the much-needed confidence, then he left, halfway through the fucking championships, not only was I gutted, I was shitting myself as well. This was not good.

Soon it was coming up for the semi-finals, and I was facing a London kid who was supposed to be a bit tasty, up to now it had been fairly straightforward, some boxers had had to take on two fights in one day in eliminators until the fight was actually on top of us. I would manage to keep it out of my mind and avoided giving it much thought until the actual day, on the day my stomach would be doing somersaults.

I had asked Billy Monagh one day in the gym, "Bill, do you get nervous before a fight?" He should know, and I didn't want to admit my bottle went before a fight, how can you say to someone, anyone, that your bottle goes before a fight.

"Fer fuck's sake, you're supposed to be a boxer, boxers bottles don't go, why get in the ring if it does?" Billy knew exactly what I was asking. "Tom, everybody's bottle goes before a fight; anyone who tells you different is a fucking liar. Often, I've had to go to the toilets before a fight with sickness; my stomach has been that bad."

That made me feel better, so it was normal for your bottle to go before a fight, I wasn't on my own. Wally would have assessed the opposition before the fight and told me how to handle it and how to approach it. If he were a good boxer, he would advise me to be careful, try to knock him out, if he was a knock out merchant he would advise me to keep away, just keep throwing out the jab, build the points up. I got none of that from Charlie. I'm sitting there in the dressing room waiting to be called up, Charlie comes over and bandages my hands and puts the gloves on, "Now look, kid, you ain't got a cat in hells chance against this kid, we've just looked at his form, and he's had over 130 fights."

Oh fuck, that's all I need, I wish I hadn't have been told, now Wally would not have told me that. As we get up from the room and head of to the ring, Charlie by my side, I can see the room is chock o block with people, getting into the ring and over to my corner was an effort in itself. Charlie never gave me any advice or any prep talk, just keep out of his way kid, keep throwing your left out. Well, fucking whoop, a dandy, I'm up against a kid who's had over 130 fights to my piss all, and he's telling me to keep throwing my left out, what the fucking hell am I facing.

When I finally turn around and look across, I take an even bigger gulp. Jesus, the kid, is bouncing around like he's won the fucking fight already, not only did he look good, he looked big as well. Fuck me, he looked like Terry Downes the world champion, Charlie was right, I had no chance, at the first bell I walked across to the centre of the ring and he was there before me, bouncing around, flicking his left out, and catching me every time, within seconds my fucking bonce was numb and aching. He was picking me off, and I didn't have a clue how to handle him. It was as though I was frozen, at the end of the first round, back in the corner, Charlie was giving me the same advice, keep away from him kid, just keep the jab going.

In the crowd who had come to watch was Jimmy Grogan, a mate of my dad's and a scrap metal merchant. As I started on the second round, I could hear Jimmy and the rest of the crowd shouting. Halfway through the round I got a bit fed up with taking the punches and beefed myself up, going at my opponent with a few of my own, suddenly, I caught him, and down he went on the deck, the crowd roared, and I could hear Jimmy shouting to me.

"Go for him Tommy, Knock him out."

At the end of the first round, I felt a bit punchy and waited for Charlie's advice, "Now look kid, don't try and mix it with him, he's too clever and too good, just keep back and throw the left out."

Well, he must be right, he's the expert, so out I go again for the third and final round with Charlie's words of advice ringing in my ear. Throughout the round, I kept back, letting the kid pick me off at will, ignoring the loud shouting from Jimmy Grogan, to get in there and punch him.

At the end of the fight, my opponent was declared the winner, as was expected. As I got dressed after I gathered together with the other lads who had entered the tournament from our club to go over the fights, offer each other commiserations or congratulations. The other lad from London came over to shake my hand, which was quite decent of him, but my pride had been hurt, and I didn't feel too much in the mood to play happy pals with him. The fact was, he had beaten me, I was more and more pissed off because the more I analysed it and thought it over; I knew I could have knocked him out.

Jimmy Grogan knew as well and came over. "Tommy, I was shouting to you, knock him out, you had him on the deck, you could have knocked him out."

The more I thought about it, the more unhappy I became about it, for fuck's sake, my first real title fight and I lost it, worse Wally wasn't there, I just knew if Wally had been there, I could have won it. I came home that night a bit downhearted and fed up. I just didn't know what to do, without Wally the boxing just didn't seem the same. The club was not the same, most of my mates had left, and the ABA championships were a couple of weeks later. The kid I could have knocked out won the title himself on a knockout, a fucking knock out, he couldn't even touch me, I knocked him down on his arse, and he won on a knockout, well, that takes the fucking biscuit. I needed a few weeks away from boxing to have a good think.

Worse, Billy Monagh's words were reverberating in my ears, Billy was one of my heroes, here he was having fought the world champion and yet complaining about the little money he was on, Brian Cartwright was British flyweight champion, yet what was he doing? Going round the fucking streets with a pickup truck, tatting round the houses, fucking tatting, his father-in-law Johnny Mann was also his manager. He would be walking about in a posh blazer and neatly pressed trousers, a trilby on his bonce, and a cigar in his mouth, looking for all the world like a big-time promoter, yet he lived in a little terraced house round the corner.

This always amazed me about Nechells; things were not always what they appeared. I would watch people going into Nechells baths on a Saturday morning, a towel under their arm, come out 45 minutes later, all bright and shiny, face and hair glowing, a spring in their step. It was like they'd had a battery stuck up their arse, their little noses stuck up in the air, an immediate transformation, now they were better than us.

My old man and mom couldn't put on an act, they hated falseness of any kind, how you live behind closed doors is your business. To put an act on, try to be something or someone you weren't was completely alien to them, as my old man would often say, you are what you are, sooner or later you will get caught out, don't tell lies unless you are a very clever man, because eventually you will get caught out. Dad made a good living and made a lot more than most people, he wore a suit, but nothing fancy, a pair of braces, a shirt and cravat and he was dressed for the day.

Billy didn't put on an act, what you saw was what you got, but to be frank, what I saw didn't impress me too much. Billy had had a lot of fights, the results of which showed on his face, yet he was still working for British Telecoms and living in a house not much better than ours in Rocky Lane. Yes, he owned it okay, but my logic was if I'm going to buy a house and stick my neck out, I want something a bit better than living in Nechells.

It also hit me like a ton of bricks that I had been deluding myself into thinking I was going to be a heavyweight like my hero Johnny Prescott. I was a welterweight, 10st, 2lbs. With the best will in the world, there was no way I was going to put four stone on, in the next few years. I had been kidding myself; I had also got carried away with the money side of it too. Some of these boxers were getting their brains knocked out of their skulls for £25 a fight. £25 might sound a lot when you consider the average wage was £10 per week, a surface deduction might tell you that £25 is for 24 minutes work. Sounds great when you say it that quick, but then you have to fight every week to make it worthwhile, the more fights you have, the more you get your brains knocked out. I had seen a few of the old-timers around Nechells and at the boxing matches, cauliflower ears, punchy brains, "Err, arr, alright then?" In a punchy slurred speech, then a blank look. Fuck this for a lark, one minute you see the young kid in the mirror, bouncing around the ring, good looking, fit, the next you see the 35 or 40-year-old, punchy, face battered, cauliflower ears, slurred speech, sitting in the boozer living off their glory days, cadging a pint here, a pint there.

The Germans

I was at a loose end again, aimless without any proper goals or focus when I bumped into Rudy Swarm on the Green, Rudy was a big handsome kid who lived behind the army and navy stores in Nechells Park Road with his elder brother Carl, his mom and stepdad. Rudy was a great bloke and a good mate, he stood in front of you man to man and looked you in the eye as a straight person should, some people were snide, there were shy people, but people who couldn't look you in the eye, speak straight and direct were not people I could get on with. Most of the people I knew and grew up within Nechells were like that, the Turners, Wootens, Hardimans, Taronis, you had to be straight to get on and survive. It was the same in Aston, Summer Lane.

Swarmy, as I called him, or the German just appeared on the Green, like many of us, he just moved in from somewhere else, no one asked questions, it's no one else's business. Some have been there for years; some were born there and were then given a house there by parents. You could have as many as five or six separate family members living in the same road, that's another reason it always paid to be straight and speak your mind, you just don't know if you're talking to a cousin, an uncle, or a brother of the bloke next to you.

I didn't know where the German had moved from before he came to Nechells, what I did know, without even asking was that he was German alright, I had watched enough war films, I had seen enough Germans on the telly to know a German when I saw one. Rudy was a typical German, ramrod straight, square cut head, and typically, with a crew cut, he was cut out of solid German rock alright. Fuck, it looked like he had an iron bar down his spine and he even had that German swagger, arrogance, about him, his older brother Carl was a bit softer but still a typical German, straight with long blonde hair. I would muse for hours about their background, were they English born or German, who was their father, and I pictured a big blonde German SS officer, as their father.

The first time I called in at the Germans' house was something else again; their house was one of those little mid-terraces with a small pocket garden and a wicker fence. Knocking on the door I was confronted by Mrs Swarm, the German's mom, and fuck me, she was even more German than the German was, fair hair tied in a bun, she was built like a brick shithouse. I had seen her in many German films, square-jawed, square head, big square body, just a slight mound forming her breasts, before settling into her stomach, you felt that if you hit her, she would just blink. I tried to look her in the eyes, but there was nothing there like there was a blanket over them.

She spoke with a nice soft voice, kindly, "Hello Tommy," but I knew Rudy had told me she was a terror if he got into any trouble. Every time I looked at her I felt a little shudder go down my spine, her husband Paddy, an Irishman, of course, was the complete opposite, he was small, quiet, hardly spoke and never said boo to a goose, no one knew him, he kept himself to himself, it was all very strange. Was Mrs Swarm, a former SS officer? Had she been married to a former SS officer, maybe someone like Eichmann, or Goebbels? At the war's end, she had to escape Germany, bringing her two kids with her. The possibilities were mind-boggling – worse - and it was something I didn't dwell on or like to think about, what about if she had worked in one of the death camps, fuck me, the thought didn't bear thinking about, self-preservation dictated that I didn't broach the subject with the German.

Rudy had got himself a job at Pilkington glass in Chester Street, Aston, he had told me there was a vacancy, so I went down, asked for a job, got one to start the next day. I was working alongside the German on the factory floor, and we would have some good fun together, getting a job was easy,

It was great, and there were some good jobs around, if you were happy with the wages that were fine. Eventually, you could and would get a job that would suit you, and you could settle down to a guaranteed lifetime within that company, but the wages were never going to be that good, to even consider buying a house in the future, having holidays, a nice car, kids, didn't fill my heart with optimism. The wages were low and just enough to survive on. Fortunately, I didn't smoke, and I didn't drink, but £7 per week didn't go very far. I know a couple of kids who had managed to buy a car on HP. By the time, they made the weekly payments and put a couple of gallons of petrol in the tank, they had no more money left. You would see them on the evenings, sitting in their cars, posing, outside the cafes, some might buy a coffee, but that was about it, they had fuck all else in their bin, it was all show.

I would spend my nights wondering about aimlessly, unsure what to do or where to go, my only role models were my mom and dad and brothers. Johnny was a villain, and I didn't fancy that for a living. Billy was taking after the old man, he was now opening up shops and warehouses, building stock up on credit and selling it at knockdown prices. Unfortunately, he'd also got the old man's other habit, he liked the booze, most people saw him as a character with his big, brash, loud voice. "Hear, have a fucking drink," before putting his hand in his bin and buying a round, course, he was everybody's best friend. But I always noticed, as soon as the drinks stopped, they all ducked. No, I knew I wanted better, but I just didn't know what.

One night I was on the Green and bumped into the German standing talking to his mate Billy Lovell. Now Billy was a nice enough bloke, but we all knew he had a screw loose, Billy didn't look you in the eye, he just stood there brooding, not saying much at all, you never knew if he was just going to swing a right-hander at you. The German was doing the talking for both of them.

"Ay Tommy, you're handy at the old boxing, ain't ya? You know Billy here can fight?"

Well, yes, I knew Billy could fight, I'd never seen him in a fight, but I'd heard enough - and I can look after myself, look, what about if the three of us get together and work as a team? The three musketeers like.

I looked at him and wondered what he was getting at, "Like what?" said I.

"At protection Tommy, at the old protection. Look at all those shops on Nechells Park Road? We just go along, offer to look after their shops for them, lean on them a bit. Tell them, it's a couple of quid a week, it'll be easy money."

I said, "Oh, and what if they don't pay up?"

"No problem, Tommy, we'll just throw a petrol bomb in the shop window, it will spread around like wildfire, within 24 hours they'll all be queuing up to pay us."

Well, I had a right fucking job keeping my expression as normal, fucking protection? Round Nechells Green? Was he fucking barmy? I looked at Billy Lovell, who hadn't moved his head to look at us or nothing, I then looked at the German who was dead serious, they're both fucking barmy, both of them.

"Rudy, think about it, you see the shops there? Well, just down there, the other side of Nechells Green Island is Bloomsbury Street nick, and I tell you, our feet won't touch the fucking ground. Who's going to go in and ask for the protection? Because every shopkeeper along here will know one of us."

That ended the discussion, I didn't see the German with Billy again, and the German never brought the subject up again. I admired Rudy's nerve, I knew he would have the bottle to do something like that, no doubt, as would Billy, but there was just no way that was going to work, the days of Al Capone and the Chicago gangsters were over. We knew about the Krays in London, we had heard stories, but this ain't London.

British Rail

There was plenty of jobs and plenty of work, but Pilkington glass was a bit of a dead-end. I decided to try British Rail down Lawley street, this was interesting and enjoyable work, as the train would bring the loaded trucks into the loading bays, the big sliding doors would open, and we would empty the rail car on to a conveyor belt. There would be four or five conveyor belts with a line of rail cars on either side, each line consisted of some eight cars. Two or four of us would be unloading these cars onto the roller belts, the goods would go along these rollers to the far end of the buffers, then carry on until the bays either side of the rollers were filled with three-wheeler Scammel trucks. Another three or four people would be loading the goods we had placed onto the belts and stack them on to the lorries. As each lorry was filled up, the Scammells would be driven off to other bays waiting for the drivers to turn up in the morning, these would then be driven making deliveries to shops and houses around Birmingham.

I aimed to become a driver of one of the Scammells, but first I had to serve six months on the line until a vacancy became available. First I had to pass my test, British Rail arranged that and we were taught on the three-wheeler Scammells. In the meantime, I was enjoying the work, all kinds of goods were being delivered from all over the country, most you couldn't tell because it was all boxed or packaged, communion wine for the church was easy to spot because it was marked fragile. Once a box came in broken, and we helped ourselves to a drink, but as it was very low alcohol, so we didn't bother again. The system was all very simple and straightforward.

Now and again big money boxes would come down the line, fucking big money boxes, these were big chests, measuring some 2ft x1ft x 1ft. Now we knew they carried money because they were addressed to the banks, I wasn't a thief, but this seemed a bit ridiculous. I decided to mention this to my brother Johnny and Ray Kirby the one night, but they dismissed my suggestion as nonsense, after all, who would be stupid enough to transport large sums of money around the country with no security? Thinking about it, they were right, and I had to agree with their logic, who would be stupid enough to transport large sums of money like that, but they did. I suppose it was that simple no one thought about it.

The foreman came up the line one early morning and came over to the bloke next to me. This bloke had started just a few days earlier and seemed pretty educated to me, he reminded me of a teacher, quite, well-spoken, educated, a little bit hippy because he had a beard, the foreman told him to collect his cards from the office he could no longer work for the company. The bloke never said a word, just walked off; puzzled, I asked the foreman why the bloke had been given the sack? Well, he'd given his address as the Royton House Hotel, well? Well, the Royton House Hotel was not a hotel but a doss house; as such, he had no fixed abode. Well, for fuck's sake, here's a bloke trying to get on his feet, get a proper job, and he's not good enough. Talk about kicking someone when they're down. Next to him was an Asian guy, couldn't speak a word of English and ate Kit Kat cat food from a tin, we wondered if he could read English, and he was alright, Jesus, how unfair.

A vacancy became available at the driving school, and I was soon sent off to the depot at Sutton Coldfield. British Rail had a huge yard next to the train station, with a fixed supply of three-wheeler Scammells. We turned up at 9 am to be shown a truck, two of us were told to get in the truck and learn to drive, and that's what we did all day long, just took turns learning to drive, changing the gears, and reversing. The idea was great, and within a few days, I could drive quite easily. When we were judged to be ready, an examiner would take us out one at a time around the roads, when he felt we were good enough the test examiner was sent for and he would pass six or eight of us in one sitting. I couldn't believe how simple it was, we all thought some backhanders were going out somewhere.

Out the yard, a half-mile little trip around the streets and that was it, qualified, I was now a bona fide, qualified driver, bleeding hell, we never even did a hill start. Now a hill start with a Scammel was a real treat, to change gear you had to double your clutch, time you changed from first gear into second on a hill you were going in reverse. Until, I passed and got my license, and waited for my turn to be allocated a three-wheeler, it was not so simple. Again, I had to wait my turn so thought fuck it, I decided to give the job a miss, they sent me out first as a mate to get to know the routes and familiarise myself, it seemed worse than driving a bus, stop-start all day. No way, José.

I know, I'll be a train driver, now that was something else, so I applied for a transfer. This was at Tysely Train Depot, the main train depot in middle England. After a few labouring jobs around the site, loading wagons with the burnt-out coal dregs/ashes I was soon allocated a job as a fireman, the fireman was the bloke who stood on the plate and kept the fire going in the engine. It was a great and fascinating job, come rain or sun you had the fire to keep you warm, and the wind whistling through your hair to keep you cool. I loved the job; you saw a different part of the country, a different perspective. Sometimes starting at 2 am meant you saw the world differently. It was an apprenticeship, in the meantime, you learnt about the mechanics of the train, how it worked. Sometimes the wheels would come off the track; with the way the wheels were shaped you would never believe the driver could get the wheels back on track again, but a good driver could, by doing a bit of shunting back and forth, he'd get the wheels back on track again.

You also learnt about the signals, how to set out the detonators on the track and at what intervals to warn any other train driver if you were to break down, or if you came across any other danger. Yes, it was a fascinating job, but slowly it started to dawn on me that the steam era was coming to an end, the newer more economical diesel engines were coming in and taking their place - slowly, but surely the steam trains were disappearing, and the diesels were coming in. The writing was once again on the wall, my job as a fireman would be disappearing with them that left only one alternative - a diesel train driver and I just didn't fancy that, at all.

The Dirty Side of Life

One day I had decided to take a day off work, boxing was out for me, I saw no future in it, except a bit of fame, maybe, but more to the point it meant getting the shit knocked out of me and no brains left at all by the time I had finished. Having left school with no qualifications I wasn't the brightest tool in the box as it was, I didn't see a future as a diesel train driver, so I just didn't know what else to do.

With my driving licence, I then started looking around to find a car, as luck would have it, I found a tidy A 55 Austin van on a garage forecourt, down Saltley, to me, it was wheels, and it gave me my independence, a bigger bonus was I could earn a few bob out of it. My dad helped me get an extra few quid off it, the rest I paid on the HP, that's it, freedom and independence. I'd got my wings, and away I was flying, along with my mates we'd be off and away, venturing further afield, I was as happy as Larry, but still somewhat rudderless in my life.

One day the old man turned to me and asked if I wanted to earn a few quid, well of course I did. He told me that all I had to do was drive George, Fruity Tuit Fewtrell around the shops where he'd sell some gear. This was right up my street, and I was well up for it, being paid three quid in the process. The next morning Fruity Tuit turned up at 9 am, we all went into the front room - the shop, and Dad and Fruity Tuit would pick out what was saleable - six dozen mirrors - a few electric fires and three dozen teddy bears. As they picked the gear out,

I would load the stuff into the van. By 9:30 am, we were off, first stop over to Hockley and a group of shops, but before reaching the shop a stop of at a local boozer for a livener.

"Got any money?" George asked.

"No."

With this George gave me my first lesson, "Now look, always carry a shilling in your pocket, that is your entrance fee and will buy your first drink, once you're in you can always win yourself to another drink."

Following our little drink, well, George had the drink, I had fuck all, having to stand there waiting for him, off we went to the nearest shop. Well, my dad reckons old Fruity Tuit was one of the best con men, salesmen in Birmingham, it's not just what someone tells you, it's what's left unsaid for you to work out. George's son Eddie Fewtrell was becoming a big club owner in Birmingham city centre, he must have taught him something, so I reckon my dad was right, within 5 minutes he'd sold the shop owner three dozen mirrors, and a dozen teddy bears.

"My lad will carry them up," Looking at me, "Driver, take three dozen mirrors upstairs, will you?"

Who the fuck is he talking to? Driver, indeed, anyway I started carrying the mirrors upstairs when George blags me on the side, take the lot up, I'll sort it later. So, up I bleeding goes carrying six dozen mirrors, but Fruity Tuit's scam didn't work. Well, okay, the guy had four dozen, which meant I had to carry two dozen back down again, and there were a lot of fucking stairs. By 12:30pm we were back down the Beehive, the old man came out, bunged me £3 and that was it, I'd earned a day's wage in two hours, Fruity Tuit ducked in with the old man, wages for the day made, well, I liked this fucking life, much better than going into the factories or on the building sites.

But you have to find what you're good at and stick to it, the problem is, if you don't know fuck all, how do you find what you're good at? But as each door opens, you have to see it as an opportunity, and if nothing else I was the eternal optimist. The old man turns to me one day, "Son, go over to Georgey Stevens, ask him for my money and if he doesn't give it to you, smack him." George owed the old man 40 quid, like the others, he would call over every Saturday morning, pay the old man then have another load of gear off him and sell it in the car factory where he worked. This worked great for a couple of years until he got into difficulties then he stopped turning up.

George lived up Great Barr, and on Saturday, I called around to see him and get the old man's 40 quid. The only problem was George wasn't looking too prosperous.

"I'm sorry, Tom, will you tell your dad, I'm sorry, but I'm totally skint?"

Well, how could I give the poor fucker a smack? I'm deciding what to do when George comes up with a solution.

"Look, Tom, you've got the van, Becky Harrison the scrap dealer down Six Ways has got a load of tinned tomatoes he's selling at dead right money, we'll both make some dough, and I can make your dad his money back."

It seemed fair enough to me. So off we go down to Becky Harrison, it seems Becky had been down to Southampton docks on business when he had these tins of tomatoes offered to him, tons of them, hundreds of cases containing two dozen tins, or three dozen small ones, two and a half pence for the small ones or threepence for the big ones. They were Mara tomatoes, I'd never heard of them, but for fuck sakes, tomatoes are tomatoes, right? Seeing as the big ones were selling at a shilling a tin, it meant we could double our money and still sell them cheap. We were onto a winner.

Our first plan of action was how to go about selling them in the greatest amounts in the shortest possible time, easier said than done. First, we would just drive out at random, picking out any small grocery shop we came across, as we were white, we kept ourselves to the white shopkeepers, well, we have to be a bit loyal.

Very quickly the differences between the races became glaringly obvious, the English bloke will look at the boxes and ponder on it for half an hour, this is why we need fucking salesmen. He'll if and butt, get his pen out and do his sums, how much he's paying at the wholesalers, against what we are charging, then he starts looking for the con, are they out of date? Are they on date? Are there holes in the tins, are all the tins there? For fuck's sake, this is hard work. After hitting half a dozen or so small shops with white English owners and only selling half a dozen cases, we returned to the van depressed and thinking we'd made a right cockup. We'd still got a full van load of Mara tomatoes with half the day gone. No doubt about it, this selling game is hard fucking work.

We couldn't just pack up; we were both skint. I'd laid out too much money, and I still had to get my old man's 40 quid back, so it was onward and upwards. Then we got our first break, passing an Asian shop I was about to carry on, now already we all knew Asians were a pain in the fucking neck to deal with, notorious in fact, they hoarded money worse than Jews. Offer them something for a fiver they want it for three quid, but what the hell, we'd got nothing to lose. Leaving George in the van, I carried a case into the Asian shop. Putting on my best smile, I said. "Good afternoon sir, would you be interested in our Mara brand tomatoes? We're selling them at dead right money as they are end of stock?"

Well, the Asian comes from around the corner, opens the box, pulls out a tin and says, "How much?" When I told him, his brain went into overdrive, working out the costs as against the potential profits. "How many have you got?"

When I told him, he said. "I'll have the lot."

Well fucking whoopee. When I walked outside and told George he couldn't believe it either, he was out of the van like a scalded cat, it took us all of 15 minutes to get the cases into the shop, collect our money, and back to the van, it took us another 15 minutes to get back to Becky's yard and reload the van. We'd made 40 quid profit in the space of 15 minutes, double the average wage. We had found the way forward; we'd got to target the Asians.

Yes, the Asians were a pain in the neck to deal with. They would ring you up, ask you to do a job for them, then cut you right down to the bone, the problem is it all comes down to what you are worth, the Asian will work out how much you are making and because he doesn't charge or expect so much he will knock you down. It's ingrained in their culture. Back home, they have to work for two quid a week, over in England they have to work for 15-20% less than the white man. In the corner shop, they very quickly recognise the benefits of piling it high and selling it cheap, so when it comes to spotting a bargain, they are up there with the best, no doubt about it, the Asians will be running the country.

So off we set, targeting only Asian areas and Asian shops, Alum Rock, Balsall Heath, Sparkbrook, only this time we were only doing a minimum six cases for the discounted money they were flying out of the van. We were doing four to five van loads a day and were at it for five days when we hit a little problem. We'd never checked these tomatoes, after all a tin of tomatoes is a tin of fucking tomatoes, ain't it? So, calling into this one shop up the Adderley Road, I never gave it a thought when the Asian asked if he could open a tin. "
Course you can." So back behind the counter he goes and comes back with a tin opener, as he opens the tin I'm standing there without a care in the world.
"Hi, hi, what's this?" There's no fucking tomatoes, it's just shreds of bits and tomato juice, I was dumbfounded, I didn't know what to say.

"Oh, look, you're bound to get the odd tin with broken tomatoes; it would be the bouncing about on the ship. Obviously, that's what's happened."

"Ok, can I open another one?" At that, my eyes shot open. "No, no, no, I'm sorry; we can't go opening every tin." Despondent, I walked out, well, for fuck's sake, no wonder the tins were so cheap, there were no tomatoes in the tins, just juice, and you couldn't sell them as dips only. No, we'd come to the end of the line, our only course now was to milk it until we could get rid of the rest of the stock and get out as quick as we could. With that, we set off up the Soho Road with Asian shops on both sides of the road stretching for miles, we planned to make a killing and get out. Well, we almost made a killing all right - ours!

George and I agreed that we would do one side of the road each, him keeping to the left, and me crossing over to the right and off we went. By the third or fourth shop, I could see we were too late, the first couple just scowled and gave a curt no, by the fourth shop the shopkeeper pointed up to his top shelf, there, running the whole length of the shop stacked four high were our Mara tomatoes. Oh fuck, the Asian never had to say a lot, but fuck, it was easy to understand in any language.

Out the shop, I walked and away up the road, I was despondent, I know I'm wasting my time. As I'm wondering how George is going, I catch him running up the other side of the road, eyes bulging, panic-stricken, with an Asian running after him carrying a meat cleaver. "For fuck's sake," the guy was balling and shouting in his language, but I could get the message, so could George. I could tell by the sweat on his brow, the Asian had proved his point. After a bit, he pulled up and did an about-turn, George never stopped until he got to the van where I caught up with him, my tomatoes hidden in my coat pockets.

Sitting in the van, it was obvious we had come to the end of the road, we weren't the only ones who thought we were on to a good deal. Others had been going into Becky's yard and buying up dozens of cases of Mara tomatoes, even the market traders in the bull ring. Now they were the ones who came unstuck, they couldn't escape, for days after customers were coming back to the barrers screaming, most had brought three or four tins, those barrow boys were not a happy bunch, but nothing could be done. As far as Becky was concerned it was buyer beware, how come he never checked them I don't know, but if he did, he never let on. We got rid of the last few cases, said our ta ras and went our separate ways.

This was the story of my life, find a little deal, have a crack at it, earn a few quid, then it comes to an end. This selling game is hard work, get a run, and it feels great, hit a brick wall and it's like banging your head all day long I started to realise that you've got to have the stamina of a bull elephant to persevere at selling, and I ain't got that stamina.

My brother Billy would sometimes hire a stall on different markets days around the midlands, he'd take stuff out of his shop and flog it on the stalls, well, some of it, even that was hard work if you didn't have the right lines at the right price you struggled to sell anything. Next to us was a mate of Billy's named Chalky, he lived up Lea Village and had a shop down Six Ways selling second-hand clothing. He was telling us he had got himself registered as a charity, every Sunday he would drive down to London and buy a whole load of gear spending £100, by Monday morning there were queues outside his shop fighting to get in, he got all his money back. Monday morning and a bit more on top, the rest of the week was all bunce, the scrag ends he'd throw on the stalls around Brum, people were fighting for a pair of shoes off him, all he did was bung a few quid to the charity every week, nice if you can get it.

Larking About at Butlins

One day Roger the Dodger said he was going to hitchhike up to Butlins in Skegness and get himself a summer job. At a loose end, my brother, Kenny, and I decided to give it a go. The old man gave us a few watches to sell to make ourselves a few quid. So off we set with Dodger, on our new venture. Not only was Dodger a bit older than me; he was also a bit of a free spirit, Dodger didn't like work too much. Oh, if he got stuck in he'd crack on for a bit, he just didn't like work too much and got fed up. He'd worked at Butlins before so knew the ropes. Driving just outside Leicester we got pulled by the coppers, I was all legitimate, with my tax and insurance, so wasn't bothered, the cops wanted to look in the back and when I opened the doors, their little eyes lit up when they saw the watches.

"They're my dad's," I explained, but they weren't happy with that, and demanded we went back to the police station with them.

After two or three hours they told us we could go, straight away Kenny clocked that two watches were missing and copped the hump. The coppers denied any knowledge of them insisting we must be mistaken—fuck me; even coppers in quite little places like this were bent. I knew the coppers in Brum were bent.

I'd had many experiences of it even at my age, more than once I'd been stopped with Billy in his van.

"Let's have a look in the back, fine, had a drink have we?" - the threat was there. "Oh, that's a nice watch?" Give em a bung, or you get nicked.

Most working pecks don't come across this aspect of the coppers. Look, you clock in at 8 am, clock out at 5 pm—12 pm Saturdays, you've just got time for the boozer or a day out, but if you think or work outside the box your fair game, simple as that. Kenny was pissed off and quite rightly too, but I knew we'd got no chance. We got back in the van and set off for Skeggy, walking through the doors we got a job straight away, Dodger, knowing the ropes got himself a job as the second cook in the kitchen, second cook? How the fuck could he be a cook?—but that was it, it's all about the blagg, I got a job as a dishwasher in the same kitchen, Dodger doing the cooking and I'm cleaning the dishes. After Kenny got a job around the camp, we all started to settle in nicely.

The only problem was I just couldn't blag a bird, the camp was full of talent, young single girls working there, groups of girls coming on holiday, and they were all looking to get banged, but I just couldn't pull. After a couple of weeks, I was getting desperate; I turned round to Dodger, who was blagging the birds like nobody's business.

"How the fuck am I going to blag the birds?"

"It's cause you're desperate, Tom, you're showing it in your eyes. Once you've got your end away, you'll be alright."

For fuck sake, what does he mean? I kept looking in the mirror for signs of desperation in my eyes, but I couldn't see it.

But Dodger was right, after another few days, and trying desperately not to look desperate, I got my end away. It was like a fucking explosion, but once that happened, it was like the floodgates had opened, I was blagging a bird every night, the birds were doing the same. Once we'd settled in we moved on to the gates at reception on a Saturday morning, from here we could clock all the fresh meat coming in, sometimes sidling over and getting in for the night. It was fucking heaven; I'd never experienced anything like it.

Even better, after a couple of weeks the head of security came across to me in the Pig n Whistle bar, Dodger had told him I was a handy boxer, so Jock asked me if I wanted to join the security team. All I had to do was turn up at security, put a yellow band on my arm and stand about in a designated bar as back up for the visible security who walked around in blue Noddy uniforms. It was a doddle, and for that, six nights a week, 7 until 12 pm, I got the princely sum of £12 a week. Now £12 a week was not a lot, but I was getting £12 a week for washing dishes. The really big bonus was the perks, and the perks were the birds, we'd be standing there at the back of the bar, and within minutes the birds, talent, would start sidling up and asking what we did. Intrigued, they'd clocked the yellow armbands, "Security love. Security?"

"Yes, love we're here to protect the guests, keep our eye on you all?" The eyes would open up. "Oh wow, do you look after us in our chalets at night as well?"

"Of course, we do, my love, what's your chalet number?" We'll be round at 12." Not only were the birds buying our booze, but by the end of the night, I'd got a list of four, five, or six chalet numbers on my arm, a little tick against the best lookers, it was like Christmas every fucking night. Off, we'd go, at midnight, give a little tap on the door to find it opened by some little dolly bird in a baby doll nightgown gagging for it. Sometimes, if my mate never turned up, obviously being busy elsewhere, I'd have to try and sort two of them out at once during the night, sometimes both together, sometimes with the one going to the toilet, it was fucking hard work.

One night one of the birds put her legs up in the air, and a beautiful pair of long legs they were too. "What do you think of my legs?"

"Beautiful," I told her.

"Yes, it's a pity my boyfriend can't see me now." As my eyebrows hit the ceiling, she explained that she was having a good blow out before getting back home and marrying her boyfriend. They lived in a small village outside Stoke on Trent, and he ran a prosperous garden centre owned by his father, she'd copped lucky. According to her, he was a right plonker, but she knew coming from a small village that she would have to behave and settle down to married life when she got back. Well, for fuck's sake.

The next morning after giving her a right good going over, I got up and set off for work, leaving my mate on the top bunk with his bird. Later on, during the day, I saw him walking up to me. "Bleeding hell, your bird's a goer, ain't she?"

"What do you mean?" I said.

"Well, after you left for work, she grabbed my hand and asked me if I wanted to drop down and have a go at her?"

"Well, for fuck's sake, and did you?"

"Yea, I jumped down and got on top, but after half an hour she got fed up and pushed me off saying she couldn't take any more and I was boring?"

"Fucking hell, did she? Well, what about your bird?"

"Oh, she never woke up. I just got up, put my clothes on and walked out."

Butlins opened my eyes up to women. I know all women ain't the same, but it reached the stage when you knew that there wasn't a fucking virgin in the place. It was one big shagathon. Husbands would send their wives there with a couple of kids while they could play away back home. What the silly fuckers never realised, was that their wives were well aware of what they were up to and set out to have a bit of fun on their own, and when I say a bit of fun I mean, they got plenty.

One night we turned up at the chalet of two birds only to find the one had her arm in plaster, that didn't stop her.

"Be careful," she said. Thinking she meant, be careful of her broken arm I made sure we gave it plenty of room, she soon put me right. "Oh, no. Take it easy."

Then I realised it wasn't her arm, she was bothered about; it was her sore pussy. Looking at the wall by her pillow, I could see the names, Dave and Deano were here. Well, I knew Dave and Deano, two cockney Jack the lads, next to their names were a few others. Fucking hell, these birds had been right at it, and it was still only midweek, was one big fucking holiday. I was lithe and fit from boxing without an ounce of fat on me, yet I still lost nearly half a stone in the two months I was working there.

There was very little trouble at night from the holidaymakers, and that was mainly from young kids having had too much to drink. Butlins didn't piss about, anyone caught causing trouble, or fighting was marched right to their chalets, their bags or suitcases packed and they were kicked out onto the streets. Few wanted that kind of treatment, when any of the others saw that, it sobered them up sharpish.

As for me? I was getting 24 quid a week, food and board included, the food was okay, and we were getting pissed up every night, the birds were buying us booze, but we were still skint at the end of the week. After a couple of months, things started to quieten down, it was coming into September, and the camp was taking the scrag ends, disabled groups on special discounts, or the winners of some singing or dancing competition who had won earlier in the year. They would get what they thought was a free holiday to take part in the competition but would end up bringing all their friends and family who would have to pay for their accommodation. If they brought their partners nine times out of ten, they would have to pay for an upgrade or a bigger chalet. No doubt about it that Billy Butlin was a clever bugger, the only ones having the fun though was us, the staff, some from around the country, some from abroad. The Swedes loved it and even made their hooch, and on our nights off if we weren't shagging we were drinking, partying and still shagging. If some of the holidaymakers clocked on to what we were up to, they'd express their envy at the fun we were having, well, to be fair, they were here for a week, by the time they had sussed it out the week was almost over, and we were chuckling our socks off.

Sadly, as with all good things it had to come to an end, some of the lads had got it so much into their blood they didn't want to go home. Some were lucky to get winter work, doing a bit of painting or decorating, others would just find some digs somewhere and go on the dole, spending the winter dossing around the town scrounging a few drinks where they could, better cold and bracing Skeggy, than some rainy shithole place in Sunderland, Manchester or Liverpool. I didn't think Brum was that bad so I was glad to head home, I reckon I needed six months to recuperate.

It was good to be home again even though Butlins and Skegness had been a great experience; certainly, I would do it again and recommend it to any young lads learning to spread their wings, but not the girls, no, not the girls, well, not your sisters anyway.

Putting on an Act

Again I was at a loss what to do or where to go, I didn't realise fully how limited my abilities were or how lacking in education I was. The problem is when you're talking to the guy next door, or some bloke down the road, your education doesn't stand out. We all speak the same language, we all know the same things, you can put a nice suit on, even a nice flash tailored one with hand-stitched lapels from Burtons, even posher from Hepworth's, with a waistcoat. Yes, you could look the part all right, but the truth be told we were all in the same boat, all of us putting an act on, you either stood there thinking you were cleverer than the next bloke, or the next bloke would be strutting about thinking he was the clever fucker looking down at you.

One of the favourite words that started to come out around Nechells and the area, in general, was the word cunt, spoken with a sneer out the side of the mouth.

"Take no notice of him, he's a cunt," or if you're in the pub, you're standing at the bar and Micky Avo, will wait until someone walks in and whisper, here he comes, the cunt. This always amazed me because Avo couldn't even read or write, he would pick a paper up and look at the pictures, trying to pretend to read - but he couldn't even spell cat. As someone walked out after an hour's drinking and friendly banter, the word cunt would slip out of the side of his mouth, "He's only a cunt," as the guy walked out the door. I went along with this for some time, thinking everyone who walked out of the door was a cunt. It's only when it slowly starts to dawn on you that we're all cunts. How many times are they saying this when I walk out the door, because for sure as fuck, at some stage, everyone is called a cunt? In truth, we were all in the same boat, in truth we should all be helping each other to get out of positions we were in, in truth, no one gave a fuck about his fellow man or friend. Your line of sight was blurred by this constant attitude, from the teachers who spoke to you like shit and looked down their noses, to the coppers on the beat, in their case most of them only joined the force after leaving the army for a regular job and a guaranteed pension, it was ridiculous.

I used to look up to a guy called Robert Taylor, a few years older than me that I met in the El Greco Café, nicely turned out, sharp suit - nice shiny shoes - always looked the part, slicked-back hair, a swagger to his walk. There were a few of them like that around Nechells, in the Teddy Boy style, but then Rob got himself a girlfriend and the next thing I know he'd got himself married. One day he'd asked me to pop round his house in Long Acre, typically he and his new wife were living in the front room, as was the way, but none of us knew any better. First, our Reggie had moved into the attic with his wife Vera as did Doris my sister with her husband George, the idea is you share the front room, get yourself on the council list, knock as many kids out as you can and build your points up. Fucking diabolical it was no different for Robert.

As I walked around the back, knocked on the door, Rob's mom opened it to let me in, her weary face pointed to the other door leading to the front room, as I opened it and walked in I had the shock of my fucking life. Far from being the sharp-suited guy I had so looked up to, there was Rob in a scruffy pair of trousers, a dirty tee-shirt, scruffy, untidy hair and a look of tired desperation on his face, fuck me, he was only a couple of years older than me, and he looked knackered. A few feet away stood his missus, she used to be quite slim and tidy, yet here she was, lank bedraggled hair, scruffy, riffy clothing on with baby sick down her front, and in a cot, a baby, screaming its fucking head off. I was fucking horrified, was this married life? They were both fucked, neither one was much over 20, yet it looked like for all the world that their life was over. I said a few words with Robert, asked how he was, what could I say? I couldn't wait to get out of there. I hardly ever saw Robert again.

Life carried on the same for my old man, he'd be in the Beehive or the Brit, the focal point of the pub and the bloke the others would come down to see, some of them just for a drink, to socialise, some to see what or if any deals were going or being done. That's what it was like, the pubs were always buzzing with something going on. Like a mate of my dad who once sidled up to him and asked him if he knew if anyone who wanted his old black Austin outside, the old man, having had a car asked him how much he wanted. Long story short - the bloke wanted a tenner, and the old man gave him the money and the logbook. Dad's mate sitting next to him offered him 15 quid for it and before the pub had closed the car had gone around the room eventually selling for 25 quid. I had no reason to disbelieve the old man as I'd seen similar incidents myself, that's how it was, everyone helped each other. It was a time when everyone was optimistic if you had a flash car, no one showed any jealousy or sought to damage it. So what, you had a nice car, if someone came around your house for a bit of marge or lard, you gave it to them. But this was old school; people had principles and strong boundaries, which they were taught within tight-knit communities.

Bent Coppers and Crooks

On a Saturday, the pub would get busy. Siddy Hobday would turn up in his Rolls Royce, the whole family, squeezing out of the doors to get into the pub. There was no resentment towards Siddy for having a flash car, a nice house in Sutton, everyone knew he worked hard and took risks. The only problem Sid had was he had a terrible temper, and he hated coppers as much as black people. The stories were repeated with awe around the town.

Sid's yard was in Gospel Street at the back of Digbeth, one day he walked into his local boozer the King's Arms to see four black blokes drinking at the bar, Sid was incensed, "What are you black bastards doing in here?" The boozer went quiet, the four men went even quieter and tried to ignore him, this incensed Sid even more and without further ado, he went over and knocked the shit out of them, they never came back again.

Another party trick was his hatred of the coppers, how a scrap yard works. It is like this; first, you have to keep a book, in the book you have to put the name, address and vehicle number of the car, if any, that they delivered the scrap in, this in itself you could consider fair enough, if it was just like that and that was all, but for the cops, it wasn't enough. First, you had to put a bung in the book ready for when the coppers came for a visit, which was about once a week, this could be anything from a tenner up to however busy you were, or how much money you were earning, in Siddy's case it was a lot. Secondly, you not only had to put a bung in the book, which was bad enough in itself, but you also had to throw a body in now and again so the cops could show they were doing their jobs properly, and they needed to show they were. How they got their jobs in the first place is unknown, but once they'd got the job, they didn't want to lose it. One cop, Sword Edge, so nicknamed because of his name was that of a famous razor blade, used to deliberately fail his promotional exams because he didn't want to lose his job. I think this might have applied to a lot of cops, not bad work if you can get it, walking around in plain clothes all day, putting the fear of fuck into anyone who was borderline, getting paid for it, plenty of overtime, plus a weekly bung and not forgetting the Christmas hand-outs. Many a time when you popped into the local scrap yard a few days before Christmas you would see the cases of booze lying around on the floor, then the cops would call in aplenty, "Hello there, how's it going?" Smiles all over, for the lowly copper a bottle of whisky, for the regulars, a case; it was merry Christmases all around. I tell you; it was like the fucking mafia.

Well, Siddy couldn't abide by it, as far as he was concerned, he abided by the law, he kept his books straight, he put in the names and addresses given to him, his only gripe was he wouldn't bung, in any shape or form, and I for one couldn't blame him. The problem was with Sid it wasn't enough, he hated the cops and the corruption that much, he used to pay the young kids in the area, a blue un, a fiver, to smash the windows of the plainclothes cop cars or splatter them with paint, while they popped into his yard to check the books. They never walked out with happy faces. Worse, they were terrified of him. The only problem was Sid was storing up problems for himself. A lot of us were, unbeknown to any one of us the coppers have memories like elephants, not only do they not forget, they don't play by the normal rules, and they have time and the law on their side.

A lot of scrap yards are or were run by ex-villains. If you're ruthless enough, dirty enough, it's an easy way of making a living. Getting a yard after the war was quite easy, the country was full of bomb sites and spare plots of land, cheap. When Harry Twink came out of prison after doing seven years for a safe robbery, he'd decided enough was enough, what bit of money he had gone into a little yard over Hockley and he never looked back. People would talk in awe of shrewd Harry, oh, he's a shrewd un that Harry, nice house in Sutton. Hmmm, very fucking clever.

Jimmy Groge, an old mate of the old man, was the same, Jimmy had a yard off the back of Broad Street, my mate Happy said, "He grassed me up, Tom." I pulled Jimmy aside in front of Happy, Jimmy protested vigorously, "Never Tommy."

"Fetch me anyone who can prove that?" That's the rub ain't it, how can you prove that someone has grassed on you? The cops ain't going to admit it, are they?

Stanley Kirby had a yard down the back of town, now Stanley, a nice guy was another ex-villain who had got his collar felt and decided enough was enough. Stanley had a nice little house in a better part of Handsworth and enjoyed a nice lifestyle, now Danny Green had a nice little monthly tickle of a half-tonne of brass that he took into Stanley's yard. He had been taking it into Stanley for the past year or so, but Danny was starting to get a bit nervous. One Saturday morning Danny asked Johnny, Rajput, Kirby and Stan's cousin, to pop down with him to give him a hand in exchange for a drink. Of course, Rajput never caught on that Danny had his own motive. Whether he told Stanley I never found out, but on the day, Danny picked Rajput up, with the scrap in the back of his little 5-hundredweight van, the Old Bill pounced, Rajput got out of the van sharpish and off he went on his toes. Amazingly, he got away, the cops never seemed much interested in Rajput, but they nicked Danny before he'd even had time to think. Danny got himself a nice little stretch in the nick, and if ever it was brought up in the boozer Rajput would get all embarrassed, bury his head and give a loud harrumph, no one wanted to accuse one of the Kirbys of being a grass.

Normally, most scrap yards got away with this because they just threw a mug in now and again, a small fry. One guy had a little perk of sweeping up the bits of scrap around the factory floor, his foreman knew all about it, his workmates knew, and no one else wanted to pick it up. It was little scraps, sweepings, no doubt the bosses knew as well, well, by the end of the week he'd built up a nice little pile that filled his saddlebag. Off he'd set on a Saturday morning for his weekly, weigh-in, this gave him a little supplement to his meagre wages, brought him a few extra beers over the weekend, no one was losing, it was a win-win all around, until one day the scrap dealer threw him in. The Old Bill nicked him, and when he protested his innocence they called around to his firm, well the foreman denied all knowledge of it, he can't be seen to be condoning theft, can he? When they called on the bosses, they had to accept the guy had nicked the metal. The guy went to court, got a 12 month suspended sentence and a fine, and lost his job, not a bad result all around. The scrap dealer's response, which was widely known, was said with a chuckle, "It was no big deal, for fuck's sake he only got a small fine and he can get another job easy enough," which in truth was the case. To me, it seemed fucking dirty and disgusting, worse in some perverse way. Many people thought the scrap dealer was a shrewd businessman, what's shrewd about putting a magnet on the scales, ripping someone off, then throwing the bodies in to satisfy corrupt coppers?

Our senior school Charlie. Charles Arthur Street. As grim
inside as it looks outside

The Bull ring Birmingham. With a typical barrow that my dad
sold his fruit and veg from

Another view of Rocky Lane with Scofield Street to the right.
Anthony's corner shop and haulage yard with builders yard mixed
in amongst the houses

A typical street scene with kids playing out until it got dark

My uncle Jimmy. -pussyfoot-. Littleford. With my aunty Hilda. Jimmy would come up with great little scams like the roulette wheel on pram wheels with a button so he could control the wheel with his belly.

A typical scrap yard of the day. Where a bung had to go in the book.
As well as the occasional body thrown in

Spion Cop Park. A favourite haunt for all us kids with the cut
behind and the dark half hour.

A typical shop of the day. A bit more than just your corner shop.

And me and my younger brother Kenny in our best clothes for my sister
Patty's Xmas factory do at Newtons

Me and my dad on my wedding day

Me and my wife Bet on our wedding day. Skint and potless

My grandad. A peaky blinder

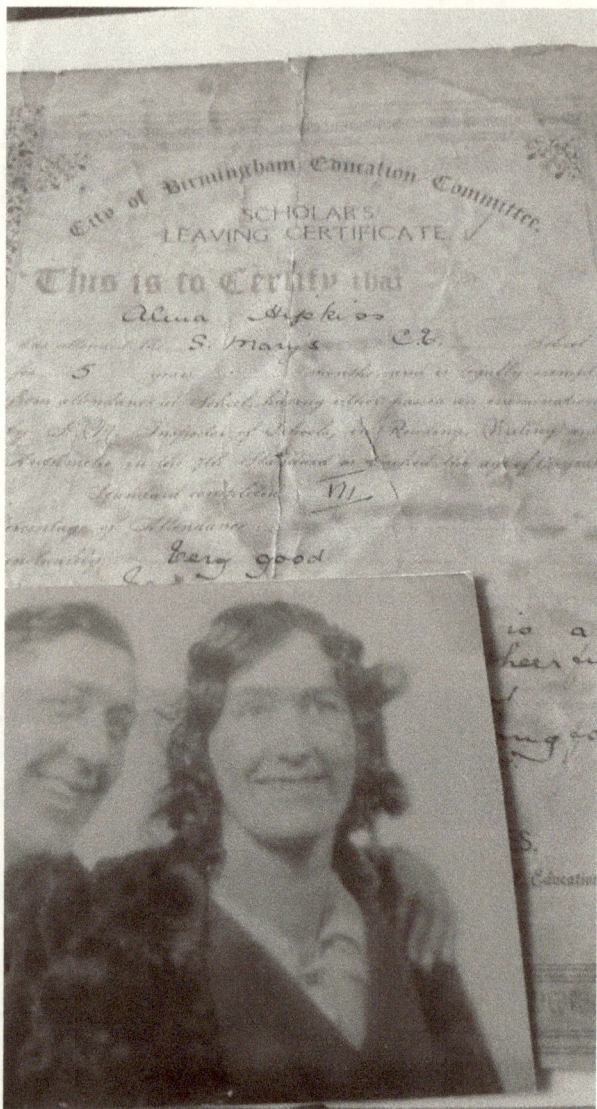

Mum and dad and my mum's school leaving certificate

A typical corner boozer. As miserable as it looks but your only option was to get drunk

A typical go cart of the day.

We couldn't afford a bike. And The Green. I don't know why it was called that as never a blade of grass grew there. Or Six Ways as it was also known

Another view of The Green or Six Ways looking towards the Beehive Pub. Where old Madge would stand outside till she got enough beer money.

And during demolition. The slums being demolished for worse slums

And The tat man. Or rag 'n' bone man...

The famous Ansell's Brewery. With the combined smells from HP sauce next door which covered the whole area and beyond.

A typical courtyard of back to backs

The gas works. The trudge back up that hill with a pram full of coke to earn our fluck money Saturday morning

Another view of The Green or Six Ways island with the notorious el Greco cafe to the left

My brother Billy. Aunt Hilda, dad and my wife Bet on our wedding day

As Fate Would Have It

I was just gone 17 years old, I'd got no money, whatever I looked at didn't suit me or what I fancied doing, working in a factory? No thanks, fuck that for a lark. I'd tried the building game, but seeing the money my old man made, made me turn my nose up at the skilled bricky earning ten pounds a week, the labourer earning eight. It was peanuts, I could do with a helping hand, a lift up, but there was no one around to help me. Then fate lent its little hand.

The front door went, and I opened it to see one of my brother's mates was standing there named Charlie Heinz. Now all I knew was that Charlie was one of the gangsters into everything and anything, as he stood looking around nervously, he asked where my old man was; well I hadn't got a clue. It was around 11 am, and I suppose he had gone uptown or to the boozer. At any rate, I invited Charlie in, and he brings out a bag of tom (jewellery). "Can you give this to the old man when he comes back?"

"Sure," I said, and in front of him, I put it in the second drawer down in the centre of the cabinet, that my Uncle David had made for my mom as her wedding present. Charlie then left the house, and I went into the back lounge.

The next thing I know is there is a loud knock at the back door leading off the kitchen. As I open the door there with his big fat pasty face is Pip the Planter, Charlie had been gone barely an hour, now I'm barely 17 and a half, and here's this Pip with a great big smirk on his sickly pale face with five of his goons around him.

"What the fuck is going on here? Who is the owner of this house?" says Pip.

Not knowing what to say, I said, "I am." Well, I'm the only one in it.

His smirk getting bigger he pulls out this warrant, "Well, this is a warrant to search this house," and with that, he marches past me with his goons, straight into the back room, then the hallway, straight into the front room and straight to the second cupboard down in my mom's china cabinet. They knew exactly where to go, so there was only one conclusion. Charlie Heinz had squealed, either that, or Charlie had told his mate Caswell the scrap dealer, and he had informed the cops. Either way, Charlie was the grass; you don't go into that much detail.

Pip the Planter was notorious in and around Birmingham. He was the top cop who everyone went to if they were having trouble nicking someone. He would just go in, nick them, then find the evidence when I say find, I mean find as in a plant, because old Pip would just find it or plant it, hence his nickname, which was a play on his name, Pip the Planter. I had heard stories of him and the rest of Birmingham CID over the last couple of years, the Old Bill would just round you up, bustle you into a squad car, or van, run you to some cop shop without telling anyone where you were going, throw you in a cell, then let you stew for a bit.

Nine times out of ten they knew who you hung around with so would nick them as well, all together, then take them to different nicks, most times they probably had done the blag they were being accused of. Either way, they started shitting because in either case they were done for, Pip would walk around to your cell," Right, is this yours?" he said, offering Dennis Woodhall a screwdriver. Dennis, puzzled, went to take it off Pip before rapidly realising the trap he had set himself up for and diving back into his cell. Dennis was lucky, for lack of evidence, they let Dennis go if he had picked the screwdriver up, he would have been fucked, the next thing would have been the statement.

"Okay guv, it's a fair cop, you've got me good and proper," and I throw my hands up. By the time it got to court, you were well and truly fucked. One, you were on legal aid, so your solicitor didn't give a shit. He knew you had a criminal record so if you were not guilty of this you had done something else, so when you screamed fit-up in the dock, your solicitor advised you to keep your gob shut, accuse the cops of lying, that gave the prosecution the excuse to bring out your criminal record, which you had.

The police were allowed to read from their notebooks word for word, the same recollections you had to stand there in the dock, like a prat, saying "No sir, sorry sir."

"Are you calling these police officers liars Mr...

"No, sir, definitely not, sir, it's a mistake." The prosecution knew they'd got you by the bollox, your defence for some reason didn't give a shit. Oh, they knew all right, they just shrugged their shoulders, went home and completely forgot about it. I'd seen this time and time again when the cops started fitting up the IRA, or people associated in any way with the IRA, or being Irish, it became a different matter, now it all opened up into the public and political domain. Villains were being fitted up and sent down by the hundreds-most had no choice but to have to take it, many had no choice but to accept it as part of the risk. It rarely stopped them from committing any further crime; all they did was become more bent, and or changed tack.

I had heard many a story of some of my dad's mates being fitted up, many were entirely innocent, as with the two guys who got eight years and ten years for a major safe robbery. When they came out, they were both broken men, (which if we must be honest, was the whole idea) The one guy got a job on the door of the Garryowen nightclub, owned by Brendon Joyce, and got his head blown off for his trouble, poor fucker.

The judges knew about all this, of course, they must have done, how many cases were going to court with disputed evidence - unsigned confessions? Either the judges were fucking stupid, or they were part of the conspiracy, each adopting the attitude, "Oh well, you may not be guilty of this, but you're guilty of something." This was a view passed on to newspapers via courtroom a journalist, one journalist in the Birmingham Mail admitted this in an article, where he had just observed a defence witness protesting his innocence and that he had been fitted up. "Har, har," laughed the copper, they all say that, but if he never did that one he's done other jobs, the astonishing thing to me was the journalist went along with this.

I was aware of some of this, not all of it, as Pip, the Planter walked in, but, as I was innocent, I had no worries. Just then, right on time, the old man walked in, that's it, nothing was said, we were both marched out, in separate cars, so we couldn't speak to each other, then driven up at speed, to Blackpool, we were then locked up for over a week in some local police station. We were not allowed to talk or see each other, it was chock-a-block and fucking bedlam, I was in with sheep rustlers from out in the country and a smart guy in a nice handmade silver suit who made his living going from hotel to hotel living the high life while bouncing cheques. It was fascinating, and I met some nice interesting characters. Without any preamble, we were then driven off to Risley Prison, my dad in the adult section, me in the youth section, it was fucking horrendous. I had no chance to speak to my dad; we were kept separate at all times. The youth section where I was, was a fucking nightmare, kids were killing themselves regularly, many of these kids were fucked up in the head, lost, and had committed petty crimes. Here they were, being locked up knowing they were going to prison, or Borstal or whatever.

Me? Well, we'd done fuck all, so it was just a case of waiting for the truth to come out.

Billy was coming up to see us regularly, but because of my age, he was mainly talking to the old man, I was just happy to leave it to them to sort it. It seemed Charlie had nothing to do with it, which was a surprise to me. According to Billy, and the rest of the family, Charlie was not a grass; it was Caswell, the scrap dealer, who had a scrap yard up Nechells Park Road. Now we all know, and it's a fact that all scrap dealers are grasses, it's the only way they can survive. It seems Charlie had dropped the jewellery into me, then gone and told Caswell but I'm puzzled when the cops came in, they went to the exact draw that Charlie had seen me put it in? How could that be? Did Charlie go back to Caswell, and tell him word for word, piece by piece where he saw I had put it? It didn't add up, but I was just a kid, my dad and brothers knew best. As far as they were concerned, Charlie was tried and tested, Charlie ain't a grass. Sadly, they didn't, it was worse, things were out of our control.

After a few more nightmare fucking weeks, we were brought up before the court in Blackpool. I'd never been to Blackpool in my life, I don't think my dad had, from what I could see from the prison van window in the drizzling rain it looked a shit hole.

I never spoke to anyone, solicitors, barristers, anyone, I don't think my dad did either. I'm just going with the flow, then Billy comes down to see us both, he'd just spoken to the barrister. He reckons we haven't got a chance of getting off with it, I'm not sure what it was, but it was either robbery of a jewellery shop in Blackpool or receiving stolen goods. Fuck me, I'd never been to Blackpool, I'd never received stolen goods.

The setup was this, whatever Pip the Planter had added to it, Dad had got done for receiving stolen jewellery a few years earlier. Some low life had come to the house, brought some stuff off my dad, the rat had then got nicked, asked where he'd got his bundle of dough, then squealed on my dad, no evidence was found, again it was Pip the Planter, my dad got sentenced to three years for receiving stolen goods. For fuck's sake, my dad was a general dealer; he bought and sold anything to earn a living, that's what dealers do.

My mom had only recently died, we were both suffering a bit, all of us were, Billy was just trying to find the best solution, he had to travel up from Birmingham to sort it out. The best solution was found, if we pleaded not guilty, the old man for certain was going to be found guilty. He had got form for receiving stolen goods, i.e. jewellery if he got done he would lose our house. There was only one solution, for me to plead guilty to receiving stolen goods; I would get a minor Borstal sentence. The old man could walk out and keep the house. It seemed simple enough to both of us, so I pleaded guilty, the old man got up, gave my hand a firm grip and walked out the dock. I'm sitting there stunned, wondering what the fuck is going on and wondering what the fuck Borstal is all about. Surely, it can't be anywhere as bad as the lunatic asylum, Risley.

Borstal

People will never understand this. Even as I put the words down now, I can see people saying, or muttering under their breath, cobblers, the cops don't do that. Well, I tell you they do, worse, it's common knowledge, but it's common knowledge only amongst a select few, the ones who are doing it, the solicitors who raise their eyebrows but do nothing, the judges, the judges know, but if the evidence is there they don't give a fuck either. As far as they are concerned the police are there to do a job, get rid of the vermin, the scumbags off the streets, and a fine job they are doing of it, ain't they? Ha, ha, funny how the prisons are getting fuller, and the crime rate is going through the roof.

As for the reporters, the journalists, well they were all good old pals with the cops weren't they, having a drink over at the press club, a G & T, or half of mild, "Oh-oh, that's another one gone down, what about all that nonsense of the baddy there screaming fit-up inspector?"

"Oh, they all do that, don't they, everyone is innocent in prison? Anyway, if he weren't guilty of this one, he was guilty of something else."

"Oh?" Yes, of course, this is your new mate telling you this, it's all jolly good fun. "What about the Birmingham Six, those little scum bags who served 20 years for a crime they never committed?"

"Well", it's obvious they were guilty in some way, what does it matter? If they didn't do this one, they did another; they deserved to be put away."

"Quite right too, another half?" It was interesting how Lloyd House was right next to the Birmingham Post and Mail, almost bosom buddies.

I had no choice but to plead guilty, from where we come from, you accept it as part of your life. So off I went to Strangeways prison in Manchester, what a fucking shithole. I'd never been to prison before, and this was mind-numbing, it was fucking horrendous, again, just a more mature version of Risley. As a young offender, you go to Risley, if you're found guilty, you're sent to a prison like Strangeways. For those experienced ones it was just a home from home, a place to get used to until you got out, for the old-timers, they shuffled along with head down, worn out and fucking defeated. Maybe some had had a last crack of the whip and got nicked trying, for others it was just a regular turnstile, get out, go on the dole, live hand to mouth, then maybe see an opportunity to nick a few quid, grab a bit off the shelf in the supermarket. Oops, collared, nicked again, so the whole cycle goes on, back to nick, lose your last few possessions, come out to fuck all, get a bedsit or a council flat, beg a bit of furniture, here we go on the merry go round again.

Then you have the special wing, or wings, for the long-termers, or lifers, those who had killed someone. There was the young guy of 24 who had been living with his girlfriend, they'd had an argument, maybe one of many, and he'd accidentally killed her by strangulation. In a panic, he'd buried her body under the floorboards, it took a few weeks, and the smell before the cops got to him. Okay, I'm not condoning murder by any degree. What the silly prat did was wrong, but we all act differently in different situations and circumstances. It was common knowledge in the prison that the guy was mentally fucked. He'd committed the most terrible act against his girlfriend, but he hadn't murdered her, it was accidental and should have been manslaughter. Even the screws knew it, it was the talk of the prison, but guilty, he pleaded to, and guilty, he was found, with a life sentence, to go with it, he walked around zombified, drugged up to his eyeballs, if he was lucky he might get out in 12 years, the first half fucked.

Then there were the two young lads of 15 and 17, who had robbed some old lady, broke into her house, killed her and stuffed her pet budgie down her throat, they were young, silent, pasty white, now they were fucking frightening. What do you do with someone like that, whatever your age, you have to be seriously disturbed to commit that kind of crime? Everyone shuffles around anonymously, we all wear shitty grey shapeless jackets and trousers and ill-fitting blue and white striped shirts. The known faces, or those who are the big shits on the outside, and maybe have contacts in the stock room and can order the newest or best fitting of the prison uniforms. The rest of us have to wear what we were given, I was given a crappy uniform, we all blend into each other, hundreds of us walking about, insignificant, bitter, chirpy, resigned to our fate, degraded, which was the whole intention.

The barons would be walking about with the smartest of uniforms, offering favours here, a pack of baccy there. Most were fucking nobodies on the outside, but in here, they were someone, keeping friends from both sides, from the big gangsters to the lowest of the scum, paedophiles mixed with nonces. It was that bad you didn't know who you were rubbing shoulders with, but that was the plan, to humiliate you, to make you realise what an insignificant bit of scum you were.

 Then you'd have the smart Alecs who made themselves feel a bit better by putting someone down or letting you know they knew more than you, "What you got, son?

"Borstal, fucking Borstal."

"Oh, you'll get your comeuppance, there; you'll get the shit knocked out of you in Borstal."

As the days went by I was shitting myself more and more, it felt like I was going to be facing a rabid mob of spitting raging fucking nut cases, I'd seen one or two in Risley.

All the time I was blithely going along totally unconcerned knowing that I was innocent, of course, it was obvious, everyone would no doubt know this, Jesus, I was too young to have done something like this, robbed a jeweller in Blackpool? Nah, people, no one in authority gave a fuck, it just passed along the chain, like a piece of meat on a conveyor belt, shove along there, you're not my concern, and off you'd be brushed. I never knew whether I had pleaded guilty to robbing a jewellery shop in Blackpool or received stolen goods in Birmingham

It's difficult for anyone to get their head around someone pleading guilty to a crime they never committed, I couldn't figure it out myself, much as I tried, why did I plead guilty? Simple, loyalty, I couldn't see my dad go to prison, even worse knowing my mom had not long died.

I know we'd all like to live our lives in a certain way, most people are brought up to get a job, put their nose to the grindstone, beaver away, with a bit of luck you get promoted, maybe a wage increase. Well, sorry, everyone I know is mainly in shit hole jobs, working for shit money, either labouring in factories or on building sites, getting to 50 with one foot in the grave and a pittance of a pension to live on. Well, cobblers to that. Thieving wasn't the way, I'd come to realise that. Worse, most of them, Johnny, the Kirbys, they all thieved and lived in the now, a little tickle, then blow it in a matter of weeks. Even my dad, I've known him to have enough money in his pocket to buy a house, own his property, his own home, yet underneath he was frightened, to take the risk, take the gamble, only a mug, buys his own house, and that was the mantra they all lived by.

Live in a council house you have a house for life, lose your job the social will pay your rent. Well, it's a no brainer ain't it? Problem is, if you live in a council house, you're fair game for anyone, money lenders, credit companies, and the cops, the cops know if your name is thrown up, they can storm in, kick the door down, do what they want with you and you ain't got a leg to stand on. No one can afford a solicitor, so it's on to legal aid, the solicitors got his nose in the trough, and as far as he's concerned, you're guilty anyway, after all, you've got a criminal record, ain't ya? Charged with stealing? Well, you've nicked before, even if you didn't do this one you'll be up for another soon enough. Dennis Sullivan, Sully, was a fighting man, well known around Summer Lane for hitting a few people. No one went to the cops, you took it on the chin, and that was it, but sadly, times were changing, we were moving into the era of the grass. The cops loved it; they thought they were being clever fitting people up all over the place, encouraging them to come out squealing and screaming like headless chickens. It worked all right for a bit, it started to work too well, now everyone was squealing at the drop of a hat - far from making improvements, the cops were making a rod for their backs. Now there was no honour, no loyalty, these were principles you were taught from kindergarten, fight your own battles, and stick up for yourself, keep your mouths shut. I was just too slow at catching on.

My dad was a decent bloke, my mom, honest and hard-working, neither were out and out crooked, you went to my dad and offered him a dozen shirts, or a few boxes of shoes he would buy them off you if he could make a profit he would sell them on. The cops knew this, he was never a problem to anyone, neither was my mom, she would buy socks, or sweets, toys, anything that would earn her a few quid to buy a few halves in the Beehive, a lot of people earned an extra crust like this. Sadly, my dad had too many major problems, one, he hated grasses with a vengeance, and two, he drank with, and associated with crooks and villains, as far as the cops were concerned, the filth, we were all one big mass of heaving thieving vermin.

No matter what anyone else knew or thought, and most people, neighbours, knew our front room was our dad's shop, by the time they nicked him for something and by the time it got to court, a whole different scenario was put forward. The old man would be claiming benefits, getting his rent paid, his council house rent paid, it's all an open book, you can't get lower than that, so while so many were at it, while so many were thinking they were being a bit clever, in reality, they were storing up problems for later on. Where my mom saw the benefits of buying that hardware shop, being all above board, being legal - my dad thought he was being clever, he was, maybe too clever. Now we were paying the price, well, I fucking was, worse, I was storing up even bigger problems for later, banking it all for ahead, as they say.

Borstal wasn't as bad as people were saying, frightening the shit out of me along the way, by the time I'd got to Thorne Borstal outside Doncaster I'd realised I'd best keep my head down. Thankfully, I quickly realised that most of the kids in there were decent kids, quite a few from respectable middle-class homes, one's uncle owned a major bedding company, another was a typical well brought up, spoilt, middle-class kid who had decided that he wanted to rob a building society of its money. Sadly, he went in and made a right cockup of it, and got himself sent to Borstal, why they were in there fuck knows. These weren't bad kids, they'd just lost their way a bit, as were most of them in there, I didn't know what a private school was, or boarding school, but this place reminded me of what a boarding school would be like. Up at 7 am, then out to various jobs, as it was summer my job was out in the fields on the farm, picking spuds or vegetables, getting a nice tan, as we went. Some worked in the laundry room, the lady who ran that had a little Jack Russell who had a dirty little habit of eating all the snot of the filthy handkerchiefs that went into being washed, she just blithely ignored it, God only knows if she let the dirty little bastard lick her face afterwards.

Everyone had their jobs, then there were some short courses you could take to get a taste of something, I volunteered for the mechanics' course, well, mechanics is simple enough, ain't it? Taking a clutch out, replacing it? Putting a new wheel on, rebuilding an engine? Well, what a fuck up I made there, I spent a week, just planning down a piece of steel, on a workbench getting it to an nth thickness, what the bloody hell was all that about, this wasn't mechanics, we were only in here for a few months, not a lifetime. Then, of course, there were the bullies, the daddies, they didn't come out at once, first of all, they tried to suss you out, weigh you up, see if you were easy meat, snidely bastards. So the one day this little prick comes over to my bed, I'm lying there minding my own business, and he gives me a bit of gob. Well, I've looked at him, and I don't quite know how to handle it, after all, he's only a little shit, so I decide to ignore him, with that he walks away; clearly, he thinks he's put me in my place, fucking unbelievable.

The next morning I'm combing my hair in front of the wall mirror when the little shit's mate comes up behind me, gives me a big push and tells me to move out of his way. With no more ado, I turned around, gave him a smart right-hander and put him on the deck. I squared up to him, but he's had enough, got himself off the deck a bit groggy and walked away. I thought that was it and went up to breakfast, by now he's realised he's made a prat of himself and wants to try and save face, over he walks and loud enough for a few to hear, but without full steam, he tells me I'm going to get it after. Oh well, so after I walk back to the dorm, and I'm waiting for him, only this time he's realised he's bitten off more than he can chew, apologises, and walks away, I'm on my guard, but he has had enough, now for round two,

The next daddy was a chap named Roberts, a big strong lad, a Geordie, I'd upset one of his little Geordie pals, so they sent him around to sort me out. Well, again, I'm lying on my bed with my socks on, he smacks me. I get out of the bed, and I'm flying all over the place on the wooden floor. I whip my socks off as I went rolling around the floor, then I'm at him when he realises I ain't so easy he gives up and walks away after I'd heard he was making a few threats I decided to confront him. Only this time he was lying stark bollock naked in the bath. As they were in cubicles, I just went marching in with a big object in my hand and asked him if he wanted some more as he was shouting his mouth off. I could see by his face that his bottle had completely fallen out. He went as white as a ghost and started trembling, no, no, no. It's a funny thing about bullies, stand up to them, show no fear, and they soon back down or bottle it, soon, I was the daddy in the camp and was invited to move my bed into the best position, a bit of a bloody joke really, all these power games.

The stupidity and pointlessness of Borstal are you don't learn fuck all, just like a prison, very few people are really bad, like the Brady's or the Moira Hindley's, most people, including myself, are just lost, or find themselves in a bad position or the wrong place at the wrong time, so what do these comics in charge do? Why just lock us away to rot that's all, so bloody stupid. So they put me on this mechanical engineering course, I had had no education at school. I couldn't even do my times tables never mind anything else. This was a 6-month taster course, the idea being to do the basic learning course, complete a written test, then when you got out to get yourself a job with an apprenticeship. I think all I learnt was to file down a block of metal to a 1000th of a millimetre. In short, I learnt sweet eff all and looking around, I don't think many others did either., it was either something like that or labouring outside on the farm, great in the summer, not so good in the winter. Yet the answer is simple really. Spot the kid at an early age, take them out the system, put them in a specialist strict but fair boarding school, like an approved school, but without the stigma of criminality, small-specialised classes concentrating on all aspects from basic education to skills needed outside the classroom. The four or five of us in that school would never achieve anything academically; our only future lay in some kind of manual skill.

In prisons, you're locked up most days unless you have a job. If you have a job, it's mainly sewing mailbags, some fucking learning curve some experience, if you were really lucky you might get a training course in bricklaying or painting and decorating. The only problem with that is then you've got to get the job when you're out, it's either low wages or shit work, who's going to send a convicted thief into a customer's house. Anyway, it didn't matter to me, I was innocent, and everyone knew it, so I was just going through the motions, wrong again of course.

So all that happens is the same old people are just regurgitated back and forth, from an approved school to Borstal to prison, then back to prison again until eventually, you realise the futility of it all, get yourself a job, or throw yourself on the dole for as long as you can. How many in that Borstal went on to re-offend, I don't know, the powers that be do know, but for all their intelligence, they don't know how to tackle the problem. Fucking amazing when you think about it, you get these judges who have got education coming out of their fingernails, ability to speak fluent Latin, yet they ain't got a clue how to treat the lower order - the working class who break the law. Yet in the majority of the cases, if most of us had had a bit of education like bricklaying, or decorating, had the error of our ways pointed out, given a proper intensive,

2 or 3-year course in some skill, most would not be going on or back to prison. I, certainly, innocent as I was, would have got myself a job when I got out, sadly, and true to form, I left there knowing fuck all and having learnt very little, but anyway, it didn't matter, I was innocent. And anyway, I'd got something to go out for.

What Now?

The old man had brought the press club opposite the law courts in Steelhouse Lane in partnership with Jack Hale. The press club used to be used by all the judges, court staff solicitors and press covering the goings on in the court. Now it was full of heavy drinkers and other rough dossers. By the time I got out, the old man had sold out his share to Jimmy Grogan the scrap dealer. Fucking great, I do 18 months in Borstal and come out to fuck all. Obviously, the old man must have his reasons and who was I to question them. Jack and Jimmy soon split up and went in different directions. Jimmy brought a club at the back of New Street Station, another rough dive, and Jack bought the Balalaika Club on Constitution Hill below Fewtrell's Cedar Club. This was quite smart and more upmarket, Jack did his best for me and gave me a gold life membership card, very nice, and it gave me a nice sense of self-importance to be treated so respectfully, but at the same time, I couldn't help but feel a bit irked that it could have been my club, oh well.

I remember the little Asian kid named Alli, he lived in a shit hole house in Small Heath. It was that dirty you couldn't tell the carpet from the floor. His dad, being a typical Asian had volunteered to host a public phone in his living room for free on the understanding that any member of the public could use it, no one did, of course. I used it once, never again. He worked as a chef in some of the top Indian restaurants in the town, and his advice was if you ever went into a curry house only ever have chicken curry. When you asked why he wouldn't say, except to insist on taking his advice, chicken is about the only meat that cannot be disguised, cat, dog, fuck knows what else can go into a curry. His son was one of about six brothers, trying to fit in at school. Being bullied a bit, he started going out thieving. Eventually, after getting a few fines that his parents had to pay, he was sent to an approved school. After a few months, the transformation was amazing. I'd see him looking spick and span; nice tie and blazer in, smart slacks, white shirt, big happy smile on his face. He loved it, did 14 months, came out and was back to his usual scruffy self within weeks, back with his gang, ingratiating himself into their company by going along with their villainy and joining in with their thieving, in the process, learning to become a professional thief, as he got older.

Yet if only these people in charge, these judges and government officials, who live a million miles from people like us, could only realise that the simplest solution would be to take that young kid, put him in a boarding school as soon as his waywardness becomes obvious, don't criminalise him before his life as begun. Better to offer him and his family the opportunity of making a new life for himself and better education. Instead, they were thrown into shit hole areas, dragged through crappy schools with not much regard for our education. At best, to become factory fodder in the local factories, fucking great, and the future for most of us feeling lucky or grateful to get a council house and a nice job, worn out by 60, zombified, even worse if you live in a pit town or a mining village, for fuck's sake. If only one percent of the population is criminals, then the majority of that one percent could have been spotted and helped from a very early age.

I was still going from pillar to post, not knowing where I was going or what I wanted to do. Coming up for the spring, I decided to revisit Butlins Skegness and get a job for the summer. Instead, I got myself a job in Margate, running a prize stall; I'd seen the job advertised in the stage newspaper, the actors' bible. The company wanted someone confident enough to draw in the customers. Well, I thought I could do the business. On the due day, I turned up for my interview and was given the job by the owner of Dreamland himself. Well, the job seemed great to me, I put my best Hepworth three-piece suit on, got myself a room in a guesthouse and started work the next day. I turned up to be met by an older guy in his 50s who was an expert at running the stall with a tasty looking young bird at his side who was about the same age as me. The job was very easy, simple to learn and easy enough. First, he would build the crowd up, come on ladies and gentlemen, get a ticket and win a prize. Once you had bought a ticket you then had to spin the big wheel behind the counter; if your number came up, you won a prize, very few people won, which is why the owner could afford to pay us to make him a lot of money. I started on Monday. On Tuesday the gaffer puts another guy on. This struck me as strange as I hadn't had a chance to prove myself. I was getting on okay with the old boy, and I thought my chances were in with the bird. I wasn't too bothered about the other bloke as I thought he hadn't got a clue and was as stiff as a board, I wasn't worried in the least. On Wednesday, the boss called me into the office and sacked me on the spot, for fuck's sake, what for? I knew the job was a piece of piss, leaving his office, I went to the stall to tell the others I had been sacked, they didn't act too surprised. Well, it seemed the boss preferred the other guy to me, and I was fucking better before I'd got the first sentence out the boss was behind me, get away and get out of dream world or I will have you arrested. Dejected and puzzled, I had no choice but to walk away, but I was sorely tempted to return later and give him a good smack. Surely, in such a small space of time, he couldn't have decided the other bloke was better. Then it occurred to me, hang about, maybe he's rung the Old Bill, who has done a quick check-up on me for him? He would have the power to be able to do that. I was perplexed.

Wondering what else to do, I went into another amusement centre. Obviously, looking the part, the boss asked me if I'd be interested in a job in a bingo hall at Butlins Skegness. Well, I'd never even played a game of bingo but what the hell, so I agreed, the guy does no more than peels of 20 quid and tells me to get the train the next day or as I wanted, report to the bingo hall manager at Butlins Skeggy as soon as I got there. The next day I got on the train, making my way up the aisle, I clocked this beautiful bird standing in front of me. Beautiful was an understatement; the bird was stunning, long blonde flaxen hair, with a French-style beret, tilted to one side. Now normally a bird like this is way out of my league, I can keep the act up for a couple of hours, but before long the slums show out of me, but cobblers to it, so over I headed and grabbed the handrail next to her, hello Blondie, where are you off to then? I'm going to Butlins to get a job, her name was Susan Khal, and she was a model from London, but was sick of the cutthroat life of modelling and of being used, well, looking at her body, I thought I wouldn't mind using you myself, sweetheart.

By the time, we got to Skeggy we got on so well, we agreed to keep in touch and meet up. Getting to Butlins Sue and I split up, her heading off for the employment office, me heading to the main office with my instructions. They were expecting me, I was welcomed in, told where the main bingo hall was and was given my key to a chalet in the camp. Letting myself into the chalet I started to unpack, for fuck's sake, I hadn't got halfway when a knock came on the door, it was security, can you pack your suitcase please and follow us? Ahhh, they must be giving me another chalet; instead, they walked me to the main office. At the desk the security chief looked at me and nodded, with that, the two security guys gave me a nod to follow them, then walked me to the main gates, fucking hell, sacked and kicked off twice within a few days, what the fucking hell is going on?

Seaside Photographer

I then managed to find a job with a photography company called Wrates; I initially went in for a job taking pictures on the seafront. This simply involved wearing a bright multi-coloured striped blazer, standing on the seafront and taking a picture of everybody walking in front of you. Mr Wrates, who owned the company, worked on percentages. For every photo taken you would hand the punter a ticket with a number on it. The very next day they could have a look in the main window of Wrates shop and view their photos. Mr Wrates worked on a take-up of 20% well, this looked like a doddle to me, and what a way to blag the birds. To blag the birds, you need an angle, and what better angle than a bright striped coat and a camera? But Mr Wrates had other ideas on his mind.

My cockney mate and I went into the interview where Mr Wrates told us he had been offered a new polaroid camera that was going down a storm in Blackpool. It was a big thing like a pair of bulls horns, inside fitted a cassette that took about 40 photos, consisting of eight photos on a sheet. The idea is you take the camera, ideally in the clubs or pubs, take as many photos as possible, walk outside, take the photos out - about 2" x 1" and insert them into a plastic keyring with a leather cover. A great idea, a permanent memento and only seven bobs for one or ten shillings for two, it was a great idea, and I was dead keen to try it out., and so was the cockney, Mr Wrates told us to call back to his office the next day after he had examined the camera in more detail.

The next day, duly calling in to see Mr Wrates I was well pleased when he informed me that I had got the contract. Even better, it was not a job; it was a contract, 50/50. Even better, Mr Wrates put at my disposal a Bedford van so I could carry the gear, develop the photos and get from pub or club to pub, I was made up. Mr Wrates also put me wise about my mate the cockney, it seems he had gone in and collared Mr Wrates after our meeting the previous day and being the typical cockney wide boy set out to put the poison down about me. These cockneys never learn, Mr Wrates saw right through him and decided that I had got the job and he was shown the door, some mate ay?

I set to with gusto, calling into the bars at night, going around taking photos. Flipping hell, they were going down a bomb; I couldn't get my arse around the places quick enough. The first night I realised I needed help, by then after a few days I had met up with Sue. Fortunately, she wasn't too happy with her job as a waitress, all the walking about was killing her feet. Without a second thought, she was well up for moving in with me into a little room in a guesthouse, now Sue was a great asset, even better than on my own. Not only was Sue a stunner, but she also had the most beautiful big tits. I could see why she had problems walking for long periods, Sue was the kind of bird that could wear a sack and look stunning, the blokes were falling over themselves to have their picture took with her, if they had wives they would sit there glaring.

We were going hell for leather; I even got a little hooter to draw the punters' attention as we walked into the clubs or pubs, bib, bib. There weren't enough hours in the night, we were rushing around like blue arsed flies. I was making a fortune, but after a few weeks, Sue decided she wanted to get another job at the red lion. To be fair, I think she felt I wasn't paying her enough, but I was keeping her and giving her a few quid. I also didn't put up too much of a fight, Sue was a lovely bird, fantastic figure, but I think she was a bit empty upstairs. Also, she wasn't the best in bed, so with no bad feeling she went off to her new live-in job, I set out to carry on with my camera.

My success with the birds never went amiss either, for starters, you could see they were interested in the lifestyle I was leading, I was a whirling dervish of energy, a big smile on my kisser as I whizzed around, okay guys, photo? While the smile was still on their faces, I clicked away and took their picture, course, if they realised how much I was blagging, they might not have been so happy. I could see the birds were impressed, I had decided to do the caravan sites during the day, people didn't want their pictures taken on the beach, I was geared up for the beachfront, my punters had to be trapped. The caravan sites weren't as busy as the pubs or clubs, of course, but I was still earning, not a fortune but quite nice. I was working 15 hours a day, but still finding time for the birds, knocking on one caravan door this pretty petite bird came to the door. "Hello there, would you like your picture taken my love?"

With that, she shuffled her two little girls outside, quickly brushed their hair, and pushed them into a pose position standing herself in the middle, intrigued I asked wouldn't your husband like to be in the picture with you? With a sad look on her face, she looked at me and said, he's not here, he's stopped back home so he can go birding it, I know what his game is, he knows I'm stuck here with the two kids and can't go out anywhere,

Well with that my ears shot up and flapped like a fucking elephant, as casually as I could muster, I said oh what a shame, look, I know it's late, but when I've finished would you like me to pop round with a couple of beers? Yes, please, her little face perked up, I couldn't wait until 12 o'clock to come, and I was around at her van like a rat up a drainpipe. A little tap on the door and she opened it to show me a little vision of loveliness. Fucking hell, she was beautiful, long auburn hair and a fantastic figure under her nighty. What a mug her husband was, the bed was pulled out and ready, she opened the two bottles, and we started to sip. That was it, the bottles went down, and we were grabbing each other like nobody's business. Fucking hell, she was a tigress between the sheets, and she knew what she was doing as well. I never got up for air. Eventually, I woke up about five to find her between my legs before getting on top of me. Jeeezzz, I couldn't take any more, she was wearing me out, I was spent, I was exhausted, fucking knackered, I was glad to leave the next morning, would you like me to pop around tonight? Yes, that would be nice. In truth, I couldn't, she was a lovely bird alright, but on last night's showing, I knew if I went around, I was never going to survive the night. A few nights later I got talking to another bird in one of the pubs, this one was a local bird who lived just outside the town, we got chatting, and I could see she was dead keen. We agreed to have a date the next night, and I duly picked her up in my little van, inviting me in she couldn't wait to introduce me to the crowded room. It seemed like everybody in Skeggy rented a room out, and this bird's mom was no exception, only this time, it was to a crowd of coppers in cheap lodgings. As she introduced me as her handsome boyfriend who was also very intelligent, I could feel the eyes boring into me, in silence. Fucking hell, coppers, sitting there like a nest of vipers, out we went after a few minutes, and off we set, popping into one of the pubs where we sat chatting in between me taking some photos and earning a few quid.

I dropped her off, and we agreed to see each other during the week, a couple of nights later, I clocked her in the ship inn, went over and she blanked me. It stunned me a bit because I knew she was dead keen on me, astonished I went up to her direct and looked her in the face, she couldn't look me in the eye, and I could see she was crying, what's up? She wouldn't answer, then I clocked it, the coppers in her house had put the poison in for me, the dirty bastards, I wouldn't mind, but the scum bags were probably only after getting into her nickers themselves. Oh well, such is life, there were plenty more fish in the sea, but what dirty bastards, putting the poison in like that.

My life went on as normal, doing the rounds, taking the pictures and building my bank balance up, it's a funny thing about making money, earn a few quid, and it feels pointless trying to save it, id tried it once on the farming, I think I saved about 40 quid in nine months, fuck all. But here, I was making big money; I was becoming Scrooge-like, saving every penny.

It was at this stage I bumped into Johnny. Johnny lived down Long Acre in Nechells and had got himself a nice little earner running the donkeys on Skeggy beach. He'd quickly worked it out how profitable it was running the donkeys. For every 12 donkey trips he ran, he put two in his pocket, even better after giving the punters the price he would short change them on giving their change back, no one checks their change when they're enjoying themselves on holiday. Everybody worth their salt had to have an edge, all the bar staff at Butlins would wait until the customers were on their second or third drink, then start gyping them out of a few bob. Some guys worked in the canteens or the cafes or shops, if anyone was having a party all the food would be supplied, most of us were having parties every night.

Johnny was a short, stocky kid and looked the spit of James Cagney, even spoke like him as well, tough and with a snarl, but I saw another side of him one day as we were walking around the fair, the gypsy fortune teller clocked him saying hello Johnny, how are you? Please, come in and sit down? Well, I saw the pure fear enter into Johnny's face, for fuck's sake, he was fucking terrified. No, no, but she had got his hand and was leading him into her caravan, he was frozen in fear as she leads him to a chair, sitting him down, she proceeded to run her fingers around the crystal ball, you have had a life of some hardship Johnny, at times you have had to fight this alone! But things are looking better for you, your future is looking bright, now cross my palm with silver, and I will tell you what's in store. Well, for fuck's sake, I'm sure she could see the cynicism on my face and patently ignored me. Johnny put his hand in his pocket, bringing out a fiver, hesitantly, he said I've only got a five-pound note, with a smart flick of her hand the gypsy skimmed the blue un out of his hand and said, that will do John. He never said a fucking word, no wonder her arms and fingers were loaded up with so much gold. After a few more minutes of telling Johnny how he was going to be very rich and finding himself a nice girlfriend, we both walked out of her gypsy caravan. In the bright sunshine, he blinked his eyes, but I could see he was still in shock - stunned, he couldn't talk for at least half an hour. I have known quite a few people stand in awe of gypsy fortune tellers, especially back in the slums, some people were terrified of them. If you didn't buy a few pegs, they could put a curse on you, many a woman has run down the hoss road later giving the gypsy some money and asking for the curse to be lifted. But we were the new generation, I thought we'd all moved on from that fear, obviously not seeing Johns face.

Scheming

At any rate, Johnny and I started to talk about what we were going to do when we got back to Brum. I'd made a right few quid, and Johnny had made a few quid, plus he had an uncle who he was certain would lend him some money if he was going to start up some business. We'd got a plan to set up a little wholesale, retail business, I'd seen our Billy doing it for years. His only problem was like the old man he was pissing it up the wall as soon as he had made it, I was determined to save my money, I assumed Johnny was just as savvy knowing the money he had saved up.

When we got back to Brum, we found some shop premises in Victoria Road, Aston, with a garage to the side and living accommodation above. Well, in truth, it was a shit hole in poor condition, but through our tinted eyes, it looked ideal. I found out Siddy Hobday, the scrap dealer, had rented it for a couple of years, but as he was now in the nick. I was given the number of the landlord, who lived in Erdington. He seemed a decent old guy with a bit of the sheeny about him, he agreed to rent it to us monthly at a fair rent, we signed the lease, and then went up with John's mother to see his uncle, her brother, who had a very nice bungalow on the Bromford Road Erdington. Johnny was an only child, and his mother doted on him, I clocked that straight away, but her brother was a bit of a different kettle of fish, having listened to us politely he offered to give it some thought. After a few days, his uncle had given it some thought and decided he couldn't put any money into our venture. In short, we got a knockback, before we'd left the house, worse, the little shit had got fuck all, nowt. Oh, he'd been bang at the fiddle on the donkeys, okay, but he was spending it as well, on the booze and the birds, not forgetting the gypsy, the prat had misled me all along, chancing it as he winged it along the way, the little prick, dejected I had no choice but to fuck him off.

I now had to rethink my position, I got a few quid, but things were now really tight. My only plan was to get as much stock as quickly as I could and start selling it sharpish. I'd got the signs up calling the company L & B, wholesale and retail toys and fancy goods, opening a business account with Barclays. In truth, I was flying on a fucking prayer. I'd got myself a 1-ton van, got myself some furniture, a bed in the place and waited for the stock to come in. It was slow, even worse, I was delusional, it came over to me the one day when yet another sales rep called in, the difference with this one as he came out with it, "Oh, you're the new owners, so you didn't know?"

"Know what?" I looked blank.

"Well, this used to be wholesale toys and fancy goods warehouse previously."

Well, for fuck's sake, no wonder I wasn't getting any credit, I was fucked. The guy took pity on me and because he felt sorry for me and realised I was a new company, agreed to sanction me 50 quid's worth of stock, fuck all really, when the few boxes of teddy bears arrived I had to spread them around the shop, and it still looked bare. Yes, I knew it, I was well and truly fucked, my only hope was in a miracle, and miracles are like hen's teeth.

I tried to keep my pecker up, putting on a front. When an old pal Ernie Trainer turned up telling me his missus had kicked him out, I was quite happy to offer him a room above the shop. Well, that's what pals do; besides, he could be helpful, and it wasn't costing me a carrot. To me, Ernie was a nice guy and the kind of bloke who you felt glad to be on your side, I'd never heard anything bad about Ernie, but he had a way about him that made you feel if he was your enemy he'd think nothing of sticking a knife in you or a hammer across your bonce. Ernie was only about 5,7, slim, and could adopt a murderous look in his eye, but I knew a lot of very short blokes and some of them could be fucking terrifying.

Having palled up, we started knocking together, keeping our eyes out for the main chance, one night Ernie took me and another pal John over to the Black Country to meet a pal of his whom he'd met in the nick. Dave was a nice guy, and very quickly it became obvious to me that he was a slick, professional villain, he drove a new sunbeam rapier and argued that he was being set up by the Old Bill regularly, the latest being a speeding charge, it was all to harass him and cause him aggravation. Dave came from Lower Gornall and told me that it was so close-knit the locals could tell what street or road you lived in by the way you spoke, I couldn't make up my mind if he was bullshitting or not. He had some good connections though, one night he took us up to his pal's country club outside Wolverhampton. The guy had offered Dave a partnership in the club that he was thinking over, it had a large roulette table in the centre and John went over to have a few spins. We were all on our last legs with only a few quid between us, much as we tried to tell John to drop it. He was insistent, after a bit he came back 40 quid up, then 50, for fuck's sake John drop it, like a typical gambler, he wouldn't have it, no, I'm on a winning streak, 20 minutes later he came over 90 quid up. Ernie and I were shitting ourselves speaking through the sides of our mouths and whispering desperately we both urged him to cash in and get over to us. He wouldn't have it, off he went again, five minutes later he was back again, "Gis a fiver," our eyeballs nearly popped out in desperation, "What the fucking hell do you mean a fiver?"

"Well, I've lost the 90 quid, but I'm on a winning streak."
We were fucking gutted, we'd barely got enough dough to get
us through the night, now he'd got fuck all, and we'd be
expected to carry him as well, we both felt like putting one on
his chin. After a short while, the owner of the club came over
to speak to Dave, he turned to John and said, you should have
pulled out at 90 quid son? Now how did he know John was
up 90 quid? He had just come directly over to us from outside
the room, he must have been watching through cameras, this
didn't go down too well with me and Ernie who had felt this
ourselves, we were both spitting feathers, John hunched his
shoulders in embarrassment.

A few nights later, Dave took us over to a little blag he was
interested in and had been observing for some time, this was a
warehouse over Colehill. The two owners would lock up every
night at nine pm, take the takings and put it in the local bank
night safe, Dave's idea was either to cop them as they walked
out or as they were putting it in the night safe further up on
the main Wolverhampton road. We clocked as they closed up,
the one partner would walk out first, carefully looking around
before opening his car door slowly, still looking around. They
were obviously and very clearly aware of the risks from
robbery. Dave thought they might have been robbed previously,
this was even more alarming. This was the best spot rather
than on the main road, but it seemed to me that the only way
to get away with this would be to creep up behind the car,
sneak out, and crack the guy on the bonce. Dave agreed,
oh, these seemed simple enough to me, fucking not, first
you've got to get to him, then smack him on the bonce. In the
meantime, his partner is going to stand there and not bang the
door on us - and what about if a bang on the bonce don't do
it? From boxing, I knew the risks of hitting someone or
knocking someone out. Besides, I just didn't fancy the idea of
smacking someone for money, principle or argument, yes, but
to smack someone just to make yourself money didn't sit well

with me. Looking at Ernie, I didn't know if it did with him either. As we both left to consider it mull it over, I got a strong impression that he didn't want to know at all, we both silently went back home, and the blag was never mentioned again. I had grown up with villains, all the ones I know had different levels or boundaries in which they would go. Rajput and Tubby Kirby never meant to kill the guy in the botched robbery all those years ago, they had simply meant to rob the place when the owner came out. It was a complete accident, but they came close to being hung, and it brought home to a lot of people the risks involved in what they were doing.

Cockney Frank, chopper - Carson had pulled me in a boozer in Aston and pointed to a bookie with a massive groin on his finger, this was my brother's mate, and Carson was trying to blag me to follow him home. Chop his finger off and nick his diamond ring!!! What kind of a fucking nut job was he? Fuck that. No, I was a ducker and diver like my old man, robbery and violence was not my cup of tea.

Meeting Bet

One day, Bobby Gough, who I had been in Borstal with came round the shop and asked if I could do him a favour, his bird had got a friend who needed a bed, she had a spare double bed so could I drop it off to her? Getting the bed onto the van, we set off over to Hockley and heading up the entry we came to this little two-up, one-down, with this bird on her knees scrubbing the doorstep. She had a very nice ass, as we got the bed in she was introduced as Betty. Well, Betty was a nice looking bird, and I thought not too bad at all. Driving back later, Bob told me to forget it, Bet had made it clear she wasn't interested. Well, that was like a red flag to a bull, and later on, I called around the house again, this time asking her for a date, she agreed, and I agreed to meet her on the cross at 7 pm the next night. As I pulled up in my van, I looked across at her standing outside the Golden Cross Pub and had the first shock of my life. There she stood dolled up to the nines with this big fucking bouffant stuck on the top of her head, the total opposite of the nice natural bird I had chatted up earlier, what the fucking hell is that on your bonce? It's fucking ridiculous, you don't need that stupid hairdo or all that crap on your face.

Course, it never occurred to me, thick as I am that she'd got this date and her sister had spent all day giving her a make-over. Oh well, we started dating and coming up to Christmas she came over to the warehouse to buy a couple of dolls for her two kids, Andrew two and Nicky one, sussing what her game might be, I made sure I charged her for the dolls. I didn't fancy any bird taking the piss with me, I'd seen a bit too much and heard a bit too much, too many women were cunning conniving fuckers, Bet seemed a nice quiet, genuine bird, but I wasn't in any rush.

A nice bird named Rose used to come around the shop. Now Rose was another lovely bird, nice body, petite. I'd met her outside the Whitehouse Pub one night in Saltley as she was heading home. As I turned and said hello darling, she told me she was just heading home and that her aunty was Diamond Lil, now Diamond Lily Hawkins, so-called for the mass of diamond rings on her fingers, had owned a chain of jellied eel shops around Aston, selling fresh seafood and jellied eels. Once we'd got the introductions over with we set up our first date, Rose was red hot in the sack, a bit older than me, married with two kids, that counted me out straight off, but she was a nice bird, and I enjoyed seeing her. I never knew why she played around behind her husband's back, but then again, I wasn't too bothered.

One day I hadn't seen her for a bit, so I decided to call around her house one afternoon down Vauxhall. She'd told me her husband was in the army, so I never gave him a thought, knocking on the door she let me in, and we started chatting. By the way, she dropped it out that she was expecting her husband any minute, so I was to pretend that I was a close friend of Diamond Lil and that I had come to inform her that Diamond Lil was ill. No sooner had she said this to me, and I was trying to filter it through my brain when the door went, cool as a fucking cucumber Rose casually gets up and introduces her husband to me as her auntie's friend with the bad news. Well, for fuck's sake, she never batted an eyelid; there stood her husband in front of me, built like a fucking brick shithouse all 6ft 2, of him. I don't know how the fuck I could stop myself stuttering and felt sure my face was as white as a ghost, I can fight, but this was ridiculous, my bottle was flapping like the clappers, saying my goodbyes. I couldn't wait to get out of the house, her husband must have been as thick as two planks, stupid, or so naïve, it was beyond a joke, women ay? They can be fucking unbelievable, I got out of there, arse tightly gripped expecting him to come chasing me at any minute, talk about a close shave? I never went around there again, and I decided Rose was a bit too dangerous for me to get involved with anymore, for fuck's sake, the girl was dangerous.

I was quite happy to get to know Bet, and we'd started seeing each other on and off. It was debatable whether it was more off than on. In the meantime, my little wholesale, retail business was not looking too well at all. I was 19, a trier without a doubt, but I was inexperienced not knowing which way to head next. Another guy had opened another similar business down on the Aston road, I went down and introduced myself hoping to pick his brains a bit, or maybe cadge a bit of help, he didn't want to know and gave me short shrift, that was a waste of time.

Nearly Stitched Up for a Jag

Opposite the warehouse some guy had opened up a little car pitch on a bit of waste ground, a garden shed for an office, he came over one day, and we got, quite pally. I'd only got the van, so he'd offer to lend me a car off his pitch any time I needed one, which was very kind of him. One day it would be a nice Ford Saloon, another a Rover, they weren't his cars, his game was to put an advert in the paper offering to sell your car, a price would be agreed the dealer would put it on his pitch, sell it, if he could, and take a percentage. The problem was we were both in more or less the same position, both on a busy part of the Victoria Road but with no passing customers, people drove up or down Victoria Road, but no one stopped or walked. In his case, all he had to do was pay a peppercorn rent and sell a car, his stock was costing him nothing, nice if you can get it, I couldn't. One day he got a nice 3,2 Jaguar S type, it looked the part and drove like a dream, it didn't do any harm that I looked the part either. For a short period during the day or night, as I drove the Jag, I could act like a young up and coming businessman, instead of the chancer I was sliding by the seat of my pants.

Nice as the Jag was, the dealer offered to do me a deal on it if I made it cash. At £500 it was a deal, I gave him the cash, and he gave me a receipt for the Jag. I was almost on the floor anyway, so it was a bit of do or bust. The next thing I know, over the next few weeks all the cars have gone from the pitch along with the dealer, a few days later the Old Bill from Victoria Road nick just up the road from us called into the shop, "Mr Lewin, can you pop over to the station please, DC Plod wants to see you."

"What for?"

"I'm sorry I haven't got a clue." Well, that makes two of us because I ain't got a clue either. At any rate, I pop across, call into the nick and introduced myself, I was led into an office to be confronted by two dicks, all nice a friendly, but my guard was up wondering what the fuck was going on.

The first cop spoke up, "You've just brought a Jaguar of the dealer opposite you?"

Straight away I thought, Oh fuck, here we go, the fucking thing's nicked! "Yes, I brought it last week,"

"Well, we've had the guy in here, and he told us you both, (me and Ernie) held him up with a gun and robbed him."

My fucking head shot up in shock, "What? You must be fucking joking; I brought it off him, and the next thing I know he's disappeared."

"Have you got the receipt?"

"Yes, of course, I've got the receipt, signed over a stamp."

"Okay, can you drop it over please so we can take a copy of it?" Well, I gave them a big smile, "Are you having a laugh?" I know enough about the Old Bill to know they could take my receipt, and it could disappear. The cops read my mind, "It's ok, we've not got Pip the Planter here, we only want to take a copy." Nervous as fuck I went back over to the warehouse, got the receipt and with a great deal of trepidation nervously handed it over, true to their word the desk cop reappeared a few minutes later with the receipt, thanked me and out I went. Ernie was waiting for me, I was relieved to get my receipt back, no doubt about it, and it would be obvious to the cops that there was no way the receipt would have been written out and signed under duress. What a snidely bastard that dealer was, he'd got himself into a fix and was trying to get out of it by throwing it on to me, but what kind of cops can boast about not being Pip the Planter? I mean, the whole of fucking

Birmingham must know about Pip the Planter, what does that make them? Dirty bastards, that's what.

If all the cops in Birmingham police know about Pip the Planter, who else must know? The solicitors and the judges for sure, nudge, nudge, wink, wink, fucking disgraceful really, the shock just wouldn't leave me. Did they know Pip the Planter had set us up for the jewellery robbery? What comes first, the chicken or the egg? Who is the worst, the thief trying to get a few quid, or the CID, fitting them up with impunity and getting away with it in the full knowledge and consent of them all? There was not only Pip the Planter, there were a few, right bent dicks in the Birmingham force that I had heard about, I didn't come across them because I wasn't into all that villainy, but I heard from others who had. It's a funny thing really and struck me as odd that these cops, with the full knowledge of their peers and the judiciary, feel justified in fitting people. Villains up, and expecting those same villains, to reform and go straight, it defies logic, okay, you might put someone away for a few years by fitting them up, but stop them being as dishonest as them? For fuck's sake, all that happens is all his kids will know, and they end up, hating the law, Pip was a filthy bastard, a fat, smirking fucker with a pasty face shaped like a football. I never saw the car salesman again, I don't know what his scam was, I can only think he'd got himself into debt and saw me as some way to get out of it. At any rate, whatever the reason, the guy must have been a bit of an idiot. My problem was, and I didn't realise it or see it in a million years, was that the Old Bill was marking all this down, in some little book deep in the archives of some dark city centre nick. There I was, knowing I was innocent, thinking nothing of it, these corrupt bastards were marking my every move then just giving me a little tug with the rope now and again, no one told me, and I never had a clue.

With the Jag we'd now started to get out and about, even more, spending money that we hadn't got, hoping for a fucking miracle. One night we picked Tony Prescott up and his mate banger, Tony was Johnny Prescott's brother the famous Birmingham boxer and a mate. I'd carry a briefcase with me in the car and a pile of papers, well, you never knew if it might come in useful sometimes to impress someone. After a drink in the Prince Rupert one night, we all set off into the town for a curry, me, Tony, Banger and Ernie Trainer. Pulling up right in front of the curry house with a roar, we walked in, in view of the staff. Tony and Banger were both 6ft tall, so we looked the part, me with my Crombie, I made sure I carried my briefcase. The manager put us at a table, ordered our meals, I got the paperwork out, and started to give the bullshit, the lads joined in the joke.

As we were finishing the meal, a couple of lads at the table in front of us were starting to whine and moan about the poor food they'd eaten. I wouldn't have minded, but they were spoiling it for us. Fair enough, if they wanted to get away with not paying their bill, I'd done it myself a couple of times, but to sit in the middle of the restaurant and start complaining loudly about the shit curry was not on. I raised my voice slightly - chided them, and said pay your bloody bill instead of creating a scene in the place as we were trying to eat. They didn't need to look back to realise it would be a mistake to argue with us, they settled down quite rapidly, paid their bill and pissed off, the manager came over full of goodwill and eternal gratitude showing on his face, I waved my hand quite royally, and told him to think nothing of it. When we asked for our bill, he again came over and informed me that no bill would be brought and that the meal was on the house. Well, knock me down with a fucking feather. Of course, I thanked him, and off we walked, the staff following us out with a big wave as we set off. I must admit to a feeling of smugness, and I could see my mates were well impressed as well. Well, I had pulled a blinder and saved them a nice few quid as well, I made a point of making that my favourite curry house if someone was paying the bill, I would insist on paying it. If

I were paying the manager would not take any money from me, mind, I never took the piss, just once a week or a fortnight, it worked out a treat. What a touch.

Derek Timberly was the son of Jack Timberly, a friend of the family who had a scrapyard down Aston. Jack was a good old stick who had brought a few items of gear off me. I had been going out with a bird name Jackie at the time and drinking up Lea Village, I'd mace a record player up, or a tent, whatever I could get. Jack and his mates would always have the money to buy from me what I had, what I never realised for a bit was that they thought I was nicking it? Fucking great, I'm a thief without being a thief, it was the same with Don. Don was a nice guy but thought he was a wide boy. He worked in the car factory but would buy anything he could get his hands on and flog it in the factory, just like George whom I'd sold the tomatoes with. Don's other little scam was running the raffle in the local boozer the tavern. He would run this maybe twice a night on the weekends and earned a few bobs out of it, he would also pick his favourites to win, I won a couple of times, partly because I was going out with his daughter, mainly because he was buying gear of me.

One night I'd called into the tavern to find Don by the bar, out the corner of his mouth, he said, got anything son? Well, as it happens, I had ten very nice and brassy women's fob watches. They were a new gimmick that my old man was buying that looked like nurses chest watches, I furtively put my hand in my pocket and brought out a few watches, all brand new and shiny, wrapped up in tissue paper, I brought them up slowly below the bar for Don to have a look, "How much?"

"£2,10s each," and without hesitating, he got his money out and brought the lot. "Can you get me some more? Get me another 20." A few days later, Don had another 20, then another 20, fuck me, I was earning nicely, and Don couldn't get enough of them, it lasted a few weeks before Don pulled me in the pub, "Ay you come here, you bastard."

"What's up, Don?"

"Them bloody watches, they're in all the local shops at £3, 10 shillings each?" well, I'm looking blank at him.

"Well?"

"Well, I've been selling them in the factories at six quid, each one bringing them back screaming."

"Well, that ain't my fucking fault, Don." It was so funny, but I couldn't laugh because he was so fucking angry. The stupid, arrogant prat thought I was selling him nicked watches. What a fucking idiot, all Jack's pals thought I was selling them bent stuff as well, while it didn't bother me, it made me wonder what they all thought of me, while they were all happy to buy what they thought was nicked gear their opinion of me gave me pause for thought. This came over to me one night when we were all having a drink in the social club in Kitts Green. A group of us were getting well pissed when I saw Jack had dropped his wallet on the floor, pissed as a newt and not being 100% sure I put it in my pocket intending to pop around his house the next day when we were all sober.

On the way home that night my Jag skidded in the snow, and I damaged the rear axle, we pulled the Jag to the side of the road, and got a taxi home, returning to the club the next day I handed Jack his wallet, it was stuffed that full you couldn't get anything in it. Jack was overwhelmed taking his wallet, he said, "Here you are, what did I say?"

I looked up, what did he mean by that? Was the suggestion that I had nicked it? Was that my reputation? For fuck's sake, Jack was so overwhelmed when he heard about my Jag. He said don't worry, I'll get it picked up, and fixed for you, and he did as well, fair play to him. In the meantime, it cemented the friendship between Derek and me, if your dads are friends, you become pals with their sons, you know each other and where you come from.

Without my Jag, we had to get about in my van, one night we went over to Bet to have a drink in the local pub in Hockley, after a few beers I gave Ernie the van telling him to drop Derek off, and I'd see him in the morning at the warehouse. The next morning, leaving Bet I got the bus home and let myself in the shop. Before I'd even got upstairs, I got a knock on the door, it was the Old Bill, "We've got Ernie Trainer across the road and Derek Timberly. It's okay, we know you were not with them last night, they've told us, but they've broken into a warehouse down the road, and we want to search your flat."

Well, I didn't feel I'd got much of a choice, passing through the shop the one cop indicated some toys on the shelf and said. "This needn't have happened." They were knocking for a bung, dirty bastards. Leading the way they went straight to Ernie's bedroom where I could see a load of bent gear on the bed, my fucking chest sunk, the stupid prats had decided to take advantage of having the van and broke in nicking a load of clothing from the shop. Worse, the idiots had decided to go back and nick another load. I wasn't fucking happy at all, it must have been Ernie's idea, Derek wasn't a thief, but worse was the fact I could easily have got nicked for it myself, thankfully I had an alibi, and they had both put me in the clear. Ernie and I had our parting of the ways, and true to form, and understandably, I never saw Derek again. No doubt I'm going to get the fucking blame for that around Kitts Green.

Hanging by My Fingernails

Sometimes the shit comes in spades, and it's difficult to know which the best avenue is to go. By now I was feeling I was hanging on by my fingernails to a lost cause in life, I was praying for some miracle, or it was a case of throwing the towel in and walking away. Worse for reasons I could never understand I was getting stopped by the cops at every opportunity, every time I went out, I was getting pulled, it was fucking ridiculous. I was 19 and was trying to earn a living, hard as it was, I was not a gangster or a villain, what was the fucking matter with these idiots, it was nonstop. One night we were in the Monty Carlo up the Soho Road, by 2 am someone came up with the bright idea of driving over to Boston and seeing a friend who ran a market stall selling flowers. It seemed a good idea at the time, so well-oiled we set off. We got to Boston at about six in the morning, knackered and looking worse for wear in our pinstriped Hepworth suits and Crombie overcoats. We were looking for King Street, where our pal lived, but none of us knew where it was. Seeing a copper over on the corner, I pulled over, got out and asked him if he knew where King Street was. Giving me directions, we set off for King Street, which was just a few roads away, we hadn't got half a mile when three squad cars pulled in front of us, hemming us in. What the fucking hell is going on here, this was sleepy Boston, not Aston Birmingham, the cops got straight to the point, "What's in the boot?" Puzzled, I was tempted to say a fucking elephant you prat, what do you think you can get in the boot of a Jag, a suitcase.

Getting out, I opened up the boot, after a cursory look they asked to see my insurance and MOT. "Okay, off you go." What the fucking hell was all that about? No reason, no justification, maybe they thought we had come up mob-handed to lay on the market trader? Maybe the Birmingham cops had put out some alert to jump on me or us at every opportunity, it was fucking blatant harassment, but I felt there was nothing I could do about it, this was the law, and the law can do what they want. Seeing our mate, we spent a few hours around Boston before saying goodbye and heading back home.

The harassment continued, and I couldn't figure out why, I know the cops harassed the known villains, they were always baiting the blacks, but only if they had got the upper hand and outnumbered them. The cops would openly boast about smacking a few black heads in if they ever got the opportunity. Wrong, but it was almost acceptable for the time, the average villain was terrified of the law and the cops in Birmingham, there was an atmosphere of fear coupled with a determination to carry on. I could never see the sense of it.

To me, the law was there to protect the public, to arrest someone if a criminal offence had been committed, that person was suspected of committing the crime, and the evidence was there to prove it. All that went by the wayside in Birmingham, the cops here think, and can, get away with anything they want, it was sanctioned by the very top, put them away by any means possible, it was utterly fucking corrupt yet it was accepted by everyone villains, coppers and solicitors alike. Everyone was complicit, my hate for coppers hadn't built up like a lot of people I know, but it wasn't being helped. On the one side, you had the villains who felt justified in nicking something to lift them up the ladder, on the other you had the coppers who felt justified in resorting to any or every criminal act to nick them, at the same time helping themselves as they went along. If someone had pulled a blag and robbed say a warehouse or jewellery shop, the cops would go steaming in, usually after a grass had given them the information. Out of the four grand in cash that was found in the house, you can guarantee two grand would be declared by the time it got into court. Any loud protestations were quickly shut up, I reckon many a copper could afford to buy a nice house in Sutton on the proceeds, to me, they were like a well-organised criminal fraternity.

With fortunate timing I happened to bump into Gerald Avery, who was the eldest brother of my mate Mick, Gerald was a nice guy who happened to be the manager for David Broad who had a steel stockholding business. David liked to see himself as a bit of a gangster wore the obligatory pin-striped suit and Crombie overcoat, looked the part and had a good business to back him up if you went to the same school and was a mate you were fine, if not he would give it the big I am over you. All in all, he wasn't a nice bloke. A couple of years earlier, he had had a fall out with someone, and this guy went down to David's office to have it out with him. Now, whether David's bottle fell out or not, I never found out, and no one spoke about it, but whatever the reasons David pulled out a shotgun and shot the guy in the legs. The guy runs out and by all accounts had no intention of grassing. But David didn't want to take chances, he did no more than dial 999, ring the Old Bill and spew his guts up, claiming he was simply defending himself.

Whether any backhanders went in no one knew, but by the time he got to court, he ended up with a two stretch and a reputation that he was not to be messed with. For fuck's sake, two years and his reputation enhanced. He was out in 14 months to money in the bank, his business doing well, and Gerry promoted to manager. Now Gerry wanted to do a deal for my Jaguar.

Gerry had a 2,2 Jaguar S type and was a year older than mine, plus he was prepared to bung me an extra couple of hundred quid, I didn't want to appear too eager but was more than happy to do the deal, my Jag was becoming an albatross around my fucking neck. Checking each other's Jags out, I agreed to drop it down to Broad's office in Watery lane the next day, turning up, David came charging across like fucking bull elephant and the bully he was. My back went up, and I stood my ground. To be fair, I was very tempted to stick one on his chin, when you're fit and can handle yourself, you weigh people up. David was big, but fat, Gerald could see my reaction and got very nervous very quickly, to be fair, Gerry was a nice bloke, it was just Dave who was an asshole. He was that busy looking for the stroke, the master con, he missed the real reason, which would have made them both pull out.

As it was, he was scrutinising my receipt and papers in such a determined way that all reason went out of the window, but Gerry wanted my Jag, and that was it. After a few minutes, honour and respect established, for fuck's sake, the deal was done, keys were exchanged the two hundred quid placed in my bin. Outside we both tootled to get into our respective cars, me driving off, happy with the deal, it just felt like the same car to me, it was a Jag, a Jag was a Jag.

I didn't see Gerry for a couple of weeks until I bumped into him up the Cedar Club, he came over all casual, "What the fucking hell have you been up to Tommy?"

I looked at him with feigned innocence, then a smile, I'm sorry Gerry, but I couldn't tell you at the time, especially in front of Broad, but the Old Bill has been fucking hassling me nonstop. Gerry was very magnanimous, "Oh, it's okay, Tom, I'm dead happy with the Jag." I just wondered what the fucking hell was going on, I got stopped four times in two days. I've had no hassle since I explained I had brought the car, Gerry was sound, and I never got stopped again, funny that.

One day my brother Johnny turned up with John McCoy. McCoy was a big bloke of some 6ft 2" fit and lithe, and Scottish, he adopted a slight stoop to appear less tall, he was like a cat, ready to pounce, the rumour was that he had a brother who played for the Scottish side Celtic. Johnny asked me if McCoy could borrow my van as he had some stuff he wanted moving. I never questioned it, my first and only concern was I would have no transport; my Jag was off the road. Immediately McCoy pointed to the car he had arrived in, an old black Austin from the early fifties, it was a fucking antique, but ok, it was transport for a couple of days and was security for my van, we exchanged keys and off they went, old as the car was it started okay and was drivable.

A couple of nights later I was having a drink in a social club in King Standing when we got involved in a scrap with some other guys, the one tried to put a glass in my face with a glass which I deflected with my left hand before putting one on his chin with my right. Within minutes it was over, and a group of us got up to the hospital to get my hand stitched up, I was pissed but didn't worry about being nicked because everyone drinks and drives. With my hand bandaged up and my arm in a sling, we started to drive back as best I could. Driving around by the markets, some copper jumped out of the shadows and put his arm out. I stopped the motor and adopted the normal conciliatory attitude, polite, respectful, "Sorry sir, we've just got back from the hospital where I've had my wrist cut as you can see, from a fall." The copper is going through the motions, and I'm trying to be as patient as possible, but the lads in the back ain't playing by the rules, they're all pissed as well and getting all impatient at this young copper who was looking for nicking. The moans and groans started, then the lip, fuck off copper, the copper caught it, "Have you been drinking sir?"

Well, of course, "I've had one earlier."

With that, he pulls out his breathalyser kit. "Could you take a deep breath and breathe into this, sir?" I took the kit off him, but said, "Hang on, I am allowed a 20-minute leeway before I have to blow into this, aren't I?" I didn't know what I was talking about, but it threw the copper, and he agreed to wait 20 minutes. The only problem is 20 minutes is a long time. While I'm waiting for a miracle to pop up, the copper is getting impatient, I'm half wishing the silly prats who started giving it the mouth in the car would just get out and stick one on the copper's chin, that way we could all get away, that wasn't going to happen. After 15 minutes the copper was getting impatient, I think it was dawning on him that there was no such rule, at any rate, after 15 minutes, he said, "Cobblers to this," and before we knew it, back up had turned up.

With no more ado, my mates were pissed off, I was nicked put in a squad car and carted off to Digbeth nick. Looking back, I saw my mates heading off, shoulders slumped, fucking great. In the nick, they asked me to blow into the bag, but I refused to point out I had just had injections, and it wasn't right for me to be breathalysed, with no further ado I was thrown into a cell where I flaked out until morning.

Four hours later they woke me up and asked me to take a breath test, oh, how about that, it's negative. Well, I could have told you that, it was the drugs knocking me about, the test was, so I could have my car back, but when I asked for it to drive away in, the desk copper came up with some excuse that it would have to be fetched from a different station and he didn't know from where. "You'll have to get a taxi, and we'll contact you to pick up your car." This was an inconvenience, but ok, I could put up with it, as my breath test had proved clear I assumed I would get my car back and everything dropped, some fucking luck. The fact is if the cops think they've got a nicking they don't like to let go, if you've got a criminal record, your fucked, they have all the time in the world to delve search and investigate if they can't get the case legally they help it along by bending the rules a bit.

I didn't hear anything for over a week, then I received a summons for stealing and driving a stolen car and being drunk while driving. Fucking hell, they'd all joined forces to get this young copper his first nicking. At the first court hearing, he was all smiles. I was directed to a solicitor who defended me on legal aid, naïve and stupid as I was I still thought that if you engaged a solicitor, his brief was to defend you to the best of his ability, whether he was paid for by you or via legal aid. Bollox, you hear stories of only the rich getting the best of defence while the poor are sent to rot in prison, but most of the emphasis is on American justice, the rich get off, the poor go to prison. In third world countries, you get shot or have a hand chopped off for nicking a loaf of bread, while us, the British, have the best judicial system in the world, our scales of justice are blind and evenly balanced. I was starting to find out rapidly that this was bullshit. I was to find out that the judicial system in England was as corrupt as any third world country; it just looks civilised. The wigs are meant to convey this sense of fairness and justice, more bullshit, its main aim is to control and intimidate. Those scales of justice ain't even-handed, trust me, they are heavily weighted down on the wrong side.

It never occurred to me that your criminal record was automatically forwarded to your defence along with the prosecution evidence, so straight off, you're fighting from a disadvantage, one arm tied behind your back and your leg cut off at the knee. To boot, not only do you have the Old Bill trying to fit you up always, your defence knows you're guilty from the start. If he's not convinced, he suspects you're half guilty, so just pulls back on any effort, if you go to one of the top criminal law firms you're just delegated to a lowly solicitor who's no more than a jumped-up clerk.

So, not knowing this, here I am sitting in my brief's office, giving him my side of the story, the facts, he was jotting them down without much comment or even raising an eyebrow, the clear breathalyser didn't even come into the equation. The fact is, I was under the influence and had no argument, fair enough. I had had a drink, my stupid fault, much as I hated the thought I had to accept a ban and a fine, but this nicked motor is another matter, for fuck's sake, it was only worth a tenner. Nicking an old banger like that. The solicitor took his notes, concluded the meeting and arranged for me to call back in two weeks.

In the meantime, I had heard that John McCoy had got nicked and was in custody on a murder charge. McCoy had been out drinking with Johnny Rajput Kirby, and John Jock Lowe. Now I knew from a run-in with Lowe that he was a big mouth How he'd never had the shit knocked out of him before I don't know, maybe he'd been some kind of hard case in his early life, but once he'd got the whisky in him, his gob started, he would spout off to anyone in the room. I can only assume people left him alone because of the company he kept, why the company put up with him I never knew. At any rate, the three of them had been drinking heavily, when McCoy decided he had had enough, everyone has their cut off point, some lose it early, at any rate. McCoy had got pissed off and made his way over to Loveless Road, Kitts Green to wait for Rajput and Jock to come home. When they did, whacked and drunk, McCoy was waiting in the shadows for them with a piece of 4 x 4, gate post. He hit Jock Lowe that hard he never recovered, dying within a short period, he put Rajput in hospital for three months, what they had done, or how far they went was only known to those three. Rajput could either never remember, or never wanted to talk about it, Lowe; yes, Lowe was a big mouth troublemaker, but Rajput? Yes, he could be, but he knew his boundaries, Rajput was harmless. I felt with the reputation the Kirbys had got, especially Raymond, McCoy would be getting payback.

At any rate, none of this was of any concern to me, McCoy had loaned me the motor. It was up to McCoy to clear me of it, there was some misunderstanding, there is no way anyone would nick an old banger like that, least of all McCoy, on the due date, I turned up at the solicitors expecting the car theft to be resolved, no such fucking luck. I've spoken to McCoy's QC, and he's refused to allow his client to appear in court as a witness, I stared at the solicitor fucking gobsmacked, and at a loss for words, trying to formulate it in my brain, how can his barrister refuse to let him appear in court? I'm thinking, why do you have to accept that? "Well there's nothing we can do, his QC, is Argyle, Argyle." Argyle is a fucking judge, and a notorious one at that every villain in Birmingham was terrified of appearing in front of him, he was ex-army and a boxing enthusiast, but rumours went around that he was robbed of his family, had suffered some mishap that gave him a hatred of all or any crooks. I'm fucked, I didn't know what else I could do, or how, except fight it. The case came up in a few days, then he put it on a plate for me, if you plead not guilty and are found guilty, you will get 18 months in prison, I would advise you to plead guilty, and you will get a three-month suspended sentence? It was hard to swallow, and I felt like a rat in a fucking trap, I was fucked either way I looked, my options were non-existent, in my mind's eye I'm looking around in desperation for someone to help, but who? Probation officers - no chance, you're on your own between the cops and inadequate, corrupt solicitors, how much they get paid to defend me, I don't know, that's between them, and the relevant bodies. But one thing for sure, if he's getting a grand out of public funds, he ain't going to give me a grand's worth of defence, oh, no, the majority of that goes on the companies' overheads, fucking great ain't it, no one ever seems to question in detail where all the billions in legal aid are funnelled too.

On the due date, I turned up at court, waiting around. Eventually, my defence turned up, all brisk and professional, business-like. You get the feeling they are in some way sympathetic to you, fighting your corner, are they fuck, they are just like the teachers I knew from school, they talk civilly, polite, but you can sense the air of superiority, towards you, the patronising manner, you're thick, you deserve no better.

Seconds before we got into court, one of the clerks came out and informed me that I was to appear in front of none other than Judge Argyle. My fucking eyes shot out on stalks. Argyle? Hang about, the same fucking Argyle that is defending my mate, McCoy? What the fuck is going on? My solicitor is in the court out of sight. Again, I was on my own, if I now fight and plead not guilty. It's odds on I'm going to get 18 months, my strong feeling through and through is I'm being stitched well up, and there's no way out. Gritting my teeth, I headed into court, How do you plead?"

"Guilty, your honour." I even have to give him his title; I was in court for less than 20 minutes. That's it, over and out, nice fucking money for those that are getting it.

As I walked out of court, still stunned, I tried to get my head around what had just happened, what I had just fucking stood for, the solicitor had disappeared, he'd done his job, earned his 30 pieces of silver and more, and gone. As I looked up, the two prosecution witnesses, came walking out of a side room, heads bowed in embarrassment, they both looked at me and the one mouthed, "Sorry," that's it. I fucking knew it, a fit-up, these two were scrap metal merchants, and McCoy must have borrowed the car off them with their knowledge or consent. For Christ's sake, the car was scrap, it was never nicked. I left court pissed off, but thankful that I wasn't doing 18 months for a non-nicked car. A few months later McCoy appeared for trial with his defence being Argyle QC, he got two years in prison for manslaughter, two fucking years, what's going on there then? Now I had no wish to see anyone get life for going a bit overboard in the right circumstances, maybe McCoy never intended to kill the Jock or put Rajput in hospital for so long, but certainly, the one never deserved to die, and Rajput, never deserved what he got, for fuck's sake, neither one was over 5ft 6". I can only assume, McCoy didn't have too much of a record, yet he was a major villain, he kept his mouth shut with his solicitor, and Argyle knew all about John Lowe and Rajput, he probably felt they both got what they deserved. The law was fucking cockeyed and slanted, so much for those level scales of justice, the courts made it up as they went along. The fact that Rajput and Lowe were old men was irrelevant, the only way to interpret something like this is the law. The cops, the judge, are looking at this as a man doing them a favour by killing them, whisper, whisper, nudge, nudge, cough, cough, what possible excuse can be given for one man, over six foot, whacking two 5ft, 6 inch drunken guys with a gate post. "Oh, my client was just in the area your worship and just happened to pick up this gate post as these two hooligans came along," how convenient.

You can dwell on these mishaps or just carry on as things are, get over them or sink into an abyss. The fact is, we Lewins was brought up with the mantra of not grassing. It was instilled in us from when we were kids, it was the simple logic of the jungle, the three monkeys, see all, hear all, say nothing. As a family, we all agreed with it, if you're a criminal committing crime, why should you squeal on your mates if you get nicked, to get yourself off the hook? What kind of a rat are you? Even the cops understood the desire of a lot of people to steal to feed your families after the war, times were hard, rationing came in, a lot of people could barely survive on the family allowance they were forced to live off. I had had cops tell me they understood why a lot of people nicked to survive, most of them themselves joined the police because of the poor pay in civvy life. Most were either nicking little bits themselves or boosting their pay with overtime, plus the fact they were guaranteed a pension, they couldn't get that in civvy street. Tim was a carpenter, by trade, he'd got his city and guilds, only to find the wages were crap, no overtime, and not much of a future. Ok, join the police, ask them why they don't go thieving to feed their families, and they will tell you; they are afraid of getting nicked. I knew a couple of coppers who were quite happy to do a bit of nicking but didn't like the idea of going to prison.

Don't give me that bollox of honour, integrity, decency and honesty, some 75 million people died or were killed in WWII. Hitler came into power from the enforced poverty imposed on the German people from the First World War, we were all told to study our history, but only what was told or advised to study. I was brought up to respect the flag, sing God Save the Queen, wave the flag, great, but then you realise the royal family got their wealth by robbing other countries. Other countries got their wealth by robbing other countries, Queen Elizabeth I got her wealth by sending Raleigh out to rob the new world, Hitler pillaged the whole of Europe, if he had won the war he would have been a hero.

All this helped formulate my thinking over the years and as I was growing up, by the time I was 17 I realised thieving was a mug's game, way before I went to Borstal for God knows what. After the war years, I saw the logic, you had the odds on your side if you robbed a shop, or a warehouse or a factory, the odds of getting found out were 90 percent in your favour. As I was coming up, the dynamics were changing rapidly, the first time you got nicked you got 3 to 6 months, the next time two stretches, then three. I used to watch my older brother Johnny and his mates boast about it. "Two stretches? Do that standing on my fucking head, yeah, of course," but then you noticed they started to drink more, before going out on a blag, then you notice how their faces go pale when they're faced with a bit of porridge. Okay, the pals rally around, dropping a few quid into the wives, but even that starts to drop off as more and more get nicked. the thieving starts to drop off, then you see them huddled up in groups talking about the big tickle, "All we need is that big tickle, just that big tickle to set us – me, for life." It was like those fucking idiots that do the pools, they spend all week, waiting for that big pools win, the jackpot. "When I win the pools, I'm going to treat myself to a nice car." They spend all their lives talking about the big win, the big tickle, but then slowly, age creeps up on them, slowly it starts to dawn on them that that big tickle is never going to come. They would never admit it, maybe even to themselves, but you can see the desire dissipate, then they just resort to cadging here or there for someone to buy them a pint, or if they're lucky having someone buy them a couple of shorts.

My generation, and the ones a bit older, was a bit of a different breed altogether, they had grown up after the war, never went through the suffering of my older brothers generation, missed or forgotten the rationing. By the time they had reached their teens the country was going through a complete transformation, from rock n roll, Bill Haley to Elvis Presley, Beatle crushers to drainpipes to velvet collars. Things were changing rapidly, people no longer automatically stood up when the anthem played before leaving the cinema, they just got up and walked out, leaving the older generation to it. The new rock and roll stars were letting us know the world was ours to grab. Then, of course, there was the Hepworth or Burton suit - the three-piece, for 30 quid, the collars were even more superior, and the hand-stitched lapel was a must. The suit of choice would be the navy or dark blue pinstriped, if you didn't have the right suit you were a nobody, then there were the gangsters, to be a gangster you had to have a three-piece suit, mohair and you were really in business.

Clubbing

Now was the time of the clubs, and Eddie Fewtrell was and became the king of the clubs in Birmingham. Eddie had managed to find the money to buy a little club in Aston that had the good fortune to have roulette table upstairs. A few people had been offered this club, including my brother Johnny, Billy Henry and another for the princely sum of two grand. While they'd had a tickle of two grand they didn't want to take the risk, the fact is, they weren't business-minded, plus, things were so good they thought it was going to last forever. Fortunately, for Eddie, he had more foresight, and he was savvier. Within a year, he had brought the Cedar Club, ringing his brother Don up, he then brought another, then another leaving first Don, then his brothers running them. In a short time, he had a clutch of very popular clubs around Brum. Everyone wanted to be seen in them, everyone wanted to go to them, they were the go-to clubs in the early 60s, and I was no exception.

With my hand-stitched three-piece suit, I felt the business, and looked the business, while most people went to the clubs paying two quid entrance in ones or twos, to see the Beatles or Tom Jones, who sometimes never turned up, we went in our little groups or gangs, made up of anything between four or ten. If there was any trouble you knew you had back up, it was a great, new and exciting time to be about, - because George - Fruity Tuit - Fewtrell was my dad's partner and friend in the business. I was automatically given free access over the door. It felt like a great honour, and this privilege was given in most of the clubs across Birmingham, "Alright Tommy?" And a little wave of the hand as we walked in, it would be out to the boozers at about 7 or 8 pm, then on to the Cedar. After that the Rum Runner, Rebecca's, maybe the Elbow Room, going piss eyed up to the Garryowen, run and owned by Brendan Joyce. If we weren't lucky enough to blag a bird, we would walk out the pubs sometimes at 6 am as there was that much going on a lot of the times it was too much to piss about wasting time on the birds. My only problem was finding the money, I was living hand to mouth, sometimes spending up to £100, in a night, when the average wage was about 25 quid.

The warehouse had gone and was rapidly becoming a distant memory, I hadn't painted myself in glory and had had to run out on a fair whack of debt, and as much gear as I could muster. The mace I'd got didn't last very long and was soon running out with how much it was costing me up the clubs trying to be one of the boys. Still, it was an exciting time for everyone in that period, everything was bustling, and as usual, you had the usual groups of people taking advantage of the normal office girls to the lads out of the factories building sites shops and warehouses. Everyone put their best suits on and hit the town, Birmingham was up and coming at the time, and there was a club to suit everyone and to suit every taste. My uncle Jeff's club the Fleur de Leys, was for the older, discerning drinker, sophisticated, with a cabaret singer and a piano, Ray Mills was on the door, a cockney who had been involved with the Krays and was at the party when Jack the hat Mcvitie got stabbed.

At most of the clubs, you could see many of the top singers and groups of the day, the Beatles, the Hollies, Alma Cogan, Dusty Springfield, all for just a couple of quid entrance fee. It was a great time, and it was a great night. Eddie would have a big splash in the mail, '*Tom Jones in person*', according to when you turned up, the singer had either done his gig and left, or was on his way. It worked a treat most time, the early birds resigned their shoulders and just carried on drinking and listening to a mediocre DJ, the latecomers just kept being fobbed off with excuses. "He's on his way, his car broke down, he's been delayed." By the time, 2 o'clock came, and it was closing time, everybody was too drunk to give a shit. If anyone complained, they were given short shrift. If anyone complained too loudly, they were given a smack on the chin, or a bang over the bonce with a truncheon, the bouncers at the clubs didn't take any shit from anyone. Sometimes you got your skull cracked before you even got into the club, it amazed me how they got away with it, there was either a lot of backhanders going on, or the Old Bill's attitude was as long as the place is being kept orderly they didn't give a shit.

I started to notice that the clubs were broken up into groups, the bulk of the people were made up of ordinary guys enjoying a night out either with their birds or mates looking to blag a bird for the night. Then you had the chancers, I suppose like me, trying to look the part while keeping one eye out for the birds and the other on any opportunity that presented itself, then you had the wide boys, the car dealers, the small business people, trying to show a front, look the part and generally look impressive. I was in awe of a few of them, imagining the glitzy lifestyle they lead, the big houses they lived in, the exciting lives they lead, what I didn't realise, of course, until I started to get to know one or two of them, was quite a few of them lived in fucking council houses or rented. Of course, that's the thing you see, you meet some beautiful bird in the club, tits sticking out, fantastic legs, nice tight arse, you spend all night trying to blag it, then offer her a lift home, and she says, "Yeah, okay then, I live over Castle Vale, oh for fuck's sake."

There was the well-known scrap dealer, who ran his dad's yard down Digbeth. You could see he had money and he knew it, not for him the Hepworth's suit, oh no, he'd have a fully handmade one-off one of the Jews up Monument Road, a silk handkerchief sticking out of his top pocket slim with it he strutted about the clubs with the arrogance of knowing he'd got the money. Usually, he had a right tasty bird on his arm, giving her the full treatment, first a meal up the Hilton hotel, then up to the overnight room, he'd booked give her a good sorting before taking her out and hitting the clubs. Fucking great, I'd take my hat off to the guy... playing it well. There were one or two like him around the town, then you had the odd actors, comedians, some hoping to be recognised, but in the mane utterly ignored. One of the actors out of Crossroads would come and stand near the bar, we used to watch him, doing his utmost to be inconspicuous, but being pissed that no one said, "Oh hello, can I have your autograph." Everyone deliberately ignored him,

Then you had the gangsters or the hangers-on, David Broad would be on one side of the bar in the Cedar, or Rebecca's, his sister Jean at the other end of the bar, each competing with the other to look the best. David would be standing there, with half a dozen gangsters giving the look, and Jean would be at the other end, giving the look. It was fucking ridiculous, really, but what can you say when they had the money. David and Jean had their own steel stockholding business and fair play to them, but their gangs were made up of people that worked for them or did a bit of villainy for them on the side, but the look was always the same. The head honcho David, or Jean would be standing there at the bar, the full centre of attention with all the others fawning around, shoulders straight, head held high, eyes everywhere, watching everything, missing nothing. Then you'd have their little gangs, smart tailored Hepworth suits, hand-stitched lapels, a double whisky in their hand, silently appraising everyone around them, heads slightly bowed in deference to their leaders, the boss, but with the same air of silent smug arrogance. As you walked passed, you could feel the look like you were a bit of shit on their shoe. I got it regularly, but the main word was mug. If you were not in their clique, not in their top ten, you were a mug, and you had to say it a certain way, half silent, out of the corner of your gob, so as you were passing you would get – the look - then a sideways draw from the mouth and an almost silent, mug. They never said it to your face mind, always behind your back, it was fucking laughable, it was pathetic, but it used to piss me off, the best part about it was most of them only lived in fucking back street council houses down in Aston, yet they looked at everyone else as total mugs.

One night I'm up Barbarella's with Micky Avo and a group, when I clocked Chrissie Lambrionou, standing up by the bar, on his tod, one arm on the bar, a whisky in the other. Three things struck me straight away, one was that Lambrionou was a good looking guy, charismatic is the word, the other was he was on his own, and third, leaning on the bar, his coat jacket was slightly open showing a fucking gun in its shoulder holster. On the other side of the bar was none other than Pip, the Planter, and his crooked crew. Well, I couldn't get my frigging breath, a well-known gangster, from London, strutting into a Birmingham club, brazen as you like, openly carrying a fucking gun, and no one was batting an eyelid. I turned to Avo and gave him a nudge, but Avo had clocked it and turned away. It made me sit back and wonder what fucking power those Krays had got down in London that could spread up to Birmingham, but then I never realise fully that it was all coming on top for all of them, including Ray Mills who was trying to keep his head down,

In the meantime, I was also noticing how the people were changing, my dad had told me stories of some of the men he dealt with, some of the tricks they got up to. Many were ex-soldiers from the war, came back to true hardship having suffered true hardship, only to think fuck it, and sought a different way of life, even the cops at the time would grudgingly admit that they could understand their motives, in truth, most of them would have done the same but never had the bottle.

Times a Changing

The people coming up today, my peers, the kids I was growing up with were learning rapidly to change with the times if you couldn't do the time don't whine. If you didn't like doing the bird get out, get a job and go straight, if you don't like work go on the dole and scrounge, a lot did, but these lot coming up today were a different breed, they were sly, many were crafty, snide. I remembered when the cops used to play it fairly straight, people would get nicked, get their collar felt, and it was fair cop FAIR COP GUV. Now the Old Bill had carte blanche to fit-up as and when they saw fit, if you only had a smidgen of evidence, even circumstantial, against you, they would just quickly find some way to make the evidence against you. First, you would be thrown in the cell and left to sweat, then you would be leaned on, the real so-called tough gangsters didn't like to be seen breaking, neither did they like the idea of doing some bird, a few years in the nick, so they would find a way to compromise. One easy way to compromise was to grass, throw a body in, even if it were one of your mates, it got you off the hook, and no one knew would they? After all, the Old Bill ain't going to tell you are they?

We Lewins were known for our soundness, not one of us would grass, it was not in our genes. We hated the Old Bill for how bent and corrupt they are, that soundness was treated with respect around Aston we were treated with respect, people would come up to me in the pub or the club, pat me on the shoulder, ahh, one of the Lewins, sound, I was quite proud of that recognition. Today it was different, I could feel it in the air, in the atmosphere, people would grass to save their skins and earn a few quid, you were only as safe as the purpose you served. I couldn't get me head around it, here they were, strutting around giving it the large buying doubles all round. Birmingham CID standing right next to them, each oblivious to the other, one group were the pepper pot gang, the fucking pepper pot gang for Christ sake, so-called because they would load there sawn offs with pepper instead of shot, the reason being to avoid getting any heavy bird once they got nicked. But they did get nicked quite often, doing a couple of eight stretches ain't a great incentive to do the villainy. I was starting to see it too many times. Thankfully I had watched my older brothers, the Kirbys, my dad's mates. I had seen the timespan from when I was five and six, seen them strutting with pride, plenty of dough in their pockets, nice suits, then getting six months, then 18 months, then three years, their faces getting greyer, etched with lines, and all the time living in a council house, rent paid by the social.

Fuck that for a game, these comics were strutting their stuff, looking down their noses at anyone else they deemed inferior. Yet they were just living around the corner, in a shit hole just the same as me, but because they were mingling with the likes of Dave and Jean, thought they were the cream, it was a bit of a fucking joke. Ok, I was on the floor, I was scratching, but I was my own man, answerable to no one, used by no one. One night in the Cedar, I was standing there, minding my own business, but who was standing next to me, but Charlie the grass who had got me and my dad nicked a couple of years earlier, and me sent to Borstal. I thought no more of it and carried on taking no notice until I happened to turn around and who should be standing six feet away was none other than Pip the Planter himself with a few of his pals. Well, for fuck's sake, right next to me, and facing the cops was the 'hump' Charlie himself, I was fucking steaming and couldn't help myself, you fucking grass, and stuck one straight on his chin, he went down like a log and out like a light bulb. Don was over in a flash with his favourite bouncer, Kelly, and bounced me out. Fair enough, I was out of order, I apologised to Don, but demanded that he threw Charlie out so I could finish him off, Don was having none of that and told me to piss off home. Fair play, I did, and I wasn't given my ticket by the club.

Another night I was in the Monte Carlo up Soho Road, a very nice upmarket cabaret club, Greeks on the door with Hercules the front runner bouncer, a nice guy but one look at him and you realised why he was called Hercules. As you walked in the door, you could lead into the bar on the right, or go into the cabaret room, have a meal and listen to the act, I just like to have a drink in the bar, as I stood there, I clocked Stan Sherrin standing at the bar with a group of guys rabbiting away. I thought nothing of it, but a few weeks earlier, I had needed a van to carry some gear out of the warehouse, Stan had very kindly offered to lend me his one-tonne transit, but then kept giving me the deaf, I thought I'd pull him and ask why? Over, I go and very discreetly ask Stan if I could have a word, then walks away. Before I know it, Stan's at the bounce and comes marching over, "Okay, think I'm a copper, do you? Outside." What the fucking hell is going on here? I had thought no such thing, for fuck sake I hadn't even clocked he was talking to Old Bill at the bar. All this going through my mind as I'm walking out. Now Stan ain't small, he's a good six foot if not more so I ain't going to hang about, as he squares up and puts his mitts up, I put one on his chin, and he goes down like a light, on the floor. His brother Tommy comes out, also at the bounce, now Tommy doesn't know what's been going on so just assumes I've put Stanley down for fuck all. He squares himself up and throws a kick at me, so I put one on his chin, this is getting ridiculous, Stanley gets up, rubs himself down, and together they walk back into the club. I'm standing there like a fucking idiot, wondering what it was all about, caution warned me not to go back in the club, so I got into my car and drove back home. What the fucking hell was all that about, the Sherrins were long-standing friends of the family from way back in Summer Lane, now they had turned on me without a second thought simply because of a misunderstanding, what kind of friends were they?

A few days later, young Mickey Kirby and I had decided to drop in to have a drink up Winston Green with Stanley Kirby the scrap dealer and Raggy Allen another scrap dealer and a pal of the old man's, who should be there as we walked in was our old pal Stanley Sherring. I looked at Stan, giving him the eye; he didn't like it, jumping up, he squares up behind the table, "What are you looking at?" I said. "Do you want some fucking more?" I'm pissed off now, Stan goes to move behind the table, as Stanley Kirby jumps up, along with Raggy Allan - panic bouncing out of their faces, lads, lads, we're all friends here. That was all Stan needed, he didn't want to risk another knockdown, pride restored, well, he did offer to have another go, we all sat down, and carried on with the conversation, talking about the good old days in the nick? Do you remember that screw on B wing when Big Johnny, pulled that con on him? Well, Micky and I looked at each other and decided to get our drinks finished and fuck off out of there. We'd had an hour of listening to the good old days in the nick, and our brains were ready to explode. I'd had a taste of prison before going to Borstal and for the life of me couldn't think of anything exciting to talk or reminisce about from your fucking time in prison. What kind of a sad life, must they lead?

Ray Corbet, the boxer, had a scrapyard at the back of Broad Street in the town centre. Ray was a nice guy and every reason why I was half glad I'd got out of boxing. Ray had boxed at lightweight and welterweight, he was built like a little brick shithouse, he never talked, he grunted, he never seemed to do fuck all, just sit in his office, or walk around the yard. He lived in a shitty little house in Sparkbrook off the

Coventry Road and every time I used to go around, he was sleeping on the sofa - his yardman Ray Braving did the dealing and ran the yard. Being on the mooch we used to go up quite regularly to see if there was anything about, there never was. Ronny Call and Graham War were in business together running a garage opposite Corbet's yard, they were nice guys but were no mechanics, they were just in it for the scam. In the corner was a classic Jensen car, stripped down, as we'd go over Ronny would give us a big smile, "Hello lads, how's things going?" Ronny was the happy go lucky wide boy, Graham, the private school, educated charmer, the garage wasn't the earner for them, it was the deals that the garage brought in or could be crafted.

I said, "What's with the Jensen, Ron?"

Open as usual, Ron just came out with it, he knew we could be trusted, the car belonged to some titled guy. "That's our wage packet, son."

Every now and again we'd phone him up, tell him it needs a new part, or some bearings, he bungs us a few quid and leaves us in peace for another few weeks until it needs summat else. Well, I looked at Avo, Avo looks at me and never says a word, I just can't make out if Ronny is pulling my chain or is deadly serious.

Looking back towards Corbett's yard, we clocked Brian Cartwright driving in with his two-tonne pickup lorry, high sided and full of scrap, my eyes popped out on stalks. Knock me down with a fucking feather, Brian was the ex-British flyweight champion in the same stables as Johnny Prescot, Billy Monagh, Wally Swift and Jack Bodell. I had sparred with Cartwright a few times together with Johnny Prescot and Billy, both lovely, straight up guys, but Cartwright was that far up his arse his nose was brown. He'd spar with me a few rounds never speak, then walk away without any words of support or comfort, and here he was driving a fucking tat wagon, jeeezzz, my brother tried that game after the war.

Cartwright lived in Nechells, his father-in-law was Johnny Mann, another Birmingham welterweight boxer who had fought Ray Corbet, amongst others, I would see them coming and regularly going around Nechells, again, giving that 'look' down their noses at everyone around. They never drank around Nechells or the Green. They'd get a bus and drive off somewhere else where they could live off the reps and pretend to be someone important, for fucking crying out loud, why do people behave this way? Ok, fair play, they were both good boxers, they should have been magnanimous, yet here they were giving it the big I am, strutting around looking down at everyone else while pretending to be someone they weren't, a fucking joke.

Dealing in Scrap

Different opportunities kept offering themselves up, but without any real bread it's hard to get off the floor, Billy the Jock had a lock-up yard down Nechells where he ran a transport yard with his brother, his brother seemed a nice enough guy and I could pick up a bit of tension between the two. I guessed it was down to Billy as his wife seemed quite frightened of him, and you could feel the air of aggression that he carried around with him. We started mooching and scratching around a bit, doing up cars, trying to earn a few quid, when Ray Bravo popped up on the scene and started hanging around, it seemed him, and Corbett had had enough of each other, and he wanted something else to do. The suggestion was made to turn the yard into a scrap yard, buying in and selling scrap. I hadn't got a clue about scrap, all I did know was most of it was bent, and you had to throw the bodies in to keep going as well as the bungs. Still, I had no money, I had fuck all, so decided to just go along with it to see what came up.

I turned up a few days later to find the two of them standing there, a four-tonne lorry to the side bay loaded with brand new brass coils, what the fuck is all that about? Ray piped up, "We've just brought the load in and the guys coming back with another two loads."

"Yeah, but how the fuck are you going to offload four-tonne of brand new brass coils?" Ray piped up he'd had plenty of experience running Corbet's yard. "I know what to do, we'll just ring the Old Bill up and tell them."

My eyeballs nearly popped out, "Tell the Old Bill?"

"Yeah," Ray said, "don't worry, I know how it works."

"Well, I don't like the fucking sound of this, and I don't want to be involved, count me out, you handle it, I'll just piss about in the corner working on the car."

With that, Ray and Billy went into the office and got on the phone, within the hour, two Old Bill turn up walking into the office, after half an hour, they come walking out, clocking me on their way. Billy and Ray followed shortly after, walking over to me.

I said, "Well?"

Ray jumped in, "It's okay, they've told me to weigh it in at a specific yard, and the cops are going to make a phone call."

I couldn't fucking believe it, that simple.

"They're going to be waiting up the road until the thieves come back with the second load and nick them?"

Again, I looked in disbelief, this is beyond a fucking joke, then Bravo looked at me and said, "They clocked you, though, asked what you were doing here?"

"Well?" They were just surprised to see your face and knowing you're a Lewin." That pleased me a little bit. "But what did you say?"

"Oh, I said you just did a bit of work in the yard." Well, thank fuck for that.

With that, Bravo and Billy drive off with the lorry loaded up with the brand new brass coils, I looked after the yard, waiting for them to come back, my brain working it all out. First, if Bravo worked for Corbet, this must have been a regular occurrence. The Old Bill was used to Bravo, you don't do a deal like that without knowing how to handle it and never having done it before. Ray was as cool as a cucumber and never even raised a sweat, neither did Billy, so it must have been no big shakes to him either, worse, the fucking Old Bill stood for it like good uns. After three-quarters of an hour, the two of them returned with the dough, and we carried on working in the yard. We watched as the unmarked car sat up the road, visible to anyone coming up or down in a road void of traffic, they sat there for three hours, as we watched, before finally giving up and leaving, before leaving the one dropped down, to see if the villains had rung up to say they were coming back another day? They hadn't, we locked the doors up at 6 o'clock, and I decided this business was no dirty game I wanted to be in. Fuck it, those coppers must be utterly fucking stupid or be confident of another game plan, at any rate, I didn't want to do business with these two. It was going on all the time, the more experience I had, the more I saw, people would fuck each other for a shilling, that was my first experience of any form of partnership, and I didn't like it at all.

I was now living with Bet up Shard End in a nice council maisonette, one day a couple of lads turned up at the door and asked if I was interested in a load of leather wallets. I recognised the two of them, one worked in Erdington Baths in the steam room, sauna. There were rumours that he used to do extras on the massage table, but I didn't know if that was true or just the usual gossip. As with everything else, you had to find an edge in whatever you did in life as the wages were so shit, maybe that was their little edge.

I was in no worries about selling the wallets if the price were right, and the price was right, and with a full lorry load, it could put me right in front. We were just getting down to prices when they dropped the bombshell, "We've got to tell you, Tom, this belongs to Collin Lawler." I kept my face straight but knew that I didn't like this too much. We finished the deal, and the guys agreed to bring the wallets around in a few days. Lawler wasn't my best mate, but I had enough respect for the bloke not to want to get involved in the deal, as well as the blokes who came to see me. One worked for Lawler, another one involved was the Beef, none other than Collin Lawler's fucking brother-in-law, this was fucking dirty and not something I would agree with.

Colin Lawler had a transport yard down Grosvenor Road, Aston, doing a bit of scrap metal as well. The guy was an earner, his dad was Wallace Lawler the liberal MP, and very well respected. His mother was an Aston girl who grew up by the Aston Picture House, she had got a job on leaving school with Birmingham city council, seeing Wallace was going somewhere as a young councillor she had set her sights on him and married him. Colin and his brother Terry had had a good middle-class upbringing in a nice house, going to private school and grammar school, before leaving and joining the navy. From what I gathered, his mother was a real snob and Collin, and Terry rebelled. Collin deliberately brought a house in Aston, due for demolition, for £500, just to get one back at his old man who was doing his level best to get the slums around Brum demolished. Quite funny really, but at the time I thought that was his business and none of mine. He had also married an Aston girl, with a gob to match, but again, it didn't warrant his business being robbed in my mind, by his own family and workers, what kind of mongrels do that?

A couple of days later I bumped into Lawler in the Grosvenor Pub, pulling him aside, I told him the strength, making it very clear not to be considering me a grass, and I was not after any fucking brownie points, to me it was disgusting, low life. Lawler thanked me, and off I trotted, okay, I was losing a nice little earner, but I don't like earning money that way. A few days later, I was down the auctions when the Beef came strutting over and blatantly called me a grass in front of his mates. I was sorely tempted to put one on his chin, but the place was crowded, and I wouldn't come out of it looking very nice, so I decided to give him a mouthful for being a fucking stroke puller, and reminding him how lucky he was that I wasn't putting one on his chin. I've no doubt that would fly around the town, but fuck it, somehow the reason would also go flying around, if that were considered a normal thing to do then I was glad not to be involved in any part of it.

Within a few weeks Lawler's yard went tits up, how I don't know, but any robbery must have affected him and the business, and with scum bags like that in the team no one is going to last very long. I was seeing more and more of this from people I was growing up with, not only would they rob you behind your back, they would grass on you without a second thought. All the time they strutted around like they were something special, clever, no pride, no integrity, no loyalty,

A few days later, I called into the Grosvenor with Bet, and the barman served us a drink on Lawler, who had popped in a few hours earlier, only a few bob, but it was his way of showing his respect. That was good enough for me, but sometimes I started to wonder I was doing myself any favours, I certainly don't think I was winning friends, and among a lot of them, I think I was being looked at as the outsider, maybe not to be trusted. That in itself said it all really, it was becoming the norm to stroke pull, pull strokes and think it was clever. Micky Avo called around one day, with his brother-in-law Sunna. I thought they were both my mates until I realised as I was getting ready, they nicked a car radio out of a cupboard. Now what annoyed me, as they must have deliberately gone on the mooch as soon I had got in the bathroom and my missus in the kitchen. A fucking two penny halfpenny car radio, how desperate or dirty do you have to be to do that? And these were mates, I didn't find out until the next day, and wasn't too happy about it. The next day I met them, coming out of Sunna's house over Kingshurst, only this time I had a glass jar on me half full of sulphuric acid, well, it was full of water, but they didn't know that. I lifted the jar to throw it in Avo's face, and I could see the sheer terror in him, he fucking runs all over the road as I threw the acid deliberately missing him and hitting the road, "Ever pull a fucking stroke like that again and I won't miss." I think they both got the message as to how far I would go in future.

227

But this is how people, my so-called pals were getting it was the new generation, and they all thought it was the norm, Sunna would once boast in the Vine in Aston that he would rob anyone to feed his missus and kids.

I said, "Do you realise what you are saying?" These were big families, and they were fucking robbing of each other like no one's business. It was widespread, one day, one of Bet's friends called around, I came back just as she and her boyfriend were leaving, not thinking much of it at the time Bet proceeded to tell me that the girl's family was a neighbour of ours in Chingford Road, King Standing. She got in all the juicy gossip about what a rough family, we were and were notorious around the area before being kicked out and evicted.

I looked at Bet with a smile, "I bet they enjoyed telling you that."

"Ay." Half an hour later Bet noticed that ten bob had gone missing off her shelf. Now ten bob was quite a bit of money for her, and as far as her mate was concerned, she was living on her own and I was only her boyfriend, I looked at her and said, "And they have the fucking cheek to slag me off?"

Ha-ha, she had to smile herself, I'd never dream of doing something, anything like that, real scumbags.

Feeling Rudderless

I didn't realise it at the time, but my difficulty was I had grown up around them all, with them all and didn't know anyone else or any other way of knowing better. I knew they were scum bags, I started to realise they were not my true friends, but I thought it was just a process they were going through, part of growing up and finding ourselves, it would all right itself eventually, some fucking hope. For many of us, thieving was the norm, from the lowest nicking off your own family, your friends, to nicking from shops, breaking into shops, breaking into factories to robbing banks. It was a natural progression, once you reached the stage of robbing banks or factories you were amongst the elite, providing you could avoid getting yourselves nicked. Today, too many were getting nicked, very few of us had had any education, so you just kept persevering until you got enough to set up a little business or your bottle started to go so much you just gradually slowed down without having to admit the fact, your bottle had gone. Quite a few turned to scrap metal, opened a yard, and turned grass, this was a win-win all round for the cops, not only were they getting villains off the streets they were nicking more people so getting good results. For me, it was difficult to know who was the worst out of the lot of them, sometimes it felt like I was in the middle of a filthy pond, trying to figure out which way to swim.

Ruth Smith tried to be a beacon of life in my life, but she was hardly equipped to help me, she did live in a different world, of course, but her life had been moderately easy in comparison, while she looked down her nose at my mom and dad's lifestyle, she had grown up as an only child. Yes, okay, living quite frugally but not knowing hardship, when her parents died, she automatically inherited the house, some fucking hardship, but maybe our Billy was right, maybe I should get a proper job. Charlie was a good mate who lived over Garrets Green, we would go out and have some good times, me, Charlie, Joe, Micky Regan, who was a cousin of another pal, John Regan, whose dad had a demolition yard in Green Lane Small Heath. Rumour had it that John's dad, John senior, had come over on the boat from Ireland before the war. Being a typical hard worker, he had got himself a job labouring on the sites and roads around Brum. Before long and having learnt a bit of tarmacking, he had nicked a vibrating roller and set up in business for himself. From that, he had built up a very lucrative demolition business.

John's old man had built himself a bungalow on an acre of land in Earlswood Solihull, as soon as his old man shot off back to Ireland, we'd be over John's for a party. His bungalow was a beautiful big place, but it was furnished straight out of a typical Irish house of the 40s, big stuffed sofas, nothing fancy, and the ugliest of slobbering bulldogs, snorting all over the place. There was no shortage of food in the fridge, which was stocked with steaks, yep, dead down to earth, scruffy but comfortable with no airs and graces. John's dad was perfect proof if needed that you didn't need the best of educations to get on in life. I heard these stories regularly, the Gallagher brothers came over from Ireland the same now they were one of the biggest house builders in the country, yet the story was they couldn't even fucking read properly.

Pushing Grommets at Rover

Charlie worked for the Rover company and had offered to get me a job there, but first of all, I had to join the union, up he takes me to the union office in Bordesley Green where for half a crown I'm now a fully signed up union member. Being a Saturday, me Joey and Mick had agreed to meet up at Charlie's house before going out for a few drinks. His mom and dad had a very nice house, immaculate inside all laid out very comfortable and homely, we were invited to come in and sit on the sofa while Charlie got himself ready. His mom was busying herself around the house, and their little pooch would meander around at the sniff, on me I had a plastic turd and a few stink bombs, quietly I snuck the turd around the back of the sofa, and cracked a stink bomb. The smell started to waft about just as Charlie's mom came back into the living room, her little nose went up in the air, and she caught it straight away, Mishy, Mishy, she shouted to the dog. Mishy recognised the tones straight away and with guilt written all over him did a runner, right behind the fucking sofa. That was it, Charlie's mom saw the turd and went fucking berserk, her little Mishy had shit on her carpet, in front of her son's friends. She was humiliated, out she shoots coming back with the fucking broom, jeeezzz, this is getting out of control, I didn't expect it to go that far. Now she's chasing little Mishy around the sofa smacking it when she can. Poor Mishy, he hadn't done a fucking thing, and here he was scattering all over the place, trying to avoid the belting of his life. I picked the turd up just as Charlie came in the room all smartened up and ready to go. We got out of there quick sharpish with Charlie looking

perplexed, what was all that about? No one said a fucking
word.

On Monday Charlie took me up to the Rover in Load Lane
in Solihull, into reception and with my newly printed
membership card. I was offered a job as a semi-skilled fitter,
on the line, at 22 quid a week, which was about six quid
above the average wage. I was to start the next day. Turning
up the next day I was taken over to one of the lines showed
what to do and left to it, my job was to push plastic grommets
into the underside of the cars, the line travelled so far, and I
just had to keep up with the track inserting these grommets,
semi-skilled? A fucking monkey could have done the job; still,
it was a job, it was regular, and it was a decent wage,
sometimes I would rush up the whole line doing about six cars
in quick succession, then slowly walking back to the start and
doing it again. Sometimes I'd just flick one in one at a time,
pacing myself along the line, this was hard fucking work, now
I started to realise why Charlie didn't talk a lot, he was fucking
zombified, within two days I was becoming zombified.

Whether you brought your sandwiches or brought a
subsidised dinner you ate in the canteen, where everyone sat
around like zombies, after half an hour heading back to work,
shoulders slumped. At 5 pm, the horn went, and that was it,
everyone made a fucking mad dash for the doors, the car park
squealing with tyres as they rushed to get out. On the third
day, everyone was told to walk out on strike, we were out
until the following Tuesday. "Why are we out on strike?"
"Dunno mate, shop stewards called us out, when we're
called out we get out." I looked in disbelief, this seemed
fucking stupid, two days' pay lost, and no one said a word. It
happened the following week, again, no one said a word, and
no one questioned it, this time we lost three days' pay. The
following week was a full week, thank fuck for that. The
fourth week we were called out again, oh for fuck's sake, this

time I was determined to find out what it was all about. After several attempts and a dozen dunno mates, I found out why we were out on strike. On another line across the way, a man had not turned up, through illness, probably fucking zombified. The foreman asked the guy next in line to do part of his job, which was to put the knob on the gear stick, the bloke refused. "I'm not doing another bloke's work." The foreman said, "But you've got to, the man's called in sick."

"No." The next thing the bloke's called the shop steward over, straight away, the shop steward listened to the foreman, agreed with the bloke on his line, blew his whistle, everybody out, well, I couldn't fucking believe it. A couple of nights later, I was talking to Charlie in the pub, as I was telling him, open-eyed and in disbelief, Charlie put his hand up.

"No, Tom, that's exactly right."

I stared at Charlie, not knowing what to make of his comments. "What?"

"Look, Tom, it's them and us, if that bloke had agreed to do the other man's job management would have said we don't need that man. They would have then sacked that man."

"Well, so what Charlie? He wouldn't be needed; anyway, there would be a simple solution to that. That's where the steward comes in, negotiates a bit more pay for the bloke doing a bit more work, it's a win-win all around."

Charlie was adamant. "No, Tom, it doesn't work like that, it's them and us." Fucking hell, I couldn't believe it, I packed up at the Rover straight away. Ok, the wage wasn't bad if you could pick up a good week, but you could never pick up a good week. I suppose the only plus was a strike plan helped you to dezombify yourself for a couple of days, but fuck that, it was not for me, it also didn't do much for our friendship either, I just couldn't understand Charlie's thinking, we drifted apart from that moment on.

Star Studded

The Star Pub in Aston was so-called because it was opposite the ITV studios on the Lichfield Road. It attracted some if not all of the stars and celebrities of the day who were appearing there, some of the Hollies, the pop group, Noel Gordon and some of the stars from Crossroads. We would go down on different nights in our best gear hoping some of the stardust would rub off if it ever did it sure missed me.

My mate, Hughie Murry, was a great singer and was always getting up in the boozers. Noel Gordon had invited him onto her daytime news show, but he never turned up.

When I asked him, he just looked aside, downcast. "I just lost my bottle, Tom, couldn't go through with it."

I was gobsmacked, Hughie was big, brash and confident, but that was just the front that he put on, underneath he was quite shy and lacking in confidence, that's what Nechells does for you, the schools do for you.

Most of the celebrities looked just like us, nothing special, not what we were lead to believe by the films and news. Pat Phoenix was different, she was an actress in Coronation Street and would often appear at the ITV studios, she would flounce into the Star Pub, big white expensive coat, silk scarf flowing behind her as she bounced up behind the bar surrounded by her minions.

"Hello dahling, a large G and T, please."

We would stand there looking mesmerised, course we couldn't show it, oh no, we had to act all nonchalant, like this was all quite normal for us. If you displayed any kind of fawning and you would be looked on as a bit of a prick, so we would stand there trying to look as normal as possible, stiff as boards, and utter pricks.

Dodger Hardiman and I decided we could do as good a job as many of these actors, we watched enough of Crossroads to know the actors were crap, so we decided to go into the studios and front Reg Watson, the producer of Crossroads and ask him for a job. Across we go, leaving it until lunchtime thinking that would be the busiest, walking through the gates the security guard shouted out to us as we wafted past arses tight, eyes dead ahead and as stiff as a board, as we waved regally to the guard as we passed. After ten yards we heaved a sigh of relief, it had worked, I knew it if you had the balls and the bullshit, you could get away with anything. Walking around the studios we tried to get our bearings, the café sign jumped out first, so we decided to head into that. The café was just like any we had seen in the major shops in Birmingham city centre, a long buffet bar with plenty of food on display, the usual tables and chairs spread around. We got ourselves a coffee, found a table and sat down, looking around, we expected to see some female pop star or actress around, or that we would give them the look. With a bit of luck, they would clock us, take a fancy and from then on, get a date and we'd have cracked it.

No such fucking luck, we sat there like dummies wondering what to do next. That's it, we might as well bite the bullet and go sort out Reg Watson, this was our moment, off we go looking past different studios, asking on the way, excuse me, do you know where Reg's room is?
"Yeah, just down there on the right."
Off we go and find it, looking through a window we could see Reg and his colleague going through film clips on a screen in front of them. Without further ado, I opened the door and

walked in, Dodger behind me, his bottle clapping as bad as mine.

As Reg turned around, he looked at us. "Yes, lads, what do you want?"

"Well, Reg, no disrespect, but we've watched a few of your shows, and we reckon we can act better than some of your actors!"

It went quiet for a bit, Reg looked at his colleague, looked back at us, then looked at each other again, and burst out fucking laughing.

"What's so fucking funny?"

"Okay, lads, nice try, you've won your bet, now fuck off." "

But Reg," I said, "we're serious."

"Okay guys, if you feel that confident, go to drama school, do some training, then come back."

Well, for myself, I thought it might be good advice, out we went, as we gave the security guard a casual wave he looked at us puzzled, trying to work out who we were. Okay, we'd got a knockback, of sorts, maybe Reg's advice was sound, I decided to give it some thought.

Looking through the stage paper, the actors' bible, I could see that there were plenty of drama schools in London, which was the place to be. Off I go to an appointment at the offices of an agent who also had a small drama school, in Chiswick. At length, the agent calls me into her office, "What makes you think you can act, Mr Lewin?"

"I've been acting most of my life miss, this should come easy to me."

She then spoke to two other applicants, one a lad named Dorian, she gave them both a rough ride, telling the one he wasn't suitable, to Dorian, he had to relax his jaw, as we walked back out to Oxford Street, having been accepted, we decided it made sense to pal up and share digs to cut costs.

The following month I set off, Avo and Sunna giving me a lift, I met up with Dorian at digs, we had found and in we moved with our little suitcases. The drama school was just a normal, school, that took young people in from junior to 20 or so years of age, in the adult section there were about 15 of us, we were met straight away as we walked in with the typical, "Halloo dahlings."

I quickly started to realise this wasn't one of the top drama schools of London; also, I found it difficult to settle in, although these kids were about the same age as me, they were far younger in life experience, they were just like school kids themselves. Quite a few had already appeared on telly and were treated like minor celebrities around Chiswick. Sally Thompson had just got a part in the Railway Children and George Georgio, had had a decent part in Dear Sir, funnily enough, he was Maltese but played the Asian in the class.

Being in a film might have been great, but George needed some money, so we decided to go into business together cleaning windows around the immediate area. I started to find Chiswick was the main hub of the acting community in London with some of the most famous actors living there, but the place would be a bit of a contradiction. You would be walking along, no one giving a shit about anyone, everyone a stranger to each other, then along would appear Tommy Cooper, the comedian, and everyone would put a spring in their step, give a cheery wave, "Hello Tommy," like he was a long lost friend. Tommy would give a cheery wave back, "Hello there," then back to normal, no one speaking to each other, everyone strangers.

I didn't like London at all, well not much, it all seemed like a rat race existence. Worse, I was a Brummie, anyone north of Watford gap was looked on as a carrot cruncher. Worse, walking around Chiswick, it started to dawn on me what I was up against. Chiswick was teaming with glamorous models, handsome actors with velvet voices, working as waiters or bar staff in the local pubs, restaurants and hotels, all working while waiting for the big break. You could be walking around Chiswick, and you'd see some guy walking around with a billboard over his shoulders, advertising eat at Easy Joe's Café.

I turned to George, "His face looks familiar?"

"Yeah, that's so and so, out of The Prisoner." For fuck's sake, the guy was handsome, a good actor, and here he was, walking around with a fucking billboard, doing the window cleaning. I came across a few actors, one miserable old git out of a regular series on the telly, Dad's Army, as miserable off it as he was on it, another guy was a family man in one of the block of flats I was living in. Chatting to him for advice he informed me that he was what's called a jobbing actor, I had seen him in a few films and television programmes like Coronation Street, he would be the one sitting in the bar visiting a relative or drinking a pint in the background while the camera focused on the main character. He informed me that while he wasn't famous or rich, he earned a living through regular work on television or theatre.

I quickly started to get the reality of the real world of television and being an actor, at any one time, 85 percent of actors were out of work, most of them I think around Chiswick. I started to question what chance I would have at my age when walking all around me, were beautiful models, and men who looked like six-foot Adonis's who had been trying to make the break for years. I gave acting a try for nine months before realising I was on a loser, worse, acting is debilitating, knockback after knockback for years before you get a break, fuck it, I threw the towel in and got a lift back to Birmingham, with the help of Ruth Smith.

Back in Birmingham, I palled back up with Avo, only to find they had told everyone about my little excursion into acting and it was flying around the town.

"Oh, oh, oh, that Tommy Lewin, a fucking actor? Oh, oh, oh, how funny, what a mug."

It never failed to amaze me how people's minds worked, they were just so fucking petty, none of them ever stepped outside their self-imposed boundaries for fear of making a mug out of themselves, but were dead quick at taking the piss out of anyone else that did. They never made a mistake because they never took any risks, if someone made a statement and they couldn't understand the word or sentence they would never query it or ask what it meant. Oh no, they couldn't risk making a mug out of themselves.

My brother Billy was polishing his shoes one day, then started cleaning and polishing the instep. Intrigued, I said," Why are you doing that?"

Puffing himself up with self-importance, he started, "well, when you're in a posh hotel, and you're walking up the stairs you can always tell if the person in front of you is a gentleman by his polished instep." With these gems of wisdom imparted he carried on brushing away at his instep.

After I'd got my breath, I said, "Posh hotel with your big gob? Every other word is a swear word." He didn't have an answer for that.

Running Sid's Scrap Yard

Siddy Hobday was still in nick with another two years to go off his seven-year stretch, no one was in any doubt that he was biting at the bit and climbing the walls to get out. In the meantime, he was losing money hand over fist, his scrapyard empty, his yardman Billy Smith, was trying to find different ways to make some money out of the yard that Sid owned outright. I caught him doing a bit of steaming around the yard, with the hope of running a commercial steam cleaning business cleaning lorries cars etc., the only problem was I don't think Billy was the full shilling and didn't have much of a clue. Chatting away, Billy asked if I would be interested in running the yard, this shook me up, they must be desperate, I was only 18 and had no experience of running a yard. I also knew sis was not the easiest of blokes to get on with, he could get upset at the slightest thing, and a backhander was the norm, Billy regularly took a backhander of him for the slightest thing.

Sid's brother Tommy had run the yard for him during the early part of his stretch and was quite pissed off with him, one day he told me, "Tom, we had the yard running, we were paying the bills, I'd even got him a nice new white Jaguar, and he still wasn't happy." They ended up having a big fall out, all this should have been warning signs to me, but I was still looking for a way of earning a few quid. I offered to have a go at running it, and Billy said he would get back to me after seeing Siddy. The word came back a week later that Sid was happy for me to run the yard, so with some excitement, I set off and opened the yard up, Billy as my gopher, and I was on 50/50, which seemed a great deal to me.

Running any business is quite straightforward first you have to work your costings out, rent, rates, utility bills, etc. Tally all that up, buy the scrap and make sure there is enough profit left over to cover those bills. The main thing is to buy your scrap at the best price you can then sell it for the best price you can get. One way to help this along is to use the magnet, every scrap yard uses the magnet, this fits onto the back of the scales and can be adjusted along with the scales as to how greedy you are. I should imagine Siddy had been very greedy, considering the lifestyle he had, a big detached house in Sutton, a freehold yard and a nice Rolls Royce. You can adjust the magnet on the arm of the scale to such an extent that if you put a hundredweight of copper on it could weigh less than a couple of pounds in weight. I was happy enough with 15% or so, the punters weren't overly bothered by that amount, and with the natural mark-up circa 20% I would be making in the region of some 35%, a third of the total amount, not bad I thought.

The main problem was getting the stuff in, the yard had been closed for some time, I didn't have money for advertising, the word was slow in getting around, it was coming in, in bits and drabs. The other problem was, which didn't give me any concern at the moment was the books, now I knew you had to keep a book, in that book goes the purchases and vehicle number of the seller, all very simple, but sometimes, due to inexperience and quietness, we would forget. Further, you had to put a bung in the book for the Old Bill, who came round to inspect them, now firstly, I didn't mind putting details in the book, but I was fucked if I was going to put a bung in the book for coppers, especially bent coppers. No, let's face it, you're expected to throw the odd body in, grass on some poor bastard whose just trying to earn a few quid, and for the privilege, bung the Old Bill as well. It was beyond sick, I mean, think about it, some of these blokes were bringing in a few pounds of copper they had ferreted out of an empty house due for demolition, maybe the copper hot water boiler, or the water pipes around the house. Okay, it's technically theft, but from who? And who's going to use it? The taxpayer has got to pay the council to remove the stuff, the same as the bricks, but you'd never get nicked for nicking a few dozen bricks of a bomb peck. To me, the law was corrupt and cockeyed.

I could understand Sid copping the needle, his attitude was if he didn't know it was bent, then he wasn't committing any offence. Sid's only problem was he was ambitious, greedy, and he hated the coppers. If he had given them big bungs in line with the money he was taking they might have accepted his books for what they were, but it all went against Sid's principles, they were bent, fuck em, he had complied with the law, he kept his books tidy, he diligently kept a record of all metals brought in. The problem was some of the phone numbers just didn't add up, all the time, the coppers were taking details from Sid's books to check against their record. Sid always had a job containing his anger, the Old Bill were terrified to come into his yard, he would slag them off to the hilt, but still, they came in. Sid always tried to find a method of filming them, with cameras set up in his office. Eventually, the cops built up a case against him. By the time it got into court, they had built up a hefty case. "But this number is a police motorbike Mr Hobday, and this one is a Welsh tractor, and this one is a police car, Mr Hobday?"

All the while, Sid's barrister was batting the answers back. "That is not for my client to know, my lud. If someone comes in with false plates, Mr Hobday would have no way of knowing."

Correct of course but neither the police prosecution nor the judge was going to accept that, and these people were very good at parcelling the evidence into a nice pile to present to the jury who will then find you guilty. The jury was made up of general Joe public, not one with a criminal record, most never been in trouble in their life, many made up probably of the zombies who worked at the car factories, never been in trouble with the police except for maybe a speeding ticket.

I knew from the experience of my old man that it's dead easy to fit someone up. Siddy had no chance, someone once said, maybe in the bible, better to let 100 guilty men go free than one innocent man guilty. I thought the laws and scales of justice acted on that principle. Bollox, if you fit the profile, together with showing your contempt and hatred for the law, regardless of how bent the law is when it suits them, then they will target you. I knew all this of course, but being ignorant of the business I just expected to learn as I went along, how fucking naïve could I be?

For the first few weeks we started stuttering along, a few batteries, a bit of alli, all normal yard tat, one day my old mates Richey Parkinson and Dennis Aziz came strolling into the yard, as they approached the main gates, they clocked two plainclothes Old Bill coming across from the opposite side of the road. It was just a coincidence of course, but Richey and Dennis assumed the Old Bill was coming in for them and legged it, showing their guilt straight away, the Old Bill legged it after them, after a few minutes the Old Bill came back, "do you know them?" Billy and I looked at each other in bemusement, "no, no," we couldn't even figure out why the silly pair of fuckers had run.

By the seventh week, it all came to an end, I was taking a couple of hundredweight of copper into a major yard in Hockley in the boot of the car, we had no other alternative as we had no money for a van when the Old Bill came and nicked me. They also decided to nick a World War II bayonet my dad had brought back from the war, I'd just taken it for re-chroming. But I suspect the cops looked at is as there spoils of war where it would end up on one of their shelves. No matter how much I pleaded they weren't interested in listening, I could not point it out in the book, I had no explanation for it, other than I had brought it in. I was charged with receiving stolen metal and released on bail, I've no doubt Sid wasn't too happy, but I realised dead rapid that the scrap business was not for me. Now I was up for another charge.

I was pissed off, to say the least, I was almost 20 and was getting nowhere, worst, I'd got a criminal fucking record I neither deserved nor have earned. 18 months in prison/Borstal for receiving stolen jewellery or robbing a jewellery shop in Blackpool, a place I had never even visited, receiving a stolen car, that was only fit for scrap, now receiving stolen metal in a business I had only been in for six fucking weeks, it was ridiculous. And yet, no one gave a fuck, no one was the least bit interested. Prison is full of people screaming, I'm innocent.

Buying the Second-hand Shop

My Uncle Jeff Eliot was a lovely bloke, as well as being a professional gambler, he had also bought the Fleur de Leys club, a very nice upmarket cabaret club. In the city centre. Naturally, he gave me a lifelong gold card, which was very handy, one day he happened to drop it out that someone had broken into his car nicked a few items and his cherished binoculars. He was more concerned about his binoculars. It so happened that a few days later, I happened to be talking to an old Nechells boy named Donald that I had had a little fall out with a few years ago. He happened to mention that he had a pair of binoculars to sell. Bingo, of all the needles in the haystack. Jeff was over the moon and bigged my effort up far more than I deserved, it was just a fluke, but I let him big me up, it's not often I get a bit of praise, so it's nice when it comes. By now we had bought a little second-hand shop in Green Lane Small Heath, Bet's mom and dad lived in Millward Street and knew the owner who had had enough. It was only a pokey little place, but Bet's mom assured me that he made a fortune. Knowing Billy's mate Chalky who had a second-hand shop in Six Ways, Aston, I could well believe it. Chalky had got himself registered as a charity, and was raking it in, he quietly let us know that by registering as a charity it opened the doors to the best charity suppliers. Every Sunday he would do a run to London, by Monday morning there was a queue outside his shop, by lunchtime, he'd made his money back, the rest of the week was all profit, he was raking it in, so I was quite optimistic that this could be quite handy for us.

Green Lane was a shithole, the rent was peanuts, and the guy gave us the contact in the town for the second-hand clothes, etc. Being as Bets old lady Peg was on the doorstep I gave her the job of running the shop, big mistake, from day one she was robbing us blind. "Fuck me Peg, I thought you said this shop was a gold mine?"

"Well," she said, "I think a lot of his customers stopped coming in." After a couple of weeks I sacked the old lady, and things picked up a bit, but I could see the real reason the shop wasn't doing any good, hadn't for a long time, the poor fuckers in the area had no money, they would come in for a pair of second-hand socks, fucking second-hand socks. One neighbour came across offering to exchange some second-hand cutlery for a few items of clothing, I think the shop lasted around five months.

Living around the corner Donald would take to popping round now and again for a chat, once or twice we would go out for a drink, hitting a few pubs, then up to the clubs. One night for some reason we decided to go up to the Ambassadors Club up the Hagley Road, the Ambassadors was an upmarket gentleman's club where you went to have a quiet drink in a refined atmosphere without any aggro. Kennedy was on the door, quiet and humble as befitted the atmosphere. Kennedy was part of an old Summer Lane family; my mom had told me a story of how the Old Bill gave him the biggest hiding of his life one night after he'd come out of the pub. He was well-known for his fighting and smacking the Old Bill, his screams could be heard from one end of Summer Lane to the other, now he had quietened down and was all respectable, as were many others of his generation.

The club was almost empty, at the bar was a solitary, Harry Twink, the scrap dealer, we both went over and joined him ordering a drink. Twink was nursing a bottle of scotch, not only was he alone, he seemed alone and a bit sad. Twink had been a safe breaker back in the day down Summer Lane. His last bit of bird was a seven stretch when he came out, he'd decided to go into scrap metal and opened a scrap yard over Hockley. Many scrap dealers were former thieves or villains, poacher turned gamekeeper, the problem is with a lot of them, they quickly forget the past, now they are respectable businessmen, right now he was drinking himself into a stupor. By contrast, I was on a high, I don't know why I hadn't got a pot to piss in, I was on the floor, again, but if nothing else, I was confident, there was always something around the corner. I think maybe my confidence depressed Twink even more, after another half-hour, he decided to leave, asking us to finish the bottle of scotch. The bottle was almost full, Donald and I were well bladdered, deciding to duck ourselves. I looked around and noticed a group of people sitting on the far side of the room, three men, two women, rather than waste it, I took the bottle over to the table asking the group to please finish it off as we were leaving. Oh, please don't go join us? Donald was almost at the door, but I was quite happy to take the offer up. The seat was quite welcoming, big mistake, down we sat, and the blonde bird started chatting to me, that's about all I can remember until one of the guys asked us to join them at their home for a coffee.

I didn't see anything unusual in this, drunk as I was, you went out, had a drink, met someone, and? Well, come to think about it, no, usually you chat the bird up, then offer to take her home. The blonde was quite friendly, but obviously, she was with her husband, taking their offer up, we all stood up together, and headed for the door, the group heading off in front of us, Donald just walking alongside me, well drunk, going with the flow.

Outside, drunk as I was the group had set off across the car park well in front of us, what it was I don't know, instinct, but something wasn't right. The three blokes were waiting in a group, two well-built big, almost six feet tall, I didn't think anything of the fact the two women were not in the group, assuming they had just carried on to the cars. The next thing I became aware of is the shortest of the group, turned on us and started giving us a load of mouth. What the fucking hell is going on here? Drunk as I was I couldn't help being stunned, which one invited us back now I can't remember, maybe it was this little prick's wife. I felt she was a bit over-friendly, but, friendly, maybe this prick had copped the needle over that? I certainly ain't going to upset someone who had just invited us for a coffee, so I couldn't figure out what his game was, whether he was Italian or had some Italian in him I don't know, but he started shouting his gob off about how he was the mafia. Donald just stood there stunned and drunk, the next thing I know he cried out in pain, this little prick had put a bottle in his face.

The next thing I know is we were all over each other, arms flailing, bottles going everywhere, all I can remember is my arms drunkenly flailing about trying to keep the fuckers off me, sober I would have been quite confident of knocking them out, drunk I was out of it. Within seconds it was over, the three of them walked off, me and Donald heading the opposite way to the Hagley Road looking for a taxi; no one saying a word. Donald heading for the hospital, the taxi dropping me off at Bet's along the way. The next day Donald came to the door, having had his face stitched up, to show a nasty circular cut to his face, obviously done with a broken bottle, the little mafia prat had thrust the broken bottle in his face. Drinking a coffee, he took it in good spirit, for fuck's sake the poor bastard hadn't said a word all night, hadn't even spoken to the people at all.

Anne Widdecombe, the politician, wrote an article for the daily mail once bemoaning the loss of the good old days when neighbours would look out for each other, look after each other, share their last bit of food, and handle their affairs with a good fight or fisticuffs followed by a handshake after, and so on and so on. Yes, those good old days and the principles of them were rapidly disappearing.

Stitched Up

We don't know whether we had won the scrap or not, we felt we had held our own against three bigger blokes, and we both looked at Donald's facial wound as battle scars, mind, he wasn't laughing too much. The three of us were trying to get our heads around the fiasco of the previous night, trying to analyse why the fuckers had invited us back for a coffee then started on us outside. They had sent the women to the car to get them out the way, which meant they had planned it. Premeditated, we had just come to this conclusion when we heard the banging on the door, the fucking Old Bill, mob-handed at the door, three squad cars and a van, our feet never touched the floor before we were whipped off over to Edgbaston nick. No niceties, we were stood at a desk, told we were being arrested, not allowed any solicitor. Neither one of us was offered the chance to explain, or the opportunity of giving our version of events, this lot wasn't in the least bit interested, one big bastard even stood close to me with a barking, snarling fucking Alsatian snapping at my heels. What the fucking hell is going on here, we were the victims, we were the ones who had been picked on. Donald had a glaring face wound, yet we were being treated like some fucking lunatic IRA terrorists, this wasn't fucking funny, we weren't even given a chance to explain or give our version of events, we were bounced straight off to Steelhouse Lane Nick, and from there to Winston Green Prison, that was it, fucked.

Winston Green was a filthy dirty, smelly fucking hell hole, full of low life with the odd one or two self-styled gangsters from up and around the clubs. On remand, you can wear your own clothes, which gave the gangsters the only opportunity to show they were above the others, by wearing their pinstripes or Crombie overcoats. I was petered up with Ronnie, who had the garage opposite Ray Corbet's yard. Graham must have got bail, but they were both up on fraud charges relating to the garage. Ronnie, cocky as ever was adamant that they would get off with the charges, swaggering around the wing in his white trench coat, a bounce to his feet. He'd say, "They've got no chance, Tom, no evidence, and we haven't done anything." Course, no one ever asked in detail what anyone else is being charged with, everyone on remand was innocent, it was just a matter of getting into court and proving it. I felt Ronnie's bounce was maybe more nerves than cockiness, but it kept him going; besides, Ronnie was a nice guy.

Within an hour of arriving at the Green, I was approached by Tommy, the Duck Irishman. I knew Tommy from on the outside as he used to come up to the old man's press club with his Irish mates, Tommy was a nice guy, but a typical Paddy, on the dole, blagging his way through life, drinking Guinness in all the pubs and clubs, a dosser. Now here he was, polished to the nines, handpicked striped uniform and pressed shirt and tie, for fuck's sake, it was tailor-made, as he thrusts an ounce of baccy in my hand.

"Have this, Tommy, I'm the baron," he said in that typical Irish accent. "Let me know when you want some more," and with that, he was gone, the fucking baron? For Christ's sake, but it all goes topsy-turvy in the nick, no one is who you think they are. You could be talking to a millionaire or a pervert unless they were on remand wearing their best gear. Ronnie would have a meal brought in every day by his wife. "I can't eat that prison shit, Tom."

I was wearing prison gear, ill-fitting at that, my only suit was with the cops. Besides, my feeling was I was in the nick, you can dress it up as nice as you want, with virtually nil chance of being found not guilty.

Ray Mills, the cockney pal of the Krays pulled out the local paper to show me the headlines. "You've hit the headlines, Tom," as though I was some kind of a fucking celebrity.

I took one look, and my heart sunk into my legs. Staring out at me as bold as brass were the three guys who had started on us outside the club, looking for all the world like dead bodies on a morgue slab, eyes closed, emphasising the crises crosses all over their faces. It looked terrible, for us, exactly as we had imagined it on the night arms flailing all over the place as we had tried to defend ourselves, but that's not how the pictures are being made to look. Here are three innocent guys, standing there, big as they are, allowing us to slash their faces, duh? No mention of the women waiting in the car. No questions being asked like, hang about, if you were being attacked, why didn't you run like normal people? What about those wounds? No stitches, they were all healed up by the court case, not a trace, it's a good job they had the full-blown up photos for the jury.

Ray Mills was also on remand for some stolen jewellery, Ray was at the murder flat with his brother when Reggie Kray stabbed Jack the hat Mcvitie. From what I had gathered it was getting a bit hot for them down London with the Krays being nicked, so Ray did a runner up to Brum, getting a job on the door of my uncles Jeff's club, the Fleur de Lis club. He also had a nice little bread and butter living with a car valeting company in Small Heath, now he was awaiting trial for the jewellery job, when his case came up Ray got five years.

After Ronnie got sentenced to three years in prison for his part in the fraud alongside Graham. I was on my own for an hour before they put this dirty little old bastard in my cell, he made my skin crawl and lying in bed on the night I could feel him crawling across the room with his hands going under my pillow to nick some mints I had there. He was out the cell the next day, the next one in was this black guy, all of six foot 3 ins, with shoulders to match, what he was in for I don't know, but I was sure that I wouldn't like to have a fall out with him, by the second night he came over all humble and friendly. It turns out he couldn't read and wanted me to write a letter to his wife, sure I said, and he handed me the paper and pen, he went to his bunk, I lay on mine writing as he dictated the words to me.

Dear Muriel,

Where it's appropriate I'm adding my own words to the letter, I am missing you very much, when I get home, I am going to make hot love to you, rip your clothes off one by one.

When he had finished, I handed him the letter knowing full well, he couldn't read it. It was only later I realised the shit I had dropped myself in, what about if the screws read it and clocked on. I was on tenterhooks all the following day expecting the screws to be knocking on the door any minute. The day after he got parole, so I heaved a fucking major sigh of relief as he left the cell. The same day I asked if I could move in with a couple of mates across the landing, Peter Beg and Ray Cromm, they were in a cell with three bunks, always better to be in with someone you knew rather than total strangers, or worse, perverts.

Pete was a nice guy on remand for a robbery, Ray was another Brummie gangster, awaiting a hearing on the Walsall co-op robbery, he had done a previous seven stretch with most of it spent in Broadmoor the nutters' prison, he had spent time and knew the Krays personally, even doing a shooting for them. He had spent time in prison with mad Frankie Fraser the London gangster, he would keep us entertained in the cell by regaling us with stories of his time in the nick. The screws got together at one time to put a stop to Mad Frank. Frank lived up to his nickname and would smack a screw at the first opportunity. They decided they had had enough of this so one night after they had locked everyone up, dived into Frank's cell, mob-handed bundled him on to a bed and deliberately broke his legs, so he had to walk with crutches for a few months. From what Ray was telling us I half felt sorry for the screws, Mad Frank was certainly a fucking nutter.

Ray also informed me that Ronnie Kray would have loved having me in the nick with him. I let Ray know quick sharpish that gangster or not, Ron would get a sharp smack of me if he tried it on.

I remembered Ray as a bouncer up the Cedar, and one or two reckoned he was a nutter when he lost it kicking punters out. On the outside, he had been into all kinds of scams, from credit cards to cheque fraud, he had been into plenty, drinking champagne with celebrities such as Cannon and Ball, Little and Large, Ray was another one who walked about the wing in his pinstriped suit, Crombie overcoat and titfer on his bonce.

In the nick, you never asked someone what they were in for unless they volunteered it. One night Ray was telling us why he was on remand, his brother had a pal whose wife worked for the Walsall co-op as a cleaner. On a Saturday night the peter (safe) was choc-a-block with the takings, the key hung in a certain hidden place. For an equal share of the pot, the guy was prepared to give them the details and tell them where the key was hidden, the estimate was 40 to 50 grand, a real nice tickle, split three ways, it was the tickle every villain prayed for, enough to set them up for life if handled wisely.

Ray's brother insisted on bringing his mate Collin in, this now took the split to four ways, then Ray wanted his pal from

Broadmoor brought in as he was on the floor and Ray wanted to give him a lift up, as he's telling us this I'm looking across at Pete with raised eyebrows. Now it's five ways, for fuck's sake, soon there will be nothing left. At any rate, the four of them went streaming in on the appointed Saturday night, the cleaner none, the wiser, a window cracked, the key found, the safe opened, the bags of notes bundled out leaving all the silver back in the safe, but why leave the cash in the safe? Well, Ray looked up at me as if it was me who was stupid.

"Well, we felt we had got plenty enough with the notes, Tom." They got back from the job and counted out the dough, 25 grand in cash, they had left a further 25 grand in silver, but couldn't be bothered with hauling it out, this was fucking unbelievable to me, but worse was to come. Divvying the money up gave them each five grand, out of that, quite rightly, they took a grand off giving the husband of the cleaner, an equal share of four grand, this four grand was given to Colin to give to the guy, all dead simple. As Colin set off home, he felt the four grand in one bin, then the four grand in the other bin, doing his sums he quite rightly worked out that put together he would have eight grand. So that's what he did, after all, he felt he was out the picture, he didn't even know the cleaner's husband, for fuck's sake. I don't know about Pete, but I couldn't get my breath, I could not get my fucking head around it.

True to form, the cleaner's husband gave it a few days when he realised he was going to be fucked he went to the Old Bill and squealed on them, but how did they all get nicked? The cleaner's husband only knew Ray's brother. Ray was adamant; it was Colin who had squealed on all of them, but it didn't weigh up right with me, something was not right. There we go, 50 grand split three ways gives them a nice touch of 16 grand each split three ways, what a touch and they fucked it, gangster? I was looking at Pete, Pete was looking blank back and not saying a word, fucking amazing, and here was Ray strutting about the nick, given full respect by the screws who I noticed treated him like a bit of a celebrity.

The next month Ray shook our hands and with the best wishes and good luck from us went off to the start of his trial. I don't think things were going to go too well, sure enough, the trial was over quite quickly with Ray getting a seven stretch, Colin a five. The whole sorry saga just convinced me even further of the futility of crime, it was fucking stupid, people like to say the odds are with the thief, but it seemed to me the odds are stacked against the thief. First, you have to do the job, then get away with it, that's partly the easy part, then you've got the odds of being grassed on against you for a variety of reasons. The great train robbers were a prime example of that to me. They pulled off the perfect blag, but for a variety of examples from being let down, fingerprints being left all over the place to grasses throwing them in after and being robbed, the lot of them ended up with fuck all to show for it except a lot of porridge.

In my disbelief, I turned to Ray in the cell, "Ray? How much does four grand work out at over five, seven years? It's less than the average fucking wage?"

"Oh yes, Tom, but you've got to remember all the other scams I was into?

Oh well, fuck that, I couldn't see sense in it unless it was a big tickle of at least 50 to 70 grand each which is unlikely. I didn't see the sense of it. Slowly, inevitably our case was coming up for hearing, I hadn't seen or talked to my solicitor, apart from our first meeting after instructing his company, someone in the nick had recommended a QC, who was supposed to be brilliant, I asked my solicitor if he would be prepared to act for me? I never knew until the day before the hearing whether he would or not. Neither Donald nor I was seen or spoken to before the trial began, we had never had a chance to put our side of the story, or given the opportunity to have our story considered, given any advice or any suggestions at all. I was starting to feel very keenly that we were fucked and going to be thrown to the wolves, we were. Worse, I had drastically lost weight, I was slim anyway and fit weighing some ten and a half stone, but I'd caught fucking worms from contaminated food, I'd only just managed to get rid of them with treatment days before the trial, I was zapped.

Inevitably, inexorably the day of the trial arrived, trial. It was a fucking fit-up, and I knew it, but still, I held out some hope, maybe my solicitor is doing all the work behind the scenes with my barrister, and they will come down to see us before the start, advise us and guide us through the whole process. Up to this point, I'd had no real experience of court cases or court procedures. I'd been into magistrates courts as a kid, in Blackpool it all went on over my head, I just accepted what was being put before me, ether I pled guilty, or we both pled not guilty, and at least one of us would be found guilty, and we knew that would be the old man, it was a no brainer. With the scrap car, again the odds were set against me, the guy who loaned me the car, McCloy was not allowed to appear in court or even give a statement clearing me. On my own I had no fucking chance, plead not guilty I would be found guilty and get a two stretch, my back was against the wall, I took the suspended, now it was all coming back to bite me in the arse.

Let's make no mistake, the law is corrupt, it always has been, it's weighted against the poor, the plebs, people like me, it goes back centuries to when the nobles ruled the land, and the peasants were left to grab what scraps they could
Poach a bit of rabbit or a fish, you get hung, nick a loaf of bread you get burnt at the stake, even a 150 years ago if you got caught thieving you were carted off to Australia. Fucking hell, the very letters QC, says it all, QUEENS FUCKING COUNCIL, not my council, the queen's council, and like a prat, I thought I was getting the best of the best, what a

fucking idiot, the closer the time came, the more I realised we were doomed.

With minutes to go before the trial was to start, there was still no show, no solicitor, no QC, not even a fucking clerk. People think, and we English even boast about how we have the best legal system in the world. Bollox, "Oh look at those Americans, they persecute the blacks." In the deep south, the white man is not guilty of killing the black man for walking on his land. People are sent to prison, then executed, tortured with appeal after an appeal before going to the electric chair only to be found innocent six months later? What a fucking shame.

Then you have the Muslims, if they're caught nicking a loaf of bread they get their hand chopped off, a loaf of bread, the other hand, you've got Indians hopping about in India with no legs and no arms, very civilised. But at least you know where you stand, or don't stand if you've had every limb chopped off if your wife's caught having an affair, they stone her to death. The fact is, very few countries have a fair, unbiased, impartial legal system, in every instance; it's weighted against the poor. England was no different, those arms holding out those scales of justice, are, in reality, leaning over like the Tower of Pisa.

We were charged with malicious wounding, no alternative. Just straight up straight forward malicious wounding, summarised as any person who maliciously shoots, stabs, cuts or wounds with the intent to maim, disfigure, disable or kill, the filthy bastards had certainly piled it on, this was a simple fight, of self-defence against three blokes who for whatever reason, having asked us back for coffee had then turned on us. But we are now living in the age of the grass, encouraged by the police it's spreading throughout society, having problems with your neighbour? Ring the cops and squeal on them - don't like your neighbour who's drawing the dole? Simple, wait until you see them doing a bit of work, then squeal on them. The country is being encouraged to become a nation of grasses, years ago people had some honour, as I thought, in my naivety, or stupidity, whichever way you want to spill the dice. I was brought up to understand there was honour among thieves, the people I thought who used to come to our house would not dream of grassing, they knew hard times, they had two or three options, they chose their life and how to lead it, but they would never have dreamed of squealing once they got their collar felt. Now all this was changing, the cops had found the perfect way of dealing with them, fit them up, bring in a little army of Pip the Planters, they would squeal and scream, knowing they were going down come what may, unless they started squealing, now, squealing was starting to become the norm.

So, you go out on the town, have a nice night out but have a fall out with the guy in the pub, give him some lip, come unstuck, ring the Old Bill and squeal on them. The law works based on the first to squeal is telling the truth, from that point on the system works against the accused, it's subtle, it's barely noticeable to those other than the ones affected. So, it was with us, that's why I knew we were fucked. We weren't just being put on trial for the crime we were accused of, we were being put on trial for who we were, what we had done in the past, the charges being loaded up accordingly.

Eventually, we were called up into the dock, jury to the left, press to the front, and our defence team immediately in front of us. Defence team, who were they? I'd never met any of them or knew them, we sat there shivering, well, it felt like shivering anyway, Donald next to me, resigned as I was, there was no time wasting, the first witness was brought forward, I recognised him, no marks on his face, "What do you remember of the night Mr…?" He walked out with his friends, we attacked them for no reason. Then the next witness, I never recognised him but accepted he was there, same question, all innocent we were attacked, pointing to us, now the next one jumps up, it was the little mafia gangster with the big mouth's wife, she is shaking like a leaf? Why is she shaking like a leaf? She couldn't remember anything; it was dark. Okay, thank you - hang on, why was she shaking so badly? She knew. Was it because she had fancied me? I vaguely remembered her being very friendly, But why was my QC not questioning her? Why was no one asking where the women were? Two women? Why did they leave and go straight to their car? Why was no one raising their eyes in wonder? The next one was the little gangster, he got up, the same story, vague, just walking out, but he remembers it was me who attacked him, pointing at me, and accusing me of stealing his wallet and money. Fucking hell, he was determined to stick the knife in; it was that little bastard that had caused it,

But no cross-questioning, no asking pertinent questions, these fuckers are sitting next to us, in the witness seats, all innocent, we were in the dock, surrounded by prison guards, looking as guilty as fuck, innocent until guilty? Bollox, we were guilty, everybody knew that. The witnesses are given an easy ride, they can shake like a fucking leaf, frightened your honour, they can tell lies, they can exaggerate, while we in the dock are guilty. You read of someone being arrested, taken to court for trial, a thousand people crawl from under a stone to throw rocks and stones at the van, yelling, shouting and bawling, all played out in the public eye, and he's innocent until proved guilty? You're having a fucking laugh, and all this helped along by the Old Bill.

I was called up first. "Mr Lewin, could you lead us through the events of that night?"

"Well, I explained how we'd got to the club, Harry had left us a bottle of scotch, I took the bottle over to these guys. The wife seemed very friendly, we were invited back, as we walked out this one started shouting his mouth off about being the mafia the next thing I know we were all over the place, that was it."

The barrister stood up, wafted his gown around him, knowing he was on centre stage, "Oh, oh, oh, mafia? Mafia?" In the loudest stage voice, you could imagine. I could feel the atmosphere in the court, fucking hell; I just wish I could have sunk through the fucking floor, the mafia? Here in middle England? That's it, at that precise moment I knew we were fucked, in truth it did sound ridiculous, who the fuck threatens you with the mafia in England? Why the fucking hell ain't our QC like this one? Why didn't my defence ask this question in the first place? But that's how the legal system works in England. Poor you, you get the crap defence, the emphasis is on finding the accused guilty, that's it.

Next up was Donald, he shuffled around to the dock, now Donald had nothing to remember, he was in the background. He never even spoke to the people, he hadn't got a clue what was going on at all, in every sense of the word he was innocent, the only thing I had said to him was to not shy from hitting out at them. His suit was covered in blood, he's got a very nasty stab wound to the face, he was simply defending himself, but when he answered the question, he replied, quite truthfully, that he could remember nothing. "

Oh," jumps in the actor onto the stage, and in his best theatrical, loud voice screamed out, "well who caused the damage then? Marley's ghost?"

You could almost feel the whole fucking court laughing, I knew it, we were fucked, we were double fucked. Donald made his way back to his seat in the dock; my suit had been produced, although there was no blood on it, buttons had been wrenched off the jacket, obviously by the innocent victims, trying their hardest to get away from us. Another bollox, the cops had deliberately wrenched them off in their efforts to worsen the case.

The judge looked at our defence, any further questions? My QC, who I now realised was my QC, waved his arm limply, gave the look and murmured, "No, your honour."

The jury was sent out, was back in less than an hour, guilty, guilty, guilty, the judge had advised the jury, not to consider the stolen wallet full of money, but why not? If the little mafia Don was telling the truth about the fight, why wasn't he telling the truth about the stolen wallet? Because the judge could see the little prick was lying, but if he was lying about the wallet, why was he not lying about his version of events, about the fight?

The Years for a Fit-up

This was a fit-up from the start; I knew it. The judge passed sentence of three years each on the charge of malicious wounding, nine years in total - to run concurrently. Plus three months suspended on the top for the stolen car, then our records were read out, making it fully clear to the jury that they had done a wonderful job, and they were fully justified in finding their verdict. As we were being led down the stairs, the cops gave a big satisfied smile, sitting next to the poor innocent victims, most at least have the humility, to keep their head bowed in shame, filthy bastards. As we were being led to the stairs, the one screw turned to us and said, "I can't believe you were found guilty against three of them?" It was small consolation, but I was grateful at least someone saw it. How the fucking hell do you define self-defence or assault? How can someone somehow magic up the word malicious, without being at the scene, did the witnesses say, "Oh no officer, they meant to scar us for life," it was malicious intent?

Every situation is different; I was threatened in my own house by two drunken thugs who had knives. You don't just flick out a punch and wait to see if that does the trick. The cops assault someone regularly, quite a bit known to be unjustified, but we all have to turn a blind eye to it and accept that the officer was just using natural defence tactics. No, the cops pick and choose according to what their chances are of getting a case proved. So if your unfortunate enough to be picked on by some bully or low life while going about your normal business, which I have quite a few times, and hit him two or three times giving him a few bruises making him go squealing to the cops, and you're unmarked, there is a good chance you will be charged and found guilty if you have a criminal record? You're fucked.

I was as sick as the proverbial pig with swine flu, not only was I sick, I was fucking angry, a fight, three years for a fucking fight, and we were thrown to the wolves by a bent defence team, it was fucking disgraceful, why did they even offer to defend us? How much were they getting paid for this? I swear legal aid is one of the biggest cons perpetrated on the British taxpayer, over one billion pounds a year is paid by the taxpayer, submitted and claimed by parasitic solicitors who do fuck all for the money, how much had this team of legal eagles, barristers, lawyers, submitted for this piece of none work? How much actual work had gone into our case by the defence team because as sure as fuck we never spoke to them? They were in court a maximum of three hours, and this is countrywide. No one is questioned; no prisoner is ever sent a questionnaire asking if you were satisfied with the defence, you had received. No one ever has to submit a report, confirming the hours spent, the quality of the defence, the efforts made, this must be the only profession in the world where it is accepted that payment is asked for in advance, and gets it. It's the only profession in the world that such payments are made, we get shit returns, and were expected to doff our caps in the process.

Solicitors are being paid thousands to defend some young kid who has shoplifted, robbed a factory, nicked a bike, guilty without doubt, guilt admitted. But a solicitor employed or engaged in putting forward the simple plea, "My client admits he's been a foolish young man your worship, he is also prepared to accept he is fully deserving of spending three months in prison" - Kerching, money in the pocket.

Birmingham must have the most corrupt judicial and police service in the country. How many people, judges, solicitors, top police officers, are in or belong to the Masons? Why would so many need or want to be in the Masons? Why is no one questioning it? The Birmingham law courts must be the biggest Masonic lodge in the country. Donald and I never went into that court to get or expect a fair trial, our guilt was decided before we even went in. We were led down the stairs of the court to the holding cells below. The holding cells on both sides of the landing were left open, probably to give us our last vestige of the feeling of freedom, we were led to an open cell where we sat trying to get our heads around the years ahead spent in prison, Donald looked like I felt, fucking brain dead.

Outside I saw Sword Edge Wilco strolling along, maybe inspecting his captures for the day. Wilco was the DS who had nicked me just a few months earlier for a hundredweight of copper. As he came to me, I couldn't help but ask him why he and his men were persecuting me for fuck all. He stood there and offered me his pearls of wisdom. "If you had have reported that fight at the time you would all have been done for affray and got a fine." So, he knew all about it, so because I do the right thing, which used to be the accepted way, and took it like a man, they do the fucking squealing, aided and abetted by the Old Bill, who are gleefully rubbing their hands. They get treated like the poor victims, awarded a few hundred in compensation no doubt, and come out smelling like roses.

He then put the killer punch in as calmly as you like, you could have had a nice little earner in that yard and made £300 a week, forgetting to mention, of course, that not only had I got to throw bodies in, I'd also got to put a bung in the books for them. "You know I couldn't do that," I said. "I'm a Lewin."

He stopped looking ahead, turned and looked straight at me. "Well, if you can't do that, then I suggest you get out and far away because you are one of the last mugs in the town."

That's it then, that was his advice to me, little did I realise at the time, it was to be, partly, the best advice I was to receive.

Before the day was out we were shunted back to Winson Green, home from home, the shit hole, I was put in a cell with Tommy Gordon, the gambler, he had just got a three stretch and couldn't believe it. Like us all, gambling I realised is a very haphazard business to be in. I knew a few professional gamblers and most lived in rented or council housing, one minute they could be up the next down. Tommy and a couple of mates had been offered some twenty-pound notes by a London gang. They'd gone down to London having rustled up enough dough for 20 grand worth of notes, to be cleaned back in Brum The message that they left with was don't grass, or else, so on the motorway coming back, they had called into a garage filled up with petrol and then set off, trapped on the motorway going north.

Within minutes they saw the flashing lights behind them and knew it was on top, desperately they tried throwing the twenty-pound notes out of the car as the whizzed along at breakneck speed before eventually getting stopped. He fell into the hands of the Birmingham cops, who told him to throw the cockney's in, or he would get a three stretch With the cockney's words ringing in his ears, Tommy and his lads were certainly not going to be doing any squealing, looking at me in bewilderment, Tommy said, "How can they say that, Tom? How can a copper guarantee I'll get three years?"

"But they can and do Tommy; they have it well worked out in Birmingham."

Now he knew that, but he decided to plead not guilty. The notes hadn't been found that they'd thrown out the car, but they still held a few, they argued that they had been to London gambling, and been passed the notes in payment, they were found guilty and got the promised three stretch, Tommy was still in shock, he was flabbergasted.

Another young guy was on the murder wing waiting to be relocated, he was only about 20 and had killed his girlfriend, it was widely felt that he should only really have been convicted of manslaughter even by the screws. Living with his girlfriend, they had argued, the argument had got out of hand, and he had killed her, panicked, he hid the body under the floorboards or the bed. Eventually, he reported the crime and filled with grief and guilt he admitted killing the girl, if he was given any advice, he either didn't take it or didn't want it. He went to court adamant that he was guilty of murder, where he might have got four, maybe eight years, he got life, so that was another life destroyed.

I heard or came across instances like this day in day out in prison, at any one time I would hazard a guess that 20% of the inmates could be innocent or not guilty of the actual charge. Looking deeper, I could never figure out why something in the region of 40%- 60% should not be in prison, no one gave a fuck. Bet told me that a plainclothes copper called round to her house to drop my suit off, in the process he took the opportunity to put the poison in, asking what she was doing with them Lewins. This from a copper that didn't even know me.

Bet turned around and said, "Those Lewins are more honest than you lot." Bless her little heart.

Life Behind Bars

Now I was a prisoner, I was put to work in one of the work-shops cutting and sewing jeans, it was monotonous, it was brain-numbing. I couldn't see any future at all, I wrote a letter to Bet giving her the sack. The prison was full of prisoners getting dear Johns of their birds or wives who couldn't put up with the position they were put in on the outside, many of the blokes tried to commit suicide or had mental breakdowns, fuck that, I couldn't handle the uncertainty.

Ruth Smith came to visit me; she was in shock, not being able to believe how corrupt the cops were. She came from a world a million miles from mine, the teaching profession, the only time they met a copper, was when they visited the school, she was to see it and get worse. I never knew how old Ruth was, it never occurred to me to ask, certainly she must have been getting on for 70 and had only got good intentions, but the probation service decided to see things otherwise, I was visited by a Mrs Weaver who had the biggest pair of tits I had ever seen and knew it. Her welcoming party piece was to wear a tight-fitting top, grab you and thrust her tits right into your face.

"Now, about this ex-school teacher, Tom? What is her motive? Oh, come on, are you having sex with her?"

To be asked that by a probation officer almost legitimises the question. I stared in disbelief. "No, Miss Smith is just interested in my well-being and seeing me do well."

"Come on," as she wrapped her arms around me again. Ms Weaver was having none of it; she knew I was having sex with

Miss Smith, a 70-year-old woman who had never had a man in her life. When Ruth got in touch with the probation service to ask about visiting me regularly, she was diverted to Miss Weaver, who not only led her into a trap but also made her jump through hoops. "Why would you want to see Mr Lewin? Why are you so interested in him? What about other unfortunate young men in his position?"

Of course, Ruth admitted that she was concerned for all young people in positions like mine, with that Ms Weaver gave her a list of the worst of the worst of the low life to visit and prove she was concerned about all young people. I felt bloody sorry for the woman, my former teacher who didn't have a bad bone in her body, was being treated like some sick old pervert, all for being interested in my welfare even from school days. Everything she did was being dirtied and spoilt; I could see the poor woman was shocked at what she was seeing.

"Ruth, what you are seeing in such a short time is something I've been seeing most of my life."

But even I was staggered, no, disgusted, at this new level of filth, I'm sitting here, the criminal, and I'm questioning the filth in Ms Weaver's mind. Under the circumstances, I suggested Ruth keep away from me until I got out, she was only leaving herself open to further harassment.

Looking around the prison, I could see it was a whole mix of all sorts of humanity, the little bent over 80-year-old pervert, spent most of his life in prison, for touching up girls or something, my mind didn't want to dwell on it. He was now back again doing a five stretch. I couldn't believe how cons in prison for a whole variety of offences, were just all shoved in together, from bent cops to perverts to murderers, shoplifters to bank robbers There was no dignity, that was not allowed you were all scum, and that's how we were all perceived. This came over to me one day in yet another example by one of the screws. He was recounting how well he got on with one well-known bank robber and considered him a normal guy who just happened to have chosen a different career path. He was quite taken aback, therefore, to find the same guy returned to prison, with a major prison sentence for abusing a young girl, with that he looked at us and explained quite innocently and unaware of how it came over, that he was just like us. Oh, so we're all fucking potential perverts. Great, but you start to realise that that's how we're all looked on.

The weeks continued to drag on, every day was torture and a fucking nightmare, Bet had had me back, but it was hard to see her once a month. Eventually, I was transferred to Stafford prison, a first timers prison, one of the first cons I came into contact with was Colin, who had done the co-op with Ray, Colin had got a five stretch for his part and wasn't at all happy when I told him Ray reckoned he had grassed on them? That upset Colin quite enough, no one likes being called or accuse of being a grass. He started going off on one telling me it was Ray who had done the grassing, I don't think it was sensible to argue with him, at any rate, if he had nicked the extra four grand, it seemed ultimate, whichever way you looked at it, down to him for getting them all nicked with his greed and stupidity. But this was the problem with grassing, it was all Chinese whispers, no one could prove it, the only ones who knew were the cops who were doing the squealing to, and they ain't likely to kill the goose that lays the golden egg.

At any rate, Stafford nick was full of grasses. They even had an information box so anyone could put notes in, ostensibly, it was for suggestions to the prison, but it was used to do the grassing. It was disgusting, it made my skin crawl, this was worse than I could have ever imagined. Fuck me with a bamboo pole; these are tomorrows villains, tomorrows gangsters, grassing on each other like fucking wasps. I was put into a cell with another inmate, who was a definite slime ball, shoulders slouched, head down, dirty little bastard, worse, he would shit in his pot, every night, every fucking night. It was ridiculous, it was disgusting, the cell stunk for hours afterwards, and I was having to breathe it.

I would turn to him, "Oh, for fuck's sake, can't you fucking control yourself?"

"I can't help it," he'd say in his whining voice. To be fair, he shouldn't have been in prison, he needed help, he was mentally fucked up, but that ain't no consolation to me. After a week, I could stand no more, I grabbed the wing screw, Mr Quick. Mr Quick was a nice enough guy, but certainly didn't live up to his name, "Sir, can't I have a single cell?"

"I'm sorry, there are no more available, you'll just have to put up with it. With that I'm back in with the little slime ball, he wouldn't even clean around him; eventually, it got the better of me, after yet another night of shitting in the pot I got up, went over and gave him a few smacks. It's not nice I know, and it certainly doesn't look good for me, but it was bad enough being put in the nick, now I was being pushed to the edge. When the screws saw him the next morning and asked him, what had happened true to form, he was quick to tell them. At a gallop, I was taken down to the isolation ward and put on rule 43. It was a fucking relief; I was on my own. The next day I was marched up in front of the governor, asking me what had happened, I told him, he seemed an understanding governor, "Why didn't you complain to your wing officer?"

"I did, sir, Mr Quick, he told me I'd got to put up with it." Whoops, I'd committed the cardinal sin, I'd grassed on a screw, they wouldn't like that. I was sentenced to a month in solitary, which was exactly what I wanted, isolation in my single cell, after being marched back to my cell I lay back on the bed, bliss, it gave me a chance to reflect on my position and what was in front of me.

Bet had told me that Reg, my elder brother was in custody and was being questioned about a jewellery robbery, he had denied being involved, they had no other suspects, just him, and someone had thrown him in. What no one knew was Pip the Planter was brought in and put in charge of the case. In short, unless there was a miracle, he was fucked, with no evidence to go on Pip could do fuck all, in desperation they had decided to turn my eldest brother Johnny over. Now Johnny was over 50 and had retired from his criminal career. Like many of his mates, he had had some good tickles in his life but spent it all thinking it was going to last forever. Now he was in peaceful retirement until Pip the Planter turned up, it seems that there had been a bit of a fire at some stage in the garden, and Pip went looking into the ashes, they would have been watched scrupulously searching the house everyone knowing Pips reputation, but no one thought to check outside with them. Miraculously, Pip poked into the ashes and discovered a single diamond from the robbery. Without further ado, Johnny was marched off to Steelhouse Lane Nick. I don't know if he was verballed up which would have been par for the course, but that was proof enough that Johnny was part of the robbery with Reg. They were both hauled up before the judge on serious charges of robbery, by now Johnny was looking at a good few years in the nick, at 50 he wasn't too happy in the dock he screamed that he doesn't know anything about any robbery, he can't understand how a diamond could be in his garden. Course they knew that Pip the Planter had put the diamond there, no doubt verballed them both up.

Reg was furious, sacked his barrister, a regular event by many a criminal in Birmingham court trials, they were fucked. If they accused the cops of verballing or fitting them up, then that entitles the prosecution to bring out their previous records, they were fucked if they did, fucked if they didn't. The cops knew this and were rubbing their hands with glee from the benches. I don't know anything else about how things turned from that, except miraculously the judge instructed the jury to find Johnny not guilty. Reg got eight years, funny how a diamond should be found in Johnny's garden, he's charged with being involved in the robbery, yet a deal is done, somehow, and Johnny is free. Fucking amazing how intuitive and clever, these judges are. Pip would go back to fitting people up, if things got too heavy, he would be shipped out of Birmingham to another force for a bit. The thing that never fails to amaze me is how deep this corruption goes. I would hazard a guess that every copper in Birmingham over a certain rank knew about Pip the Planter and the rest of the crime squad if they knew. How many others knew, how deep did this corruption go? Gossip being what it is, how many judges knew about it? It's mind-boggling.

In America, a film was made called the Star Chamber, about a group of cops belonging to an inner circle going out and shooting the main criminals who were getting off with crimes. That was fiction, this is a fact, its reality, if the judges and fellow cops condone it fine, say so, let's have all the cards on the table, if it's illegal, if it's corrupt, which it is, what does that say about all the others in the conspiracy?

All this and many other things were going through my mind as I sat in solitary, day after day, it was clear to me, unbelievable as it must seem, that my family were being deliberately targeted by the police with the full backing of the judicial system. I couldn't figure out why. Were we that stupid to be being caught like this on such a regular basis? Was the evidence on a knacker of an old battered car that clear that it was obvious that I had nicked it? But then I looked back to when Charlie Heinze the grass came around the house, dropped that jewellery in, then an hour later Pip the Planter turning up with a court search warrant, Was it just a simple coincidence how things turned out? Were we just in the wrong place and coincidentally grassed on so regularly? Were we being deliberately targeted? Worse, were certain known villains being set up, or blackmailed, to deliberately set us up? Both Charlie the grass and Johnny Avo were both bang at it, Charlie was doing business with Caswell a known grass and scrap dealer, he was, in fact, adamant that it was Caswell that had grassed, that he had been in Casswell's yard that morning after dropping off the jewellery.

As a family, I grew up with a feeling of respect shown to us by many people in Nechells and further afield. My dad was dealing with many people daily, shopkeepers, businesspeople, Reg, the security guard who had a shop around the corner. Yes, my two elder brothers were professional thieves, villains, my dad was far from it, he was a general dealer who was savvy enough to make a living from it, he never hurt anyone, he never pulled a stroke on anyone, he was the Arthur Daly of his time. Before Arthur Daly, there were dozens of Arthur Daly's around the country after the war, del boys who lived off their wits to make a living. One neighbour even tried to emulate my dad by copying him; it never bothered my dad he used to smile at it.

My dad was a good, decent man with strong morals, along with my mom, paramount among everything was 'thou shalt not grass'. If anyone of us had grassed we would have been disowned, this was taken on by all my family, what didn't help was Johnny and Reg, would slag the coppers off to bits. Knowing how bent they were, was one thing, calling them all the dirty bastards under the sun, was another. Unwittingly, they were building up scores with the Birmingham police that was putting them on a big list. One by one, that list was diminishing with the planting that was going on. As villains were being fitted up, they quickly learnt the only way was to start throwing bodies in. That was bad enough, but now I had a strong suspicion we were being deliberately targeted and thrown to the wolves, the more this happened, the more people were starting to distance themselves from us, even the known villains or those on the periphery. Fuck me, it was self-protection, the more they hung around us, the more likely it was that they were going to be dragged into the net, our popularity and respect rating had sunk to near zero.

All these things were going through my mind on a regular daily basis, while I was in solitary, poor Reg, facing another eight years in the nick. If anything, Reg needed help, when he was young he got married and had trained as a carpenter, he had been one of twins, and only he survived. My mom was adamant that he had taken all the badness of the other, but Reg wasn't bad, he was ill and diagnosed with schizophrenia in prison when little was known about it. My mom hadn't got a clue, but back then there were lots of disturbed kids around and growing into adulthood, many affected by the harsh upbringing and the effects of the war, every street had a nutcase in one form or another, it was acceptable it was the norm. Reg had married Vera, she was a nice girl, but she simply couldn't cook, this in itself would be no problem, but she was married to a bloke who hadn't got a clue either. When I first met Bet, she couldn't cook at all, but she learnt as we went along, Reg was going out to work as a chippy coming home to fish fingers and chips, everything with chips, worse, he was working his nuts off five and a half days a week, for peanuts. The wages of skilled men were little more than that for the labourer. Even worse, he would turn up on a Saturday to have a drink with Johnny and the rest, at the local pub the Beehive or the Brit. They would all be standing around, pulling rolls out, buying drinks all round, fighting to buy a round, and he was struggling with a couple of quid after paying his missus the rent and housekeeping.

Back then no one thought of bank accounts, you carried your bank in your pocket, when the average wage was eight, ten pounds a week, my old man would pull out his roll of five hundred quid to buy around if you'd had a tickle you would carry your wad in your roll, everybody was rich, except Reg. I could see how pissed off he was, worse again, if you were a working peck you were looked down on, you would get 'the look', the half withering put down, "oh hi." He's only a working peck, oh, oh, oh.

None of my brothers was big, the better things got after the war, the later ones like Kenny and me grew the extra inch or so, but Johnny and Reg were only 5ft 6,7, inches, both strong wiry for their age, and they had plenty of bottle, but their shortness left them open to being picked on outside their circle,

One Saturday Reg had got home from another hard slog on the sites, Vera reckoned she had been pestered by a neighbour in the courtyard where they lived. Without further ado, Reg went steaming round to the neighbour, and it went off, someone called the cops, a cop turned up to deal with it, but Reg was steaming, he ended up laying on the copper, for that Reg got a four stretch. Inside, he was picked on by some guy who was a lot bigger. What he should have done was go up to the bloke, give him the biggest smack he could, go for it knowing the screws would break it up within minutes, but Reg must have been pissed off, he took a broken jug and give it the bloke in the face. For that little mistake, he got his sentence doubled to eight years, and he was sent to Wakefield prison, the lifers' prison, it was only there; eventually, he was diagnosed as schizophrenic. But he was still never helped. British prisons are full of disturbed and schizophrenic cons.

I also began to recognise how easy it would be for me to go on the same path as Reg, I was pissed off, I was angry, and a fair bit bitter at the hand that I was being dealt. Facing three years and three months in prison was fucking daunting at the least, spending it in prison with this bunch of nut jobs and low life was beyond me, I also knew I was going to find it very difficult to keep out of trouble, without a doubt, prison makes you violent, if not physically, then in thought.

The next day the governor popped in to see me as part of his duties, "Any requests, Lewin?"

"Well, yes, sir, now that you mention it."

"What's that, Lewin?"

"I'd like to stop down here, sir, if I might."

The governor nearly fell back in shock, "You, you can't be serious? No one in any nick volunteers for isolation."

Well, I could, and I did, the other purpose was to let them know that if this was punishment, I wasn't being punished. After a couple of weeks, I was taken back to my cell, on Mr Quick's landing, all alone and on my own, for a few days. Then another young con was put in with me. This time it was a nice kid who was in for his first offence, he was also an artist and painted a portrait of Ruth Smith that I had asked him to do for me. Ruth was highly pleased, I got on fine with the kid, except for his music, now I used to like my music, but since getting done, I just couldn't abide it, my nerves were shredded, and all I wanted was peace. He'd play his little cassette player until late at night, sometimes pushing me to the very edge before turning it down, or off.

Mr Quick would ask him every other day, "How are you getting on with Lewin?" Fully expecting the kid to say something, but fair play to him, all he would say is "Fine sir, fine," then he'd come back and tell me.

My job was the landing cleaner, it was a good enough job, all it entailed was the cleaning of the toilets and the landing of my section each landing had a recess with a toilet piss bowls and a big sink for slop outs. Every cell had a slop bucket, mainly for a late-night piss if you were caught short, many would shit in a newspaper placed on the floor, roll it up, then throw it out the cell window as a parcel. A team were permanently employed on yard duty picking up parcels, others like my former cellmate, would shit in it every night, then take it out for slop out the next morning, tipping the contents into the big sink, all fucking degrading and disgusting really.

I had just mopped up all the floors looking nice and pristine where I'd just mopped when this black guy comes strolling casually as you like with his slop bucket, messing all my floor up. "Excuse me mate, can't you wait for the floor to dry - look?"

Well, for fuck's sake, the bloke went right off on one, shouting and screaming and waving his arms around like a fucking lunatic. I put my left hand up to keep him well back, but he did no more than grab my hand and start to bite my fucking fingers. Astonished, I gave him a right-hander putting him square on the deck. When he got up he was more subdued, but I stood cautious of him, as I'd heard that a lot of blacks had got some sort of hereditary mental problems and you never know how they are going to come at you, they grow up thinking a machete is a normal tool to carry. But no, off he went quiet as a mouse. The guy across the landing asked what had been going on, and I leaned over the railing to tell him, "the guy's a fucking nut job."

I saw, too late, his eyes rise as he could see behind me. The nut job had come back from his cell with a bowl hiding a tomato sauce bottle behind it, and with all his strength, he whacked me on the bonce. I felt my legs buckle, but stood my ground, with that he walked away straight to the screw who was standing a few feet away, he was carted off to isolation.

The next day I was taken down in front of the governor, for questioning, the screw had seen the black guy bouncing the bottle off my head but nothing that had happened earlier. "Right Lewin, what went on?" I told him, missing out a little bit of course.

"Well," he said. "You punched him in the jaw, breaking his false teeth?"

"No sir, as I said, I put my hand up to keep him back, he bit my finger, the only thing I can think of is with the exertion of pulling my finger out of his mouth, maybe it broke his false teeth."

One thing I found in prison, at least you got a fair trial without being fitted up like on the outside, I was again put in isolation, but now realised what rule 43 was about, not only was it just about punishment and isolation it was about protection, for the nonces and paedophiles. Our food was brought to us on a tray, breakfast, lunch, dinner, after the second day my brain was working overtime hang about, those cooks in the kitchen don't know me. All they know is they're sending meals down to prisoners in rule 43, now if I was in their position I would take the opportunity of throwing anything on their food, snot, gob, anything, they are perverts, maybe my food is full of shit? Fuck it, I stopped eating, there is no way I'm eating that fucking food, it might be contaminated. After three days of not eating I was taken to the hospital ward, lovely, clean, comfy, that'll do me, after a further week I was taken to the magistrates hearing to tell my side of the story. The black guy was found guilty and got three months on top of his sentence. Quite right too. I got 15 stitches in my bonce for the trouble, it was almost worth it as I was finally given another single cell on the opposite side of the prison wing well away from the black and his mates. I made a deliberate effort for a few weeks to keep alert for any blacks or mates of the black guy coming near me, surprisingly, none did.

The first year went, slowly, I could begin to see the light at the end of the tunnel. I was sent a form to apply for parole, considered it, then realised it was a waste of time, I'm marked as violent, no, I've just got to get my head down and do my sentence, prison is a waste of time and taxpayers money. I saw it in Borstal, I've seen it in various prisons, these police, judges and magistrates should be made to serve a few months in prison to see the effects of it on the prisoners and their families themselves. One or two bent cops in Stafford had been that blatant they had been caught out, boy don't you see the difference then in their demeanour, pasty frightened faces, shoulders hunched over, eyes focused on the floor, much as it made my skin crawl to see them it was also a lovely sight to see. But anything they learn is not passed on, they serve their time, then crawl off somewhere like the slugs they are.

You learn nothing in prison; fortunately, I loved reading and avidly read book after book. I also made model galleons which gave me a great deal of pleasure and kept my mind occupied and distracted from the monotonous daily boredom, you wake up at 8 am, with a loud banging on the doors and shouts to slop out. Then it's down for breakfast, then you're sitting around all day with a break for lunch, then for dinner, it's back to your cells for the night, unless you have some evening class hobby, I had signed up for a woodworking class, these classes are run by skilled tradesman on the outside who simply wanted to earn some extra money. That's fine, none of my business and none of my concern, but more than a couple of occasions the tutor would show his resentment for having to be there, as soon as the session ended and the clock hit 8, or 8:30 pm. God help you if you were immersed in finishing off a piece of work, they had done their two hours, and were desperate to get out. "Come on, hurry up," as nasty as you like, reminding me of those factory workers at the Rover company a couple of years earlier. For fuck's sake, if it's that bad that you're only in it for the money, find another fucking job, how desperate are you? When you're finishing off a delicate bit of work that needs an extra few minutes, and you've got some irritable prat who's not in the least bit interested in being there it can be bloody frustrating, after another couple of times I threw it in and never went back again.

To be a screw is only a few degrees different to being a cop, it's said that a percentage pull out within the first few months. As a cop you have to be prepared to nick your next-door neighbour, you even have to sign and agree to arrest your mother if you catch her stealing, whether you would or not, in reality, is a different kettle of fish. The fact is you have to be prepared to do that, as a screw you have to sign a contract that you're prepared to give the birch to a prisoner if so ordered, whether you agree with it or not. In the prison service, a fair few applicants pull out within the first few months, who wants to do a job like that? How desperate do you have to be?

One screw admitted to me that he had tried haulage and drove his own lorry, but he couldn't make a success of it, in prison, there was plenty of overtime plus the really big draw, the pension, guaranteed. It's the same magnet that draws people in to the police, the overtime plus the gold plated pension at the end. I don't suppose any one of them would look at it as a failure.

A three-month basic decorating course came up, run by a Mr Lumb, I was running after it like a rat up a drainpipe. Desperate to learn something, desperate to give me something to do away from the daily boredom, after a few nail-biting weeks, I was offered the course, great, it gave me something to focus on. There were about eight of us on the course, and we began to learn from scratch how to prepare a piece of wood or a door, rubbing it down, then rubbing it down some more until it was perfectly sanded, then undercoated, checked again, rubbed down again, then undercoated. It was brain numbingly boring at times, but it was useful, the one major lesson it taught me was the preparation,

Everything was about preparation, in boxing, you trained and trained before a fight, any type of work was the same if you didn't do the preparation properly, your whole effort was wasted. It was a valuable lesson that was to stand me in good stead in the future. Mr Lumb wasn't a bad guy at all, he quite enjoyed the job, telling me that he had joined because of the security it offered and guaranteed income, plus the pension. He wasn't a screw, but a civilian worker but he had to abide by and follow the prison teachings, the time on the course passed quite quickly, and by the time I had finished the course, I at least knew how to decorate a house, how to paste fold and paper a wall. For myself decorating was not for me, it could be mind-numbingly boring, and I could well see where that expression watching paint dry came from, but at least I knew I could decorate a house. Finishing the course, I was now left with only a couple of months to serve.

Opposite me was a black guy named Robert, Rob was one of four black guys serving six years for an armed robbery in Wolverhampton. He and his pals were a nice bunch of lads, and we would spend many a day chatting. The biggest percentage of people in prison were losers and wasters, most in for a bit of petty nicking, having learnt nothing they would go out, try to get some menial work, and if not, go on the dole where with a bit of luck avoid any more nicking. Rob was a different kettle of fish, he was a professional if he couldn't get his money one way he would try another way, his end goal was to set himself up in business, as such he would try to feel me out, "What are you doing when you get out, Tom?"

Hoping I would turn and say maybe find a bank to rob, most villains in nick learnt their trade from each other, discussing options, potential tickles, whether it be factories banks or security vans. I let Rob know very quickly that any kind of thieving was not for me, I'd seen too many fuck ups, too many grasses to even consider any kind of villainy. To me, being in prison for a fight was stupid enough, looking at the robbery scene was a no go for me, I'd seen too much, that was my biggest advantage over all these guys. They'd not had my life experience, they were starting fresh, I had seen the pitfalls, the negatives, the failed attempts, worse id seen the grasses, and prison was not something that sat well with me, prison was a fucking misery, a drudge. I had more confidence in my ability than to allow to spend time in prison, the professionals accepted it as part of their life, well it wasn't for me.

No, I'm getting into transport when I get out, I'm going to buy myself a lorry and do transport. Rob didn't say a word, one day I said, "What do you think of old Enoch Powell's speech then Rob?"

I was expecting him to throw a load of vitriol at me, but no, in measured tones, he said, "We agree with him, Tom, who do you think voted him in? We did, in 20 years we will run this country."

"How do you get that then?" I asked him.

"Simple mathematics, Tom, you white's knock out 2.2 kids, we knock out eight without a seconds thought." It was a sound assessment, and I could see he believed it, Rob was no mug, he was a clever kid.

Starting Again on the Outside

Coming up to my release I started planning in earnest, filling Bet with my plans and getting her excited, Ruth Smith had offered to help me out with a car, and a mate of Ray Kirbys offered me a job at his taxi firm in Bordesley Green, I was focused and determined to turn things around. When the day of my release came I was given a few quid and a ticket to Birmingham by train. Getting up in the morning I was out of the gates by 7 am, the fresh air hitting me like a bolt. Okay, we were allowed out for fresh air in prison, but no matter where you walked in prison, it was still filthy, dirty, like a heavy cloak around you, I had a spring in my step, hope in my heart, determination in my head.

Bet was a sight for sore eyes, she had got herself a nice little council house up in Kitts Green. She had managed to find some furniture, clean it up and make it nice and homely. Typically, of me, I had a quick look around, a nod, commented on how nice she'd made it, little did I fully appreciate what an effort she must have made, how hard she must have suffered to make such a nice home. Billy would pop in now and again, smoke her fags then piss off, Reg would drop in and bung her a few quid, but she had to do it mostly on her own. It was only in little bits and drabs that she told me about what she had had to do, how much she had put aside to buy me a pair of slacks and a blazer. The least I could do was marry the girl, so within days we had booked ourselves into the Birmingham registry office, just inviting the odd few, to witness the event, I had no money, not a pot to piss in, I saw it as no big deal, to

284

Bet it meant everything. As well as growing up in the slums of Birmingham, which in itself hardens you up, prison blunts your feelings, your emotions, even further, you watch someone getting the shit kicked out of them, so what, see someone getting stabbed hard shit. Bet was as happy as Larry, she idolised me and I never even saw it, I was cynical about everything and anyone. My sole focus was on making us money and getting out of the environment we were in.

The taxi business was quite lucrative, the main reason being it was all cash going straight into our bin, I also quickly learnt that the most lucrative times were the night, day times were bread and butter, but the nights, at weekends, was nice money with tips and drunken passengers. The downside was the spew you had to clean up, and the drunken toss pots you had to put up with, but it was money, and it left my days free. Another positive was that after seeing the drunks coming out of the clubs, paralytic, reminded me of how stupid I had been, I didn't want a drink, while they were getting drunk I was making money. Within a few weeks, I had enough money to pay for a lorry off of old Sid, the scrap man, who had now finally realised he was on a loser with the scrap metal, but knowing how good a yard can be had got himself one and was scratching to earn a living out of anything he could, except scrap. He'd got a ten-ton tipper and sold it to me for a good price, well, I thought so at the time. Only I never realised he'd brought it in as scrap, but it seemed like a sound tipper, and he even put me onto a contract with Amy Roadstone delivering gravel around Birmingham. It wasn't the best of contracts, and it knocked the crap out of the lorries, but it kept me going, Sid's brother Tommy was on the weighbridge and looked after me, some job runs were better than others.

Tony Hawks had a scrapyard down Livery Street and used to offer me little tickles in which he'd sell me a load of copper wire. I'd take it to a farm, a friend of his had then burnt the rubber off, then take it back to Tony's yard and sell it back to him. Most times, I'd get fuck all on the weight, but it was another door. Tony also had a big Drott that he wondered, could be useful to me, I said I'd take the Drott and see if I could find work for it, I did, straight away with Amy Roadstone, shifting gravel around the site.

In Tony's yard one day, two gypos came over, on introduction, the older gypo asked how much I charged for the day and when I told him offered me a few days contract. My job was to drive over to Willenhall, follow behind them in an eight-ton lorry they already owned, the two gypos were brothers, and the older one put me in the picture, "We were 5% away from making a million, Tommy." How they had fucking done it I don't know, but somehow they had got a contract with this major metal foundry to buy all the aluminium in the compound in which we had driven our lorries. The real plan was the money they thought was in the ground, all the metal filings dropped over the years, that had seeped into the ground, they had taken samples of soil from around the yard and took it for analysis, it was just one to five percent away from making it a viable venture, and it was a big compound. I knew they were telling the truth because the guy next to Ray's yard up town held a few tons of soil in his yard, the same thing. I had to take my hat off to these gypos, who were into every trick in the fucking book.

My job was a doddle, the pikeys had brought all the alli at rock bottom price, within weeks the price had shot up, the foundry wanted to buy it back. All I had to do was sit there in the cab, reading my newspaper while their bunch of lads casually loaded both lorries up with aluminium. What a treat, I was using hardly any diesel, and getting paid more money. Once loaded I would be given the shout and had to follow them a few hundred yards away to the foundry, over they would go on the weighbridge, me following behind, down a dusty track, tip the metal up to the bay, then of again back to the compound, everyone was smiling, everyone was a winner. This was going on four or five times a day, and I was spending a fiver in diesel, a treat. Fair play to the lads they paid me up each day, and this went on for a couple of weeks, in the end, I got a thank you and went back to my normal contract work with Amy Roadstone.

Down at Tony's one day, he gave me a quizzical look, "how did your job with the paddies go then?"

"Great," T said, "paid me up proper, every day, nice lads."

"Oh, you never clocked on then?"

"Clocked on to what?" Where had I been fucking conned, where was the scam? Everything was right about the pikeys except the lorry. They had brought an eight-ton tipper, with low sides, took it to a specialist who had then taken the back off, put a false chamber in the bottom of a fuel pipe and a tap on the rear, hidden away. The chamber held exactly one-ton of water, as I followed them onto the weighbridge they would go in to collect their ticket, come out and I'm now on the bridge, they would turn the tap on as I got my ticket, the ton of water would run out of the back. I was following behind them kicking up the dust, fucking brilliant, they were making a fortune every single day, and they hadn't even touched the metal in the compound, I burst out laughing with Tony, fair play to them, ha-ha.

When you get sentenced for a crime, the punishment was supposed to be the end of it, not that I was guilty anyway, this again is bollox, when a citizen picks the paper up and reads about the police sending criminals postcards, or visiting them after they have paid for the offence they have committed, they just assume the police are doing their job, the villains are out there committing further crimes.? Good on you officer, keep on to the bastards, well they ain't, its fucking harassment.

I was parking my ten-tonne lorry on the car park of the tavern in Kitts Green, the Drott on the back, I'd got another flatbed lorry outside my house doing casual work, one morning I woke up, was getting ready for work when a knock came on the door, it was two old bills, plain clothes, "Yes?"

"Where were you this morning?"

"What do you mean where was I? I've just got out of bed."

"Can we search your house?" I was entitled to tell them to fuck off, but shouted to the kids, "Where have I been this morning, kids?"

"Nowhere." Still, the filth had to look, it was only cursory, they knew it wasn't me, they told me the post office at Marston Green had been held up that morning with a group carrying shotguns, well,? What the fuck has that got to fucking do with me? Well, we've been informed that you have been asking around town for guns. Hahaha, I tell you these coppers are fucking thick, without grasses and fitting people up, they would be bolloxed.

A few weeks previously I had been up a certain Irish club in town, the Irish owner was a friend of mine, as I thought.

"How are you going, Tommy, nice to see you back, what was all that about back there?" So, I told him. "The dirty bastards, that would not have happened here, Tommy."

"I know. I'd like to shoot the bastards." That's all I had said, it was a throwaway statement, but it was told to the Old Bill, you scratch my back, I'll scratch yours. It was fucking unbelievable, a few nights later I'm in the tavern when the landlord pulls me over. "Tommy, just to mark your cards, but the cops were in here yesterday asking all about you."

I looked puzzled, "asking about me. What for?"

"Oh, just asking about your lorries and if I knew how you had got them?" Fucking hell they ain't going to leave me alone.

Bet told me a copper named Dave had grabbed a young kid, outside her house while I was inside. Now Dave was based in

Stechford Nick and was the cousin of Jackie, a girl I used to go out with. Dave used to work on the building sites with a bricky mate of mine Paddy Martin. As a labourer, he was always nicking stuff of the sites, it was a joke that he was now a copper. The young lad was eight years of age and a friend of my son's, his father, Johnny Mac was also a friend of mine, not a close pal but a pal.

He was also a known villain. Dave had grabbed Mac's son by the neck and was giving him a bit of a whack around the face, Bet ran out, grabbed the boy and gave the copper a kick for good measure, telling him to leave the lad alone. Dave did know more than ring his station telling Bet she had assaulted a police officer.

Within minutes an inspector had arrived and said, "You do realise I can arrest you for assault on an officer?"

Bet was shitting herself, but stood her ground. "Well, if you arrest me, I'm pressing charges against him for assault on an eight-year-old child."

The inspector was taken aback, and it shook Dave right up, it was so obvious he couldn't deny it. The inspector gave Dave the look, apologised, and off they both walked. This was getting beyond a fucking joke picking on an eight-year-old kid that kid later went on into crime, serving life for murder, did that treatment or any subsequent treatment by Dave the cop have any lasting influence? I wonder.

It wasn't to end there, I was employing my neighbour Fred to drive the ten tonner, and I was doing jobs with the small flatbed, advertising for work in the Birmingham Mail. One day a guy rang up, all friendly asking me if I'd be interested in doing occasional pickups for him from around Birmingham This would involve my picking up one of his lads from the Soho Road who would take me to the site over Walsall, smack in the town centre, at 7:30 am and going around the building to check with the foreman. He came back told me it was fine and to start loading up with scaffold poles and boards. With a full load we set off for Hockley and the company yard, went in to see his boss and he then came back with my cash plus a bit on top, very nice too for just over a two-hour job. Just over a week later he rang up again, by now we were like pals, we had struck up a rapport, he was happy with my reliability, I was happy with his cash, now I was to meet him down Snow Hill, by the WMCA hostel, on another building site. I turned up at the usual time of 7:30 am before the main workers turned up, loaded the lorry up and set off to the yard in Hockley, off with the load and he paid me up, and off I go with my wages in for the day.

A week or so later, I got a phone call out of the blue. "Mr Lewin?"

"Yes?"

"Can you pop up to Steelhouse Lane police station?"

My brain went into fucking overdrive. "What for?"

"I don't know Mr Lewin, do you own a lorry?"

"Yes."

"Ahh, that's it," dead calm, dead casual.

"Maybe you've had a light out or broken lens?" I looked at Bet, what the fuck is all that about?

"Yes, it must be one of my lorries." I said to Bet, "you come with me if I ain't out in ten minutes get round the solicitors and fucking scream."

Off we set to Steelhouse Lane Nick, Bet sits in the waiting room, I'm ushered into an office where I'm greeted by two old bills, "You picked some scaffold up from Snow Hill last week?"

"Yeah?" I could feel myself stiffening up.

"Where did you take it?"

"To a yard over Hockley."

"Could you be able to take us to the yard?"

My natural instinct was to clam up at this stage, but before I could get the words out, the one dick reminded me of my position, and I could be looking at another prison term.

"Of course, I can take you to the yard, look, go outside and ask my wife, she takes the calls. I picked a load up from Walsall as well a couple of weeks ago." This must have convinced them, as with no further ado, they whipped me out to the car park, and we headed over to Hockley.

On the way to the yard, the one dick asked, "Do you know Harry Gee?"

"Yes of course I do, he's an old family friend from Summer Lane, don't tell me he's set me up?"

They never answered once I pointed the yard out we did an about-turn and set off back to the nick where Bet and I set off back home. We then dissected the circumstances, of how I was had in the net, okay, it was early in the morning, light, but early enough to get in before the workers, there was nothing that could have aroused my suspicions. I got onto the phone sharpish to my friend Tommy Hewston who was also running a transport business, his wife Sheila answered the phone, "Oh thanks, Tom, I'll tell him when he gets in."

The only problem was she never told him, she forgot, a few days later Tommy was nicked and bundled off to Steelhouse Lane Nick. He told me later he was shitting himself as they threatened him with the lock-up then prison. Eventually, he was let go, they had told him it wasn't just him; these comics were ringing different transport yards up all over Brum, they had been getting away with tons of it. If they had asked Tommy Hewston if he knew me, and naturally, he would have answered yes, no wonder they would have gone heavy on him, how much is that a coincidence? Both in transport, both picking up the scaffold, worse, me knowing Harry Gee, for fuck's sake.

A week later I popped into one of the boozers in the town to have a drink with the old man, propping up the bar was

Rajput Kirby with a bloke who left a few minutes after I got in. After a few minutes, Rajput casually turned around and said, "Oh, by the way, that was Jimmy, he's asked me to apologise to you, he was the guy ringing you up but swears he never knew it was you he was ringing up."

I looked at Rajput in disbelief, in his dogma of not being a grass he had made sure the guy had got out of the boozer and away before telling me. I was stuck for fucking words, here I was facing a fucking nicking, and Rajput's worried about his mate and not grassing on him. I was fucking dumbfounded, Rajput, where's your fucking loyalty?

A few weeks later, Harry Gee was taken to court, I'd seen him a couple of weeks earlier and set out to assure him that I hadn't grassed on him but was in no position to keep my mouth shut. He assured me that he didn't blame me, he got a two grand fine, I thought he got off well light. I turned round to Bet, we've got to get out of here; otherwise, I'm going to end up back in the nick.

Planning a New Life

Seeing Mac's son being victimised like that by a bully copper, having my house turned over by the cops, then this lot with the scaffold was getting beyond a fucking joke, I was just trying to get on top, I'd hardly been out of nick six months, we had been offered the chance to buy our council house in Kitts Green, for two grand, it was great value, Ray Kirby lived opposite and had brought his house for 15 hundred quid, but my worry, and I turned to Bet, and said, the problem is, we might own it, but it's still a council house, it will always be a council house we've got to get away from here.

Plus, I was starting to feel that my name, my reputation was at ground zero, people who knew me knew I wasn't the person being touted. How can a lifelong friend not tell me some guy in the pub had almost cost me a load of bird, all in the name of not wanting to be considered a grass? I felt some people were looking at me like I was some kind of a fucking monster. This came over to me when I put an 8-ton lorry up for sale, there was nothing wrong with the lorry except it was two-ton short of what I needed. I got several calls. One guy named Eddie apologised to me a few months later telling me he was out of order, but when he heard my name, it made him nervous to view the lorry.

Henry Taroni rang me up. "Oh, hello there, I'm Henry Taroni I'm ringing about the lorry."

I said, "Yes, when do you want to look at it?" Henry ain't shy about using his name as he is so well-known, "I'll tell you what Henry, I'll drop it down your yard tomorrow."

That threw him. "Who's that?"

"Tommy Lewin, Henry." I felt the little pause on the other end, the next day I took the lorry down to Henry's yard; going into his office, we had a nice chat before he got his yardman to try the lorry out. His yard man then told me Henry didn't want the lorry, this was a fucking liberty, and I called back into Henry's office to give him a bollicking. "If you don't want the lorry, Henry, don't send fucking lackeys to tell me." Henry looked embarrassed. What never fails to annoy me, is the bloody hypocrisy of many of these people, I noted it was the same with the people my parents moved away from the slums with, once they had a nice house with a tidy front garden they forget who they were, where they came from, I'm not knocking some of these guys, but they forget, I know many of them have criminal records themselves.

Stanley was a bully who carried a knife, if they haven't thrown bodies in, they have fucked people all over the place to get in front. That's fine if they can live with it, but don't act all fucking high and mighty, like my brother Johnny. Ray Kirby swore by Charley Heinze, as long as he was useful to them, they would turn a blind eye. "Charley ain't a grass."

Oh yeah, that's why the cops went to the exact drawer, in the end room of three. Prison hadn't made me bitter, what it had done is taught me who my friends were, and they were getting thinner on the ground than ever.

I knew what it was, they couldn't bear the thought of buying a lorry off Tommy Lewin, only to find there was something wrong with it, and they had been had in the net. Pat Roach, the actor, wrestler also rang up unknowing to me, only to tell more than a few people all over town that I had been trying to sell the lorry, the prat. I'd put it up for sale, simple as that. He spoke to Henry and threw up their excuses, what they forget, what they don't like to mention is I know them as well, I know the moves they got up to.

I was becoming more aware on a day-by-day basis how fickle such a lot people are. How easily they can be manipulated by the media, it's like they ain't got a fucking brain of their own, sometimes council house people can be their own worst enemy, buy a new car and they can be out in force wanting to know where you'd got your money. I was already getting questions asked, yet the simple truth is, most people spend all their fucking wages without saving anything.

After doing our sums, we worked it out that we could afford nine grand, this could give us a nice semi in Walmsley or Great Barr, nice enough, but I didn't fancy the idea of a garage down the back of the garden. In the meantime, Bet had clocked a nice house in Sutton looking over the park, let's have a look for a comparison, okay, we know we couldn't afford it, but at least we would know. Big mistake, as soon as we looked around the house, we both fell in love with it, looking at Bet's face; I knew we had to have it. Sid's brother, Tommy, was still on the weighbridge for Amy Roadstone, he agreed to give me a headed letter if I asked the mortgage company, giving Amy as the company I contracted for. They duly sent a letter to Tommy on the weighbridge, Tommy kindly gave me the blank letter, which I duly filled out myself, simply doubling my wage, that gave us the mortgage to buy the house, which we had already put the offer in for.

We were on our way, but the knives were coming out, my brother Billy called me the biggest '*George Hunt*' in the world. "buying that? How fucking stupid are you? You could have your council house for two grand." Susan, Ray's wife across the road, came over one day and asked us if we thought we were better than them? I looked puzzled. "Why would you say that?"

"Well, why don't you buy a house around here, or up Elmdon?" She just never got it, Bet's brother, John came round one day with his wife Marie, she barked it out, "What I'd like to know Tommy, is how you can afford to buy a house in Sutton Coldfield when you've only just come out of prison? When John and I have been working for years him in the jewellery quarter and me doing hairdressing, and we can't afford a house?" The jealousy was clear I was doing something bent.

John sensibly intervened. "Marie, how much has your old man fiddled the books for out of his hairdressing shops?"

But I could see she wasn't happy at all, her dad owned a chain of hairdressing shops, and they were still living behind the shop, and they couldn't afford to buy a house in Sutton. The simple fact is I couldn't afford to buy a house in Sutton, I was working on a wing and a prayer, I was taking on board my dad's mantra, you can do anything in life if you set your mind to it. Even better, the people we were used to growing up with lived mainly in council houses, hardly anyone had the experience of buying or owning a house unless it was a council house, I was sticking my neck right out taking a hell of a risk with my family.

Within a few weeks, we were off, everything packed on an open-topped lorry, just like the fucking Nesbits, the future bright and optimistic, we were on the road of a wild adventure, where it would lead us we had no idea, where we would end up we had no idea, but it was going to be a rollercoaster ride, leading us to hotels, caravan sites, shops, pubs, it was going to be far more exciting than we could ever have imagined, BUT THAT WILL COME IN MY NEXT BOOK, how anyone can do what I have done, achieve even more than I have done, with no education, no prospects and a criminal record.

Even worse was the constant harassment from the police for over 40 years. There has been victimisation and interference at every opportunity to blight my prospects with customers and potential customers in the private and business sector, from building, landscaping, to guests in our hotels. An example of blatant harassment from a local police officer on a guest and his wife in our first hotel – led to the guest (a serving police officer himself) feeling obliged to write a formal letter of complaint to the Chief Constable. That guest and his wife never returned to our hotel, yet my wife and I survived – and I'm still smiling.

But back to the present. On our first night of settling into our dream home, we finally got to bed, the kids all excited at living in a nice area and looking forward to starting their new schools. As we lay in bed, I turned to Bet, I was fucking shitting myself, ay? "How the fucking hell are we going to pay the mortgage?" I could feel Bet stiffen next to me, but as calmly as anything she just said, "oh well, no problem, we'll just go back to a council house." Fuck me, I couldn't believe her reaction, she felt as calm as anything, yet I knew she must have been equally as frightened.

The day we moved, we were cut off...

www.ingramcontent.com/pod-product-compliance
Lightning Source LLC
Chambersburg PA
CBHW022002090426
42741CB00007B/864